アドベンチャー

日本語辞書

Adventures in Japanese

Dictionary

Hiromi Peterson

Cheng & Tsui Company

D1089392

Copyright © 2005 Hiromi Peterson

All rights reserved. No part of this publication may be reproduced or transmitted in any form or
by any means, electronic or mechanical, including photocopying, recording, scanning, or any information
storage or retrieval system, without written permission from the publisher.

Cover and title page illustration: Michael Muronaka

10 09 08 07 06   8 7 6 5 4 3 2

Published by

Cheng & Tsui Company
25 West Street
Boston, MA 02111-1213 USA
Fax (617) 426-3669
www.cheng-tsui.com
"Bringing Asia to the World"™

Printed in the U.S.A.

Adventures in Japanese Dictionary
ISBN 0-88727-448-X

Companion textbooks, workbooks, hiragana/katakana workbooks, flashcards,
audio and software products for all levels of the
Adventures in Japanese series
are also available from the publisher.

ADVENTURES IN JAPANESE

DICTIONARY

CONTENTS

Abbreviations of Grammatical References

A		い Adjective: *atsui, takai, shiroi*
Adv		Adverb: *totemo, amari, sukoshi*
C		Copula: *desu, de, na*
D		Derivative
	Da	Adjectival Derivative: *-tai*
	Dv	Verbal Derivative: *masu, mashoo, masen*
Exp		Expression
N		Noun
	Na	な Adjective: *kirei, joozu, suki, yuumei*
	Nd	Dependent Noun: *-doru, -han*
	Ni	Interrogative Noun: *dare, doko, ikura*
	N	Noun: *hana, kuruma, hon*
PN		Pre-Noun: *donna, kono, ano*
P		Particle: *de, e, ni*
Pc		Clause Particle: *kara, ga*
SI		Sentence Interjective: *anoo, eeto*
SP		Sentence Particle: *ka, yo, ne, nee*
V		Verb
	V1	Verb (group) 1: *ikimasu, hanashimasu, nomimasu*
	V2	Verb (group) 2: *tabemasu, nemasu, imasu*
	V3	Verb (group) 3 [irregular verb]: *kimasu, shimasu*

Japanese	Volume-Lesson #	Word type	English
<A>			
Aa ああ	2-13	SI	Oh!
abunai あぶない＝危ない	2-4	A	(is) dangerous
abura あぶら＝油	2-14	N	oil
achira あちら	2-5	N	over there [polite equiv. of あそこ]
achira あちら	2-9	N	that one over there [polite equiv. of あれ]
agaru あがる＝上がる/あがります	3-7	V1	(to) step up
ageru あげる/あげます	1-15	V2	(to) give (to equal)
ai あい＝愛	2-15	N	love; affection
～aida (ni) ～あいだ (に)＝～間 (に)	3-5	N+P	While ～
aida あいだ＝間	2-2	N	between
aisatsu (o) suru あいさつ (を) する＝挨拶 (を) する	4-1	V3	(to) greet
aishite iru あいしている＝愛している/あいします	2-15	V1	(to be in) love
aisukuriimu アイスクリーム	2-4	N	ice cream
aji あじ＝味	2-14	N	taste; flavor
ajiwau あじわう＝味わう/あじわいます	4-6	V1	to taste
aka あか＝赤	1-5	N	red
akachan あかちゃん＝赤ちゃん	2-2	N	baby
akai あかい＝赤い	1-6	A	(is) red
akarui あかるい＝明るい	2-11	A	(is) bright
Akemashite omedetoo (gozaimasu).あけましておめでとう (ございます)。＝明けましておめでとう (ございます)。	2-7	Exp	[New Year's greeting]
akeru あける＝開ける/あけます	1-13	V2	(to) open
Akete kudasai. あけてください。＝開けて下さい。	1-2	Exp	Please open.
aki あき＝秋	1-12	N	autumn; fall
Akihabara あきはばら＝秋葉原	3-9	N	Akihabara [a city in Tokyo]
akikan あきかん＝空き缶	4-9	N	empty can
akirameru あきらめる＝諦める/あきらめます	4-7	V2	to give up
(～ga) aku　(～が) あく＝開く/あきます	4-4	V1	(something; place) opens [int.]
akushu (o) suru あくしゅ (を) する＝握手 (を) する	4-1	V3	to shake hands
amai あまい＝甘い	2-14	A	(is) sweet
amari + Neg.　あまり + Neg.	1-5	Adv	(not) very
ame あめ＝飴	1-2	N	candy
ame あめ＝雨	1-1	N	rain
amerika アメリカ	1-3	N	U.S.
amerikajin アメリカじん＝アメリカ人	1-3	N	U.S. citizen
ana あな＝穴	2-11	N	hole
anata あなた	1-2	N	you
anatano あなたの	1-2	N	yours

ane あね=姉	1-3	N	(own) older sister
ani あに=兄	1-3	N	(own) older brother
annai (o) suru あんない (を) する＝案内 (を) する	4-8	V3	(to) guide
annaisho あんないしょ＝案内所	4-8	N	information booth
ano ～ あの ～	1-2	PN	that ～ over there
anoo . . . あのう . . .	1-2	SI	let me see . . . well . . .
anshin (o) suru あんしん (を) する＝安心 (を) する	4-8	V3	(to) become relieved
anzen あんぜん＝安全	2-4	Na	(is) safe
ao あお=青	1-5	N	blue, green [traffic light]
aoi あおい=青い	1-6	A	(is) blue
arau あらう=洗う/あらいます	2-7	V1	(to) wash
are あれ	1-1	N	that one over there
Arigatoo. ありがとう。	1-1	Exp	Thank you.
Arigatoo gozaimashita. ありがとうございました。 ＝有難うございました。	2-9	Exp	Thank you very much. [used after one has received something, or after a deed has been done.]
Arigatoo gozaimasu. ありがとうございます。	1-1	Exp	Thank you very much.
aru ～ ある ～	2-11	PN	(a) certain ～
aru ある/あります	1-10	V1	there is (inanimate object)
aru ある/あります	1-11	V1	have (place de)
arubaito(o) suru アルバイト (を) する	2-2	V3	(to) work part-time (at ～)
aruku あるく=歩く/あるきます	1-7	V1	(to) walk
asa あさ=朝	1-4	N	morning
asagohan あさごはん=朝御飯	1-4	N	breakfast
asatte あさって=明後日	1-11	N	(the) day after tomorrow
ashi あし=脚	1-6	N	leg
ashi あし=足	1-6	N	foot
ashita あした=明日	1-4	N	tomorrow
asobu あそぶ=遊ぶ/あそびます	1-15	V1	(to) play; amuse [not used for sports & music]
asoko あそこ	1-2	N	over there
atama あたま=頭	1-6	N	head
atarashii あたらしい=新しい	1-10	A	(is) new
atatakai あたたかい=暖かい	1-14	A	(is) warm
(TA form) ato de -あとで=-後で	3-6	N+P	After S1, S2.
(～no) ato de (～の) あとで=(～の) 後で	1-12	P+N+P	after ～
ato ～ あと～=後～	2-10	PN	～ more
atsui あつい=暑い	1-1	A	(is) hot [temperature]
atsui あつい=厚い	2-14	A	(is) thick
atsuku suru あつくする=熱くする	2-14	V3	(to) make hot; (to) heat
atsuku あつく=厚く	2-14	Adv	thick
(place de) (person ni) au あう=会う/あいます	1-12	V1	(to) meet (someone) (at a place)

(～ga) atsumaru （～が）あつまる＝集まる/あつまります

                                  4-3   V1   (animate subjects) gather [intransitive]

(～o) atsumeru （～を）あつめる＝集める/あつめます

                                  4-3   V2   (to) collect (something) [transitive]

ayamaru あやまる＝謝る/あやまります 4-7 V1   (to) apologize

<B>

～ba, ～hodo ～ば、～ほど	4-6	Vd+P	the more ～, the more ～
baggu バッグ	2-3	N	bag
Baibai. バイバイ。	1-14	Exp	Good bye.
～bakari ～ばかり	3-8	Nd	only ～
- ban - ばん＝- 番	2-10	Nd	Number -
ban ばん＝晩	1-4	N	evening
bangohan ばんごはん＝晩御飯	1-4	N	dinner; supper
bangumi ばんぐみ＝番組	3-6	N	(TV) program
- banme - ばんめ＝- 番目	2-13	Nd	[in order]
- bansen - ばんせん＝- 番線	3-9	N	track number -
Banzai! ばんざい！＝万歳！	2-10	Exp	Hurray!
baree(booru) バレー(ボール)	1-5	N	volleyball
basho ばしょ＝場所	2-10	N	place; location
basu バス	1-7	N	bus
basuketto(booru) バスケット (ボール)	1-5	N	basketball
basutei バスてい＝バス停	2-13	N	bus stop
beddo ベッド	1-10	N	bed
beigun べいぐん＝米軍	4-3	N	American military
beikoku べいこく＝米国	4-3	N	U.S.
(Dic.) beki da/beki dewa nai べきだ／べきではない	4-4	N+C	should/should not do ～
bengoshi べんごし＝弁護士	1-3	N	lawyer

Benkyoo (o) shinasai. べんきょう (を) しなさい。＝勉強 (を) しなさい。

                                  4-3   V3   Study. [polite command form]

benkyoo (o) suru べんきょう (を) する＝勉強 (を) する 1-4 V3   (to) study

benri べんり＝便利	3-7	Na	convenient
bentoo べんとう＝弁当	1-14	N	box lunch
beranda ベランダ	3-7	N	veranda
betsu(betsu) べつ (べつ)	4-9	N	separate
besu(betsu) ni べつ (べつ) に	4-9	Adv	separately
bideo ビデオ	1-4	N	video
biiru ビール	2-4	N	beer
bijutsu びじゅつ＝美術	1-11	N	art
bijutsukan びじゅつかん＝美術館	2-13	N	art museum
bin びん＝瓶	4-9	N	bottle
binboo びんぼう＝貧乏	2-11	Na	poor
biniiru ビニール	4-9	N	vinyl
bira o maku ビラをまく/まきます	4-4	V1	(to) scatter handbills

biru ビル	3-9	N	building	
boku ぼく＝僕	1-1	N	I [used by males]	
bokutachi ぼくたち＝僕達	1-12	N	we [used by males]	
boorupen ボールペン	1-2	N	ballpoint pen	
booshi ぼうし＝帽子	1-2	N	cap; hat	
borantia ボランティア	4-7	N	volunteer	
bukatsu(doo) ぶかつ（どう）＝部活（動）	3-2	N	club activity	
bukkyoo ぶっきょう＝仏教	4-6	N	Buddhism	
bun ぶん＝文	3-4	N	sentence	
(yon) bun no (ichi) （よん）ぶんの（いち）＝（四）分の（一）	4-2	N	1/4	
bungaku ぶんがく＝文学	3-1	N	literature	
bunka ぶんか＝文化	3-2	N	culture	
bushu ぶしゅ＝部首	3-4	N	classifier (*kanji*)	
buta ぶた＝豚	1-10	N	pig	
butaniku ぶたにく＝豚肉	2-14	N	pork	
butsudan ぶつだん＝仏壇	4-2	N	a Buddhist (family) altar	
butsuri ぶつり＝物理	3-1	N	physics	
byooin びょういん＝病院	1-3	N	hospital	
byooki びょうき＝病気	1-12	N	illness; sickness	

\<C\>

(o)cha （お）ちゃ＝（お）茶	1-4	N	tea	
chadoo ちゃどう＝茶道	4-6	N	tea ceremony	
chairo ちゃいろ＝茶色	1-5	N	brown	
chairoi ちゃいろい＝茶色い	1-6	A	(is) brown	
(place) chaku ～ちゃく＝～着	4-8	Nd	arrival at (place)	
Chakuseki. ちゃくせき。＝着席。	1-1	Exp	Sit. [ceremony]	
- chan - ちゃん	2-2	Nd	[Used instead of - さん when addressing or referring to young, small or cute animals or children.]	
(o)chashitsu （お）ちゃしつ＝（御）茶室	4-6	N	tea ceremony room	
(o)chawan （お）ちゃわん＝（御）茶腕	4-6	N	tea bowl; rice bowl	
(o)chazuke （お）ちゃづけ＝（御）茶漬け	3-8	N	tea poured over a bowl of rice, eaten with garnishes	
chi ち＝血	4-4	N	blood	
chi ga deru ちがでる＝血が出る/でます	4-4	V2	(to) bleed	
(o)chichi （お）ちち＝（御）乳	4-4	N	mother's milk	
chichi ちち＝父	1-3	N	(own) father	
chichi no hi ちちのひ＝父の日	1-15	N	Father's Day	
chigau ちがう＝違う/ちがいます	2-2	V1	(is) wrong; (to) differ	
chiimu チーム	1-12	N	team	
chiisai ちいさい＝小さい	1-6	A	(is) small	
chiisana ちいさな＝小さな	4-3	Na	small [formal use of 小さい and used only before a noun]	

chika ちか＝地下 2-9 N basement
chikai ちかい＝近い 1-10 A (is) near; close
chikaku ちかく＝近く 2-2 N vicinity; nearby
chikara ちから＝力 2-11 N power; strength; ability
chikatetsu ちかてつ＝地下鉄 1-7 N subway
Chikoku desu. ちこくです。＝遅刻です。 1-1 Exp (He/She) is tardy.
chikyuu ちきゅう＝地球 4-9 N the earth
chippu チップ 2-5 N tip
chiri mo tsumoreba yama to naru ちりもつもればやまとなる＝塵も積れば山となる
　　　　　　　　　　　　　　　3-1 Prov Dust amassed will make a mountain.
chizu ちず＝地図 2-13 N map
chokoreeto チョコレート 2-5 N chocolate
choojo ちょうじょ＝長女 4-2 N an eldest daughter
choomiryoo ちょうみりょう＝調味料 3-11 N seasonings
choonan ちょうなん＝長男 4-2 N an eldest son
chooshoku ちょうしょく＝朝食 3-1 N breakfast
chotto ちょっと 1-4 Adv a little [more informal than すこし]
Chotto matte kudasai. ちょっとまってください。＝ちょっと待って下さい。
　　　　　　　　　　　　　　　1-1 Exp Please wait a minute.
Chotto ukagaimasu ga . . . ちょっとうかがいますが . . . 2-13 Exp I have a question.
chuugaku ちゅうがく＝中学 1-3 N intermediate school
chuugaku ichinensei ちゅうがくいちねんせい＝中学一年生 1-3 N seventh grader
chuugaku ninensei ちゅうがくにねんせい＝中学二年生 1-3 N eighth grader
chuugaku sannensei ちゅうがくさんねんせい＝中学三年生
　　　　　　　　　　　　　　　1-3 N freshman; ninth grader
chuugakusei ちゅうがくせい＝中学生 1-3 N intermediate school student
chuugoku ちゅうごく＝中国 1-3 N China
chuugokugo ちゅうごくご＝中国語 1-4 N Chinese language
chuugokukei ちゅうごくけい＝中国系 4-2 N (person of) Chinese descent
chuukyuu ちゅうきゅう＝中級 3-4 N intermediate level
chuumon (o) suru ちゅうもん (を) する＝注文 (を) する 2-5 V3 (to) order
(Go) chuumon wa. 2-5 Exp What is your order? May I take
　(ご) ちゅうもんは。＝(御) 注文は。 your order?
Chuuoosen ちゅうおうせん＝中央線 3-9 N Chuo (Central) Line [orange colored
　　　　　　　　　　　　　　　 train line in Tokyo]
Chuusha (o) suru. ちゅうしゃ (を) する。＝駐車 (を) する。 4-3 V3 (to) park
Chuusha (o) suruna. ちゅうしゃ (を) するな。＝駐車 (を) するな。
　　　　　　　　　　　　　　　4-3 V3 No parking. [negative command form]
chuushajoo ちゅうしゃじょう＝駐車場 2-13 N parking lot
chuushoku ちゅうしょく＝昼食 3-1 N lunch
<D>
da だ 2-11 C [plain form of a copula です]
dai～ だい～＝第～ 4-2 PN [counter for naming sequential numbers]

JE 6

- dai - だい= - 台	1-10	Nd	[counter for mechanized goods]
daibutsu だいぶつ=大仏	4-8	N	a big image of Buddha
daidokoro だいどころ=台所	2-14	N	kitchen
daigaku だいがく=大学	1-12	N	college; university
daigakuin だいがくいん=大学院	4-2	N	graduate school
daigakusei だいがくせい=大学生	1-12	N	college student
daihachiguruma だいはちぐるま=大八車			
	4-4	N	carriage (with two wheels on the sides)
daiji だいじ=大事	1-12	Na	important
(〜o) daiji ni suru （〜を) だいじにする=(〜を) 大事にする			
	4-6	V3	(to) value 〜; take good care of 〜
daijoobu だいじょうぶ=大丈夫	1-12	Na	all right
daikirai だいきらい=大嫌い	1-5	Na	dislike a lot; hate
dainijisekaitaisen だいにじせかいたいせん=第二次世界大戦	4-3	N	World War II
daisuki だいすき=大好き	1-5	Na	like very much; love
daitai だいたい	2-5	Adv	generally
daitooryoo だいとうりょう=大統領	4-3	N	president (of country)
Dakara だから	2-11	SI	Therefore [Informal]
〜dake 〜だけ	2-3	Nd	only 〜
〜dakedenaku 〜mo 〜だけでなく〜も	4-6		not only 〜, but also 〜
dakiau だきあう=抱き合う/だきあいます	4-3	V1	(to) embrace each other
dame だめ	1-2	Na	no good
dandan だんだん	4-4	Adv	step by step; gradually
dansei だんせい=男性	3-6	N	male
danshikoo だんしこう=男子校	3-2	N	boy's school
dansu ダンス	1-5	N	dance; dancing (Western)
dare だれ=誰	1-3	Ni	who?
daremo だれも ＋affirmative ending	4-6	N	everyone
daremo だれも ＋negative ending	1-4	N	nobody
daroo だろう	3-1	C	probably is [informal form of でしょう]
Dashite kudasai. だしてください。=出して下さい。	1-2	Exp	Please turn in.
dasu だす=出す/だします	1-13	V1	(to) turn in; hand in
dasu だす=出す/だします	2-4	V1	(to) stick out; submit; take out
(gomi o) dasu （ゴミを) だす=出す/だします	2-7	V1	(to) take out (the garbage)
(V-stem) dasu (V-stem) だす=出す/だします	4-3	V1	to start doing 〜
datta だった	2-11	C	[plain form of a copula でした]
de で	1-14	C	[te form of copula です]
〜 de 〜 で	2-9	P	between 〜 ; among 〜
(place) de (+ action verb)	1-4	P	at; in (a place)
(counter) de で	1-14	P	[totalizing particle]
(tool) de で	1-14	P	by; with; on; in [tool particle]
(transportation) de で	1-7	P	by (transportation facility)
(reason) de で	2-6	P	because of (reason)

(〜 no naka) de （〜のなか）で＝（〜の中）で	2-9	P	among 〜
(noun) dearu (noun) である	4-6	C	[formal writing form of だ]
(noun) degozaimasu (noun) でございます	4-1	C	be [polite equiv. of です]
deguchi でぐち＝出口	2-13	N	exit
(place o/kara) dekakeru でかける＝出かける/でかけます	2-4	V2	(to) leave; go out (from a place)
(〜ga) dekimashita （〜が）できました＝出来ました	2-14	V2	(〜 is) ready; (〜 is) done
(〜 ga) dekiru できる＝出来る/できます	2-6	V2	(be) able to do 〜
dekirudake できるだけ＝出来るだけ	4-7	Adv	as 〜 as possible
(〜de/kara) dekite iru （〜で／から）できている/出来ている	4-6	V2	is made of/from 〜
Demo でも	1-4	SI	But [used at the beginning of a sentence]
〜demo 〜でも	4-1	C+P	(〜 or) something
denchi でんち＝電池	4-9	N	battery
denkiseihin でんきせいひん＝電気製品	3-7	N	electric goods
densha でんしゃ＝電車	1-7	N	electric train
denshimeeru でんしメール＝電子メール	3-3	N	e-mail
denshirenji でんしレンジ＝電子レンジ	3-7	N	microwave oven
dentoo でんとう＝伝統	3-7	N	tradition
dentooteki でんとうてき＝伝統的	3-7	Na	traditional
denwa でんわ＝電話	1-4	N	telephone
denwa o kakeru でんわをかける＝電話をかける/かけます	2-6	V2	(to) make a phone call
denwabangoo でんわばんごう＝電話番号	1-15	N	telephone number
depaato デパート	1-7	N	department store
(shiai ni) deru （しあいに）でる＝（試合に）出る/でます	2-10	V2	(to) participate in a (sports) game
(place o) deru でる＝出る/でます	2-4	V2	(to) leave (a place)
〜deshoo 〜でしょう [falling intonation]	2-7	C	probably 〜
〜deshoo 〜でしょう [rising intonation]	2-7	C	Isn't it 〜?
desu です	1-1	C	am; is; are
Desukara ですから	2-11	SI	Therefore [formal]
Dewa では	1-14	Exp	Well then [formal]
dezaato デザート	2-14	N	dessert
dezain デザイン	2-9	N	design
- do - ど＝- 度	2-6	Nd	- degree(s); - time(s)
doa ドア	1-10	N	door
dochira どちら	2-5	Ni	where? [polite equiv. of どこ]
dochira どちら	2-9	Ni	which (one of two)? [polite]
dochiramo どちらも + neg.	2-9	N	neither; not either
doitsu ドイツ	1-3	N	Germany
doitsugo ドイツご＝ドイツ語	1-4	N	German language

dokidoki suru ドキドキする	2-10	V3	(become) excited; (become) nervous
doko どこ	1-3	Ni	where?
doko e ittemo どこへいっても＝どこへ行っても	4-8		No matter where (you) go
dokodemo どこでも	3-1	Ni+P	anyplace
dokoemo + neg. どこへも + neg.	7-5	Ni+P	(not to) anywhere
dokusho どくしょ＝読書	1-5	N	reading
dondon どんどん	4-4	Adv	rapidly
donna～ どんな～	1-5	PN	what kind of ～?
dono～ どの～	1-13	Nd	which ～?
donogurai どのぐらい	2-6	Ni	about how long/far/often?
Donogurai arimasu ka. どのぐらい　ありますか。	2-13	Exp	How far is it? [distance]
Donogurai desu ka. どのぐらいですか。	2-13	Exp	How long/far is it?
Donogurai kakarimasu ka. どのぐらい　かかりますか。	2-13	Exp	How long does it take? [time]
Doo desu ka. どうですか。	1-11	Exp	How is it? [informal]
Doo itashimashite. どういたしまして。	1-1	Exp	You are welcome.
Doo iu imi desu ka. どういういみですか。＝どういう意味ですか。	3-4	Exp	What does it mean?
Doo shimashita ka. どうしましたか。	1-12	Exp	What happened?
Doo shitara ii desu ka. どうしたらいいですか。	3-3	Exp	What should I do?
doobutsuen どうぶつえん＝動物園	2-13	N	zoo
Doomo どうも。	1-1	Exp	Thank you.
doon to oto ga suru ドーンとおとがする＝音がする	4-4	V3	(to) boom
dooshite? どうして？	1-11	Ni	why?
dootoku どうとく＝道徳	4-7	N	moral
dootokuteki どうとくてき＝道徳的	4-7	Na	moral
dooyatte どうやって（＝どう）	3-9	N	how? [informal]
Doozo kochira e. どうぞこちらへ。	2-5	Exp	This way, please.
Doozo yoroshiku. どうぞよろしく。	1-1	Exp	Nice to meet you.
doraibaa ドライバー	2-4	N	driver
dore どれ	1-13	Ni	which one?
dore どれ	2-9	Ni	which one (of three or more)?
doroboo どろぼう＝泥棒	4-2	N	robber; thief; burglar
- doru - ドル	1-13	Nd	- dollar(s)
doryoku (o) suru どりょく（を）する＝努力（を）する	4-7	V3	(to) make efforts
dotchi どっち	2-9	Ni	which (one of two)? [informal]
doyoobi どようび＝土曜日	1-7	N	Saturday

<E>

e え＝絵	1-5	N	painting; drawing
E えっ	2-11	SI	Huh?
(place) e (place) へ	1-7	P	to (place)
Ee ええ	1-1	SI	Yes [informal]
Eeto . . . ええと . . .	1-2	SI	Let me see . . . Well . . .

eiga えいが＝映画	1-5	N	movie
eigakan えいがかん＝映画館	2-3	N	movie theater
eigo えいご＝英語	1-4	N	English
eikyoo えいきょう＝影響	4-6	N	influence
eikyoo o ataeru えいきょうをあたえる＝影響を与える/あたえます			
	4-6	V2	(to) influence
eikyoo o ukeru えいきょうをうける＝影響を受ける/うけます			
	4-6	V2	(to) be influenced
eiwajiten えいわじてん＝英和辞典	3-4	N	English-Japanese dictionary
eki えき＝駅	2-13	N	train station
ekiben えきべん＝駅弁	4-8	N	a box lunch sold at stations
ekiin えきいん＝駅員	3-9	N	station employee
emu-saizu エムサイズ	1-14	N	medium size
- en - えん＝ - 円	1-13	Nd	- yen
engei えんげい＝園芸	4-3	N	gardening; landscaping; horticulture
enjinia エンジニア	1-3	N	engineer
enpitsu えんぴつ＝鉛筆	1-2	N	pencil
enpitsukezuri えんぴつけずり＝鉛筆削り	1-10	N	pencil sharpener
(Go)enryonaku doozo. （ご）えんりょなく、どうぞ。＝（御）遠慮なく、どうぞ。			
	3-8	Exp	Without reservation/hesitation, please.
erabu えらぶ＝選ぶ/えらびます	4-6	V1	(to) choose; select; elect
erai えらい＝偉い	2-11	A	is great (person)
eru-saizu エルサイズ	1-14	N	large size
esu-saizu エスサイズ	1-14	N	small size

<F>

fooku フォーク	1-14	N	fork
fuben ふべん＝不便	3-7	Na	inconvenient
fudootoku ふどうとく＝不道徳	4-7	Na	immoral
fuhei ふへい＝不平	4-3	N	a complaint
fuhei o iu ふへいをいう＝不平を言う/いいます	4-3	V1	(to) complain
fukitobasu ふきとばす＝吹き飛ばす/ふきとばします	2-11	V1	(to) blow away
fukoo ふこう＝不幸	4-7	Na	unhappy; unfortunate
fuku ふく＝服	2-3	N	clothing
(toranpetto o) fuku （トランペットを）ふく＝吹く/ふきます			
	3-6	V1	(to) blow (a trumpet)
Fukuoka ふくおか＝福岡	2-1	N	Fukuoka
fukuro ふくろ＝袋	2-9	N	(paper) bag
fukusoo ふくそう＝服装	4-6	N	(the style of) dress; clothing; fashion
fukuzatsu ふくざつ＝複雑	3-4	Na	complicated
- fun - ふん＝ - 分	1-7	Nd	- minute(s)
fune ふね＝船	1-7	N	boat; ship
furaidopoteto フライドポテト	1-14	N	french fries
furansu フランス	1-3	N	France

furansugo フランスご＝フランス語	1-4	N	French language
furu ふる/ふります	4-7	V1	(to) jilt; leave/reject (a boyfriend/ girlfriend)
furu ふる＝降る/ふります	2-7	V1	(rain; snow) fall
furui ふるい＝古い	1-10	A	is old [not for person's age]
futago ふたご＝双児	2-15	N	twin
futari ふたり＝二人	1-3	N	two (persons)
futatsu ふたつ＝二つ	1-2	N	two [general counter]
futekitoo ふてきとう＝不適当	4-6	Na	improper; inappropriate
futoi ふとい＝太い	3-8	A	is thick (in width; size)
futon ふとん＝布団	3-7	N	Japanese bedding
futon o shiku ふとんをしく＝布団を敷く/しきます	4-8	V1	(to) lay out the bedding
futoru ふとる＝太る/ふとります	1-6	V1	(to) get fat
futotte imasu ふとっています＝太っています	1-6	V1	is fat
futsuka ふつか＝二日	1-11	N	the second day of the month
futsuu ふつう＝普通	3-3	N	ordinary; average; regular
futtobooru フットボール	1-5	N	football
fuusen ふうせん＝風船	1-15	N	balloon
fuyu ふゆ＝冬	1-12	N	winter

\<G\>

(subject) ga が	1-7	P	[subject particle]
(Sentence 1) ga が、(Sentence 2)	1-5	Pc	(S1), but (S2)
(Sentence) ga. . . が. . .	2-6	Ps	[Softens the statement.]
gaikokugo がいこくご＝外国語	1-11	N	foreign language
gakki がっき＝学期	3-2	N	semester
gakkoo がっこう＝学校	1-3	N	school
gakusei がくせい＝学生	1-3	N	student [college]
gaman がまん＝我慢	4-2	N	silent suffering; endurance
gaman (o) suru がまん(を)する＝我慢(を)する	4-2	V3	(to) be patient; endure
gamanzuyoi がまんづよい＝我慢強い	4-2	A	patient
gamu ガム	2-3	N	gum
ganbaru がんばる＝頑張る/がんばります	1-12	V1	(to) do one's best
Ganbatte. がんばって。＝頑張って。	1-12	Exp	Good luck.
gareeji ガレージ	1-10	N	garage
garigari ガリガリ	2-11	Adv	chew away; gnaw[onomatopoetic]
gasorinsutando ガソリンスタンド	3-9	N	gas station
- gatsu umare - がつうまれ＝- 月生まれ	1-3	Nd	born in (- month)
～gawa ～がわ＝～側	2-13	Nd	～ side
geemu ゲーム	1-15	N	game
geemu o suru ゲームをする	1-15	V3	(to) play a game
geki げき＝劇	2-12	N	stage play
geki o suru げきをする＝劇をする	2-12	V3	(to) give/put on a stage play
genbaku げんばく＝原爆	4-4	N	atomic bomb

genkan げんかん＝玄関	3-7	N	entrance way; foyer
(o)genki (お) げんき＝(御) 元気	1-1	Na	fine; healthy [polite]
(O)genki desu ka. (お) げんきですか。＝(御) 元気ですか。	1-1	Exp	How are you?
genmai げんまい＝玄米	4-7	N	brown rice
getsuyoobi げつようび＝月曜日	1-7	N	Monday
gin ぎん＝銀	2-15	N	silver
giniro ぎんいろ＝銀色	1-5	N	silver (color)
ginkoo ぎんこう＝銀行	2-2	N	bank
Ginza ぎんざ＝銀座	3-9	N	Ginza [a city in Tokyo]
gitaa ギター	1-5	N	guitar
go ご＝五	1-1	N	five
go-juu ごじゅう＝五十	1-1	N	fifty
gochisoo ごちそう＝御馳走	4-8	N	feast; a big meal
gochisoo (o) suru ごちそう (を) する	2-5	V3	(to) treat (someone)
Gochisoosama. ごちそうさま。＝御馳走様。	1-14	Exp	[after a meal]
gogatsu ごがつ＝五月	1-3	N	May
gogo ごご＝午後	1-7	N	p.m.
gohan ごはん＝御飯	1-4	N	(cooked) rice
gokiburi ごきぶり	1-10	N	cockroach
Gokuroosama. ごくろうさま。＝御苦労様。	4-9	Exp	Thank you very much (for your service). [Generally used by superior as an expression of gratitude for a service or favor done by a person of lesser status.]
Gomenkudasai. ごめんください。	4-1	Exp	Is anyone home? [Used before one enters someone's home.]
Gomennasai. ごめんなさい。	4-0	Exp	I am sorry. [apology]
gomi ごみ	1-2	N	rubbish
gomibako ごみばこ＝ごみ箱	1-10	N	trash can
Goo ni ireba goo ni shitagae. ごうにいればごうにしたがえ。＝郷に入れば郷に従え。	3-7	Prov	When in a village, do as the villagers do. (When in Rome do as the Romans do.)
(〜ni) gookaku suru (school に) ごうかく (を) する＝合格 (を) する	4-9	V3	(to) pass an exam; be accepted (by school)
goraku ごらく＝娯楽	3-6	N	entertainment
Goran kudasai. ごらんください。＝御覧下さい。	4-1	Exp	Please look. [More polite than 見て下さい。]
goranninaru ごらんになる＝御覧になる/ごらんになります	4-1	V1	(to) look [honorific equiv. of 見る]
〜goro 〜ごろ	1-7	Nd	about 〜 (time)
gorufu ゴルフ	1-5	N	golf
goryooshin ごりょうしん＝御両親	2-2	N	(someone else's) parents [polite]

goshujin ごしゅじん＝御主人	3-6	N	(someone else's) husband
gozen ごぜん＝午前	1-7	N	a.m.
Gozonjidesuka. ごぞんじですか。＝御存知ですか。	4-1	V	Do you know? [honorific equiv. of 知っていますか]
guai ga warui ぐあいがわるい＝具合が悪い	2-6	A	condition (health) is bad; feel sick
gun ぐん＝軍	4-3	N	military
gunjin ぐんじん＝軍人	4-3	N	military personnel
～gurai ～ぐらい	1-13	Nd	about ～ [Not used for time.]
gurei グレイ	1-5	N	grey
guriinsha グリーンしゃ＝グリーン車	4-8	N	green car [JR first class car]
gyooji ぎょうじ＝行事	3-2	N	event(s); function
gyuuniku ぎゅうにく＝牛肉	2-14	N	beef
gyuunyuu ぎゅうにゅう＝牛乳	1-4	N	(cow's) milk
gyuunyuupakku ぎゅうにゅうパック＝牛乳パック	4-9	N	milk carton

\<H\>

ha は＝歯	1-6	N	tooth
hachi はち＝八	1-1	N	eight
hachigatsu はちがつ＝八月	1-3	N	August
hachijuu はちじゅう＝八十	1-1	N	eighty
hadaka はだか＝裸	4-8	N	naked; nude
(e)hagaki （え）はがき＝(絵)葉書	3-3	N	(picture) postcard
haha no hi ははのひ＝母の日	1-15	N	Mother's Day
haha はは＝母	1-3	N	(my) mother
Hai. はい。	1-3	Exp	Yes. [Used in response to roll call.]
Hai はい	1-6	SI	Yes
Hai doozo. はい、どうぞ。	1-2	Exp	Here, you are.
Hai, chiizu. はい、チーズ。	1-15	Exp	Say, "Cheese."
Hai, piisu. はい、ピース。	1-15	Exp	Say, "Peace."
haiken suru はいけんする＝拝見する/はいけんします	4-1	V3	(to) look (at); see [humble equiv. of 見る]
(furo ni) hairu （ふろに）はいる＝(風呂に)入る/はいります	3-3	V1	(to) take (a bath)
(place ni) hairu はいる＝入る/はいります	2-4	V1	(to) enter (a place)
haiyuu はいゆう＝俳優	3-6	N	actor
(something ga) hajimaru はじまる＝始まる/はじまります	2-10	V1	(something will) begin; start
hajime ni はじめに＝始めに	2-14	Adv	(at the) beginning
Hajimemashite. はじめまして。	1-1	Exp	How do you do?
Hajimemashoo. はじめましょう。＝始めましょう。	1-4	Exp	Let's begin.
(V stem) hajimeru (V stem)＋はじめる＝始める/はじめます	3-4	V2	(to) begin doing ～
(something o) hajimeru はじめる＝始める/はじめます	2-10	V2	(someone) start/begin (something)
hajimete はじめて＝始めて	2-7	N	(for the) first time

hakikaeru　はきかえる＝履き替える/はきかえます

	3-2	V2	(to) change [i.e., shoes, pants, etc.]

hakketsubyoo はっけつびょう＝白血病 4-4 N　leukemia

hakkiri はっきり　　　　　　　　4-1　Adv　clearly

hako はこ＝箱　　　　　　　　2-9　N　box

- haku/- paku - はく/- ぱく　　　4-8　Nd　- night(s)

haku はく＝履く/はきます　　　2-3　V1　(to) wear [below the waist]

hakubutsukan はくぶつかん＝博物館 3-9 N　museum

- han - はん＝ - 半　　　　　　1-7　Nd　- half

hana はな＝花　　　　　　　　1-10 N　flower

hana はな＝鼻　　　　　　　　1-6　N　nose

hanabi o suru はなびをする＝花火をする　2-7　V3　(to do) fireworks

(o)hanami （お）はなみ＝花見　　4-6　N　cherry blossom viewing

hanashiau はなしあう＝話し合う/はなしあいます

	4-3	V1	(to) talk each other; discuss

hanashichuu はなしちゅう＝話し中　2-6　Exp　line is busy

hanasu はなす＝話す/はなします　1-4　V1　(to) speak; talk

hanaya はなや＝花屋　　　　　　1-13 N　flower shop

hanayome はなよめ＝花嫁　　　　4-2　N　a bride

hanbaagaa ハンバーガー　　　　1-14 N　hamburger

hanbun ni はんぶんに＝半分に　　2-14 Adv　in half

hantai (o) suru はんたい（を）する＝反対（を）する　4-4　V3　(to) disagree

ha(ppa) は　（っぱ）＝葉（っぱ）　4-6　N　leaf

happyoo (o) suru はっぴょう（を）する＝発表（を）する

	3-3	V3	(to) present (orally); announce

Harajuku はらじゅく＝原宿　　　3-9　N　Harajuku [a city in Tokyo]

harau はらう＝払う/はらいます　2-5　V1　(to) pay

hare はれ＝晴れ　　　　　　　　2-7　N　clear (weather)

haru はる＝貼る/はります　　　3-3　V1　(to) paste; glue; attach

haru はる＝春　　　　　　　　　1-12 N　spring

(o) hashi （お）はし＝(御) 箸　　1-14 N　chopsticks

hashi はし＝橋　　　　　　　　　2-13 N　bridge

hashiru はしる＝走る/はしります 1-12 V1　(to) run

hatachi はたち＝二十歳　　　　　1-3　N　twenty years old

hatake はたけ＝畑　　　　　　　4-3　N　(vegetable) field; garden

(place de) hataraku はたらく＝働く/はたらきます 2-2　V1　(to) work (at ～)

(place) hatsu ～はつ＝～発　　　4-8　Nd　departing from (place)

hatsuka はつか＝二十日　　　　　1-11 N　the twentieth day of the month

hatsuon はつおん＝発音　　　　　3-4　N　pronunciation

hatsuon suru はつおんする＝発音する 3-4　V3　(to) pronounce

hayai はやい＝早い　　　　　　　1-7　A　is early

hayaku はやく＝早く　　　　　　1-12 Adv　early [used with a verb]

hayaku はやく＝速く　　　　　　2-4　Adv　fast; quickly [used with a verb]

Hayaku. はやく。＝速く。	1-4	Exp	Hurry!
(Dic./NAI) hazu desu. はずです。	2-6	Nd	I expect that he/she will do/will not do; He/She is expected to do/not to do.
Hee. へ～え。	4-9	Exp	Really! [conversational]
heiwa へいわ＝平和	3-2	N/Na	peace; peaceful
hen へん＝変	2-6	Na	strange; weird; unusual
hen へん＝辺	2-13	N	area
heta へた＝下手	1-5	Na	unskillful; be poor at
heya へや＝部屋	1-10	N	room
hi ひ＝火	4-4	N	fire; light; flame
hi ひ＝日	1-15	N	day
hidari ひだり＝左	2-2	N	left side
hidoi ひどい＝酷い	1-11	A	(is) terrible
higashi ひがし＝東	2-1	N	east
higashiguchi ひがしぐち＝東口	3-9	N	east entrance/exit
higashikaigan ひがしかいがん＝東海岸	4-3	N	east coast
hige ひげ＝髭	1-6	N	beard; moustache
hikari ひかり	4-8	N	Light [A *shinkansen* that stops at major *shinkansen* stations.]
- hiki - ひき＝ - 匹	1-10	Nd	[counter for small animals]
hikkoshi (o) suru ひっこし (を) する＝引っ越し (を) する	4-2	V3	(to) move (one's residence)
hikkosu ひっこす＝引っ越す/ひっこします	4-2	V1	(to) move (one's residence)
hikooki ひこうき＝飛行機	1-7	N	airplane
hiku ひく＝引く/ひきます	4-4	V1	to pull; subtract
(jisho o) hiku (じしょを) ひく＝(辞書を) 引く/ひきます	3-4	V1	(to) look up a word (in a dictionary)
hiku ひく＝弾く/ひきます	2-6	V1	(to) play (a string instrument)
hikui ひくい＝低い	1-6	A	is short (height)
hima ひま＝暇	2-15	Na	is free (time)
hiroi ひろい＝広い	1-10	A	is wide; spacious
hirosa ひろさ＝広さ	4-3	N	width; space
Hiroshima ひろしま＝広島	2-1	N	Hiroshima
hirou ひろう＝拾う/ひろいます	4-9	V1	(to) pick up
(o)hiru (お) ひる＝(お) 昼	1-4	N	daytime
hirugohan ひるごはん＝昼御飯	1-4	N	lunch
(O)hisashiburi (desu). (お) ひさしぶり (です)。＝(お) 久しぶり (です)。	3-3	Exp	I have not seen you for a long time.
hito ひと＝人	1-10	N	person
hitori ひとり＝一人	1-3	N	one (person)
hitoribotchi ひとりぼっち＝独りぼっち	4-7	N	alone; lonely; solitary
hitorikko ひとりっこ＝一人っ子	2-15	N	only child
hitorimo + Neg. ひとりも＝一人も＋ Neg.	4-7	N+P	(not) even (one person)

JE

hitotsu ひとつ＝一つ	1-2	N	one [general counter]
hitsuyoo ひつよう＝必要	4-6	Na	necessary
～hodo ほど + Neg.	2-9	P	(not) as ～ as
hoka (no noun) ほか（の～）	2-9	N	other ～
Hoka ni nani ka. ほかになにか。＝ほかに何か。	2-5	Exp	Anything else?
Hokkaidoo ほっかいどう＝北海道	2-1	N	Hokkaido
homeru ほめる＝褒める/ほめます	4-2	V2	(to) praise
hon ほん＝本	1-2	N	book
hondo ほんど＝本土	4-3	N	mainland
hone ほね＝骨	4-4	N	bones
Honshuu ほんしゅう＝本州	2-1	N	Honshu
hontoo ほんとう＝本当	1-3	N	true
Hontoo desu ka. ほんとうですか。＝本当ですか。	2-3	Exp	(Is it) true/real?
hontoo ni ほんとうに＝本当に	2-3	Adv	really; truly
honya ほんや＝本屋	1-13	N	bookstore
(～ no) hoo （～の）ほう＝(～の) 方	2-9	N	～ is more [alternative]
hoogen ほうげん＝方言	4-8	N	dialect
hookago ほうかご＝放課後	3-2	N	after school
～hoomen ～ほうめん＝～方面	3-9	N	～ direction
(～o) hoomon suru ほうもんする＝訪問する	4-1	V3	(to) visit
hoomu ホーム	3-9	N	platform
hoomuruumu ホームルーム	1-11	N	homeroom
hoomusutei o suru ホームステイをする	2-2	V3	(to) do a homestaty
(～o) hoshigaru （～を）ほしがる/ほしがります	4-4	V1	(someone else) wants ～
(something ga) hoshii ほしい＝欲しい	1-11	A	want (something)
hosoi ほそい＝細い	3-8	A	is thin; slender
hosonagai ほそながい＝細長い	3-8	A	is thin and long
hotondo ほとんど	3-2	Adv	almost; mostly
hottodoggu ホットドッグ	1-14	N	hotdog
hyaku ひゃく＝百	1-1	N	hundred
hyaku-man ひゃくまん＝百万	1-13	N	(one) million

〈I〉

- i - い＝- 位	2-15	Nd	[rank]
ibaru いばる＝威張る/いばります	4-7	V1	(to) brag; be arrogant
ichi いち＝一	1-1	N	one
ichiban いちばん＝一番	2-9	Adv	the most
ichigakki いちがっき＝一学期	3-2	N	first semester
ichigatsu いちがつ＝一月	1-3	N	January
ichigo いちご＝苺	2-14	N	strawberry
ie いえ＝家	2-2	N	house
ii いい	1-2	A	(is) good
Ii desu nee. いいですねえ。	1-11	Exp	How nice! [on a future event]
Iie いいえ	1-1	SI	No [formal]

Iie, kekkoo desu. いいえ、けっこうです。 1-14		Exp	No, thank you.
ijime　いじめ	3-2	N	bullying
ijimeru　いじめる/いじめます	3-2	V2	(to) bully; (to) treat someone harshly
〜 ijoo 〜いじょう＝〜以上	4-4	Nd	more than 〜
〜 ika 〜いか＝〜以下	4-4	Nd	less than 〜
Ikaga desu ka.　いかがですか。	1-13	Ni	how about 〜? [Polite form of どうですか.]
ike　いけ＝池	1-10	N	pond
ikebana　いけばな＝生け花	3-7	N	flower arrangement
Ikebukuro　いけぶくろ＝池袋	3-9	N	Ikebukuro [a city in Tokyo]
ikemasen　いけません	2-3	V2	won't do; must not do
iken　いけん＝意見	3-3	N	opinion
ikiru　いきる＝生きる/いきます	4-2	V2	(to) live
iku　いく＝行く/いきます	1-7	V1	(to) go
(o)ikura　(お)いくら	1-13	Ni	how much?
ikutsu　いくつ	1-2	Ni	how many? [general counter]
(o)ikutsu　(お)いくつ	1-3	Ni	how old?
ima　いま＝今	1-3	N	now
ima　いま＝居間	3-7	N	living room; family room
imi　いみ＝意味	3-4	N	meaning
(〜to iu) imi desu (〜という) いみです。＝(〜という) 意味です。 3-4　Exp　It means 〜.			
imin　いみん＝移民	4-2	N	immigrant
imooto　いもうと＝妹	1-3	N	(my) younger sister
imootosan　いもうとさん＝妹さん	1-3	N	(someone's) younger sister
inaka　いなか＝田舎	4-4	N	countryside; hometown
(o)inori　(お) いのり＝(お) 祈り	3-8	N	prayer
inoru　いのる＝祈る/いのります	3-8	V1	(to) pray
inshoo　いんしょう＝印象	4-3	N	impression
inshooteki　いんしょうてき＝印象的	4-3	Na	impressive
inu　いぬ＝犬	1-10	N	dog
ippaku futsuka　いっぱくふつか＝一泊二日	4-8	N	one night, two days
Irasshai.　いらっしゃい。	4-1	Exp	Welcome. [Used when greeting others in to one's home or other personal space.]
Irasshaimase. いらっしゃいませ。	2-5	Exp	Welcome. [formal]
irassharu いらっしゃる/いらっしゃいます	2-6	V1	(to) exist; be (for animate) [polite form of いる]
irassharu いらっしゃる/いらっしゃいます	4-1	V1	(to) come; go; exist [honorific equiv. of 来る, 行く, いる]
(〜ni) ireru いれる＝入れる/いれます	2-9	V2	(to) put in 〜
iriguchi いりぐち＝入口	2-13	N	entrance
iro いろ＝色	1-5	N	color
iroiro いろいろ	2-9	Na	various
iru いる/います	1-10	V2	there is (animate object)

17

(～ga) iru （～が）いる＝要る/いります	1-14	V1	need ～
isha いしゃ＝医者	1-3	N	(medical) doctor [informal]
isogashii いそがしい＝忙しい	1-7	A	is busy
Isseki nichoo. いっせきにちょう＝一石二鳥	3-8	Prov	Kill two birds with one stone.
issho ni いっしょに＝一緒に	1-4	Adv	together
isshookenmei いっしょうけんめい＝一生懸命	2-11	Adv	(with one's) utmost effort
isu いす＝椅子	1-10	N	chair
(-te) itadakemasenka. （-て）いただけませんか。	4-1	E	Would/Won't you do ～?
Itadakimasu. いただきます。	1-14	Exp	[before a meal]
itadaku いただく/いただきます	4-1	V1	(to) eat; drink; receive [humble equiv. of 食べる, 飲む, もらう]
itai いたい＝痛い	1-12	A	is painful; sore
itariakei イタリアけい＝イタリア系	4-2	N	person of Italian descent
itasu いたす/いたします	4-1	V1	(to) do [humble equiv. of する]
itoko いとこ	1-15	N	cousin
itokonnyaku いとこんにゃく ＝糸こんにゃく	2-14	N	shredded konnyaku [grey or transparent tuber root gelatin]
itsu いつ	1-7	Ni	when?
itsudemo いつでも	3-1	Ni+P	anytime
itsuka いつか＝五日	1-11	N	the fifth day of the month
itsumademo いつまでも	4-9	Adv	forever
itsumo いつも	1-4	Adv	always
itsutsu いつつ＝五つ	1-2	N	five [general counter]
Ittekimasu. いってきます。 ＝行って来ます。	3-1	Exp	[Used by a family member who leaves home for the day.]
Itterasshai. いってらっしゃい。 ＝行ってらっしゃい。	3-1	Exp	[Used by a family member who sends off another family member for the day.]
iu いう＝言う/いいます	1-13	V1	(to) say
iwau いわう＝祝う/いわいます	4-2	V1	(to) celebrate; congratulate
iya(tt) いや（っ）	2-11	SI	No [stronger negation than いいえ]
iyaringu イヤリング	2-3	N	earrings
<J>			
Ja じゃ	1-14	Exp	Well then [informal]
jaketto ジャケット	1-13	N	jacket
jama じゃま＝邪魔	1-6	Na	hindrance; nuisance; is in the way
(plain form) janai (plain)じゃない	4-7	C	～, isn't it? [emphasis and confirmation]
- ji - じ＝- 時	1-7	Nd	- o'clock
jibun じぶん＝自分	2-15	N	oneself
jidoosha じどうしゃ＝自動車	1-7	N	car; vehicle
jigoku じごく＝地獄	4-3	N	hell
jijo じじょ＝次女	4-2	N	a second daughter
jikan じかん＝時間	2-10	N	time

- jikan - じかん＝- 時間	2-6	Nd	- hour(s)
jikokuhyoo じこくひょう＝時刻表	4-8	N	time table
jikoshookai (o) suru じこしょうかい (を) する＝自己紹介 (を) する			
	2-2	V3	(to) do a self-introduction
jimusho じむしょ＝事務所	1-10	N	office
jinan じなん＝次男	4-2	N	a second son
jinja じんじゃ＝神社	2-7	N	shrine (Shinto)
jinkoo じんこう＝人口	4-4	N	population
jinsei じんせい＝人生	4-2	N	one's (whole) life; a lifetime
jinshu じんしゅ＝人種	4-3	N	ethnic race
jinshusabetsu じんしゅさべつ＝人種差別	4-3	N	racial discrimination
jishin じしん＝自信	4-7	N	confidence
jishin ga aru じしんがある＝自信がある/あります	4-7	V1	be confident
jisho じしょ＝辞書	1-2	N	dictionary
jitensha じてんしゃ＝自転車	1-7	N	bicycle
jiyuu じゆう＝自由	2-3	Na	free; liberal
jiyuuseki じゆうせき＝自由席	4-8	N	non-reserved seat
jogingu ジョギング	1-5	N	jogging
- joo - じょう＝- 畳	3-7	C	[counter for *tatami*]
joobu じょうぶ＝丈夫	4-7	Na	strong; healthy; durable
joodan じょうだん＝冗談	2-10	N	a joke
jookyuu じょうきゅう＝上級	3-4	N	advanced level
joozu じょうず＝上手	1-5	Na	skillful; be good at
josei じょせい＝女性	3-6	N	female
joshikoo じょしこう＝女子校	3-2	N	girl's school
joyuu じょゆう＝女優	3-6	N	actress
JR ＪＲ〔ジェイアール〕	3-9	N	Japan Railway
jugyoo じゅぎょう＝授業	1-11	N	class; instruction
jugyooryoo じゅぎょうりょう＝授業料	3-2	N	tuition
juku じゅく＝塾	3-2	N	cram school
junbi (o) suru じゅんび (を) する＝準備 (を) する	4-3	V3	(to) prepare
juu じゅう＝十	1-1	N	ten
juu じゅう＝銃	3-2	N	gun
juu-go じゅうご＝十五	1-1	N	fifteen
juu-hachi じゅうはち＝十八	1-1	N	eighteen
juu-ichi じゅういち＝十一	1-1	N	eleven
juu-ku じゅうく＝十九	1-1	N	nineteen
juu-kyuu じゅうきゅう＝十九	1-1	N	nineteen
juu-man じゅうまん＝十万	1-13	N	hundred thousand
juu-nana じゅうなな＝十七	1-1	N	seventeen
juu-ni じゅうに＝十二	1-1	N	twelve
juu-roku じゅうろく＝十六	1-1	N	sixteen
juu-san じゅうさん＝十三	1-1	N	thirteen

juu-shi じゅうし=十四	1-1	N	fourteen
juu-shichi じゅうしち=十七	1-1	N	seventeen
juu-yokka じゅうよっか=十四日	1-11	N	(the) fourteenth day of the month
juu-yon じゅうよん =十四	1-1	N	fourteen
juubun じゅうぶん=十分	4-9	Na/Adv	enough; ample
juugatsu じゅうがつ=十月	1-3	N	October
juuichigatsu じゅういちがつ=十一月	1-3	N	November
juunigatsu じゅうにがつ=十二月	1-3	N	December
juusho じゅうしょ=住所	1-15	N	address
juusu ジュース	1-4	N	juice

<K>

ka か	1-1	SP	[question particle]
(sentence) ka? (sentence) か？	3-1	SP	[male informal sentence ending particle]
kaapetto カーペット	3-7	N	carpet
kabe かべ=壁	2-11	N	wall
kabukiza かぶきざ=歌舞伎座	3-9	N	*Kabuki* theater
kaburu かぶる/かぶります	2-3	V2	(to) wear [on or draped over the head]
kado かど=角	2-4	N	corner
kachikan かちかん=価値観	4-7	N	(sense of) value
kaeri かえり=帰り	4-1	N	return (home); (on one's) way home
kaeru かえる=帰る/かえります	1-7	V1	(to) return (to a place)
kaeru かえる=変える/かえます	3-1	V2	(to) change (something)
kaesu かえす=返す/かえします	2-5	V1	(to) return (something)
kafeteria カフェテリア	1-4	N	cafeteria
kagaku かがく=科学	1-11	N	science
kagaku かがく=化学	3-1	N	chemistry
kage かげ=陰, 影	4-7	N	shade: shadow
- kagetsu - かげつ= - か月	2-6	Nd	- month(s)
kagi かぎ=鍵	2-4	N	key
kagu かぐ=家具	4-9	N	furniture
- kai - かい=- 回	3-4	Nd	- time(s)
(sentence) kai? (sentence) かい？	3-1	SP	[male informal sentence ending particle]
kaidan かいだん=階段	3-7	N	stairs
kaigairyokoo かいがいりょこう=海外旅行	3-2	N	overseas travel
kaikeigaku かいけいがく＝会計学	4-3	N	accounting
kaiketsu (o) suru かいけつ (を) する=解決 (を) する	4-9	V3	(to) solve
kaimono かいもの=買い物	1-7	N	shopping
kaimono (o) suru かいもの (を) する=買い物 (を) する	1-7	V3	(to) shop
kaisatsuguchi かいさつぐち=改札口	3-9	N	ticket gate
kaisha かいしゃ=会社	1-7	N	company
kaishain かいしゃいん=会社員	1-3	N	company employee
kaji かじ=火事	4-4	N	a fire
kaji かじ=家事	3-3	N	household chore; housework

kakaru かかる/かかります	2-9	V1	(to) require; take (time)
kakeru かける/かけます	2-3	V2	(to) wear [glasses]
kakeru かける/かけます	3-8	V2	(to) pour over; sprinkle
kakeru かける＝掛ける/かけます	3-7	V2	(to) hang
kakijun かきじゅん＝書き順	3-4	N	stroke order
kakko ii かっこいい＝格好いい	3-3	A	is good looking
- kaku - かく＝- 画	3-4	N	- stroke(s)
kaku かく＝書く/かきます	1-4	V1	(to) write
(e o) kaku (えを) かく＝(絵を) 描く/かきます	2-15	V1	(to) draw; paint a picture
kakusu かくす＝隠す/かくします	2-11	V1	(to) hide (something)
kamaimasen かまいません	2-3	V1	I do not mind if . . .
kamera カメラ	1-15	N	camera
kami (no ke) かみ (のけ)＝髪 (の毛)	1-6	N	hair
kami かみ＝紙	1-2	N	paper
～kamo shirenai ～かもしれない	3-7	E	might ～; may ～
kamoku かもく＝科目	1-11	N	subject
(gamu o) kamu （ガムを）かむ/かみます	2-3	V1	(to) chew gum
kan かん＝缶	4-9	N	can
～kana. ～かな。	3-2	SP	(I) wonder if ～.
kanai かない＝家内	3-6	N	(own) wife
kanashii かなしい＝悲しい	1-11	A	is sad
kanbyoo (o) suru かんびょう (を) する＝看病 (を) する	4-7	V3	(to) take care of (a sick person)
Kanda かんだ＝神田	3-9	N	Kanda [a city in Tokyo]
kandai かんだい＝寛大	4-7	Na	generous
(～ni) kandoo (o) suru （～に）かんどう (を) する＝感動 (を) する	4-7	V3	be impressed (with ～); be touched (by ～); be moved (by ～)
(o)kane (お) かね＝(お) 金	1-2	N	money
(o)kanemochi (お) かねもち＝(お) 金持ち	2-11	N	rich person
kangaesaserareru かんがえさせられる＝考えさせられる	4-7	V2	I am made to think [causative passive form]
kanjijiten かんじじてん＝漢字辞典	3-4	N	*kanji* dictionary
kanjiru かんじる＝感じる/かんじます	4-6	V2	(to) feel
(o) kanjoo (お) かんじょう＝(お) 勘定	2-5	N	a check; bill
kankei かんけい＝関係	4-3	N	relationship
kankei ga nai かんけいがない＝関係がない	4-3	Exp	no relation; no connection
kankoku かんこく＝韓国	1-3	N	Korea
kankokugo かんこくご＝韓国語	1-4	N	Korean language
kankokukei かんこくけい＝韓国系	4-2	N	(person of) Korean descent
kankoo (o) suru かんこう (を) する＝観光 (を) する	4-8	V3	(to) tour
kankoo basu かんこうバス＝観光バス	4-8	N	tour bus
kankoo kyaku かんこうきゃく＝観光客	4-8	N	tourist

kankoo ryokoo かんこうりょこう＝観光旅行	4-8	N	sightseeing tour
kankyoo かんきょう＝環境	4-9	N	environment
kanningu カンニング	3-2	N	cheating
kanojo かのじょ＝彼女	3-6	N	she; her; girlfriend
Kanpai! かんぱい！＝乾杯！	3-8	Exp	Cheers!
kansai かんさい＝関西	4-8	N	Kansai area [region of western Honshu including Osaka and Kyoto]
kansaikuukoo かんさいくうこう＝関西空港	4-8	N	Kansai Airport
kansha (o) suru かんしゃ（を）する＝感謝（を）する	2-15	V3	(to) appreciate; thank
kantan かんたん＝簡単	3-4	Na	simple
kantoku かんとく＝監督	3-6	N	(movie) director; (baseball) manager
kantoo かんとう＝関東	4-8	N	Kanto area [region of eastern Honshu including Tokyo]
kanzenshugisha かんぜんしゅぎしゃ＝完全主義者	4-7	N	perfectionist
kanzume かんづめ＝缶詰め	4-3	N	canned food
kao かお＝顔	1-6	N	face
～ kara ～から	1-11	P	from ～
kara から＝空	4-9	N	empty
～ kara ～ made ～から～まで	2-13	P	from ～ to ～
(sentence) kara ～から	1-11	Pc	because ～ ; since ～ ; ～, so
karada からだ＝体	1-6	N	body
karai からい＝辛い	2-14	A	(is) salty; (is) spicy
karappo からっぽ＝空っぽ	4-9	N	empty
kare かれ＝彼	3-6	N	he; him; boyfriend
kareeraisu カレーライス	2-5	N	curry rice
kariru かりる＝借りる/かります	2-3	V2	(to) borrow; (to) rent (from)
karui かるい＝軽い	3-7	A	(is) light (in weight)
Kashikomarimashita. かしこまりました。	4-1	Exp	Certainly, Sir/Madam. [Used to acknowledge a request.]
～kashira. ～かしら。	3-2	SP	(I) wonder if ～. [used by female]
kashu かしゅ＝歌手	3-5	N	singer
kasu かす＝貸す/かします	1-14	V1	(to) lend; rent (to)
kata かた＝方	1-10	Nd	person [polite form of ひと]
(Verb stem) kata かた＝方	2-14	N	how to do ～
katachi かたち＝形	3-4	N	shape
katai かたい＝硬い	3-8	A	is hard; tough
katana かたな＝刀	4-6	N	sword
katazukeru かたづける＝片付ける/かたづけます	2-14	V2	(to) clean up; put away
katsu かつ＝勝つ/かちます	1-12	V1	(to) win
Katta! Katta! かった！かった！＝勝った！勝った！	2-10	Exp	(We) won! (We) won!
kau かう＝買う/かいます	1-13	V1	(to) buy
kawa かわ＝川	1-7	N	river
kawaii かわいい＝可愛い	1-6	A	is cute

Kawaisoo ni. かわいそうに。＝可愛そうに。1-12 Exp How pitiful.

(〜ga) kawaku (〜が) かわく＝乾く/かわきます 4-8 V1 (someone/something) gets dry [intransitive]

Kawarimashita. かわりました。＝代わりました。
2-6 Exp It's me. [lit., We've changed over.]

kawaru かわる＝代わる/かわります 2-6 V1 (to) change (over)

kawatta 〜 かわった〜＝変わった〜 3-8 V1 different 〜; odd 〜; unusual 〜

kayoobi かようび＝火曜日 1-7 N Tuesday

kayou かよう＝通う/かよいます 3-2 V (to) commute

kazaru かざる＝飾る/かざります 3-7 V1 (to) decorate

kaze かぜ＝風邪 1-12 N a cold

kaze かぜ＝風 2-7 N wind

kaze o hiku かぜをひく＝風邪を引く/ひきます 2-6 V1 (to) catch a cold

kazoku かぞく＝家族 1-3 N (my) family

(go)kazoku (ご) かぞく＝(御) 家族 1-3 N (someone's) family

kazu かず＝数 3-4 N amount

(sentence) kedo けど 2-6 Pc Although 〜

kega (o) suru けが (を) する＝怪我 (を) する 4-4 V3 (to) get injured

keigo けいご＝敬語 4-1 N honorifics

keikaku けいかく＝計画 4-8 N a plan

keikaku (o) suru けいかく (を) する＝計画 (を) する 4-8 V3 (to) plan

keikan けいかん＝警官 2-4 N police officer

keiken (o) suru けいけん (を) する＝経験 (を) する 3-7 V3 (to) experience

keitaidenwa けいたいでんわ＝携帯電話 3-3 N cellular phone

keizai けいざい＝経済 3-4 N economics

(person to) kekkon (o) suru けっこん (を) する＝結婚 (を) する
2-2 V3 (to) be married (to 〜)

kenbaiki けんばいき＝券売機 3-9 N ticket vending machine

kenbutsu (o) suru けんぶつ (を) する＝見物 (を) する 4-8 V3 (to) sightsee

kenchiku けんちく＝建築 4-6 N architecture

kenchiku (o) suru けんちく (を) する＝建築 (を) する
4-6 V3 (to) build (a house or a building)

kenchikuchuu けんちくちゅう＝建築中 4-6 N under construction (a house or a building)

kenchikuka けんちくか＝建築家 4-6 N architect

kendoo けんどう＝剣道 3-2 N *kendo* [Japanese fencing]

kenjoogo けんじょうご＝謙譲語 4-1 N humble language

kenka (o) suru けんか (を) する＝喧嘩 (を) する 2-4 V3 (to) fight [personal]

kenkoo けんこう＝健康 3-8 N health

kenkooteki けんこうてき＝健康的 3-8 Na healthy

kenkyo けんきょ＝謙虚 4-7 Na humble

kenpei けんぺい＝憲兵 4-3 N military police [MP]

(sentence) keredo けれど 2-6 Pc Although 〜

kesa けさ＝今朝　　　　　　　　　1-12 N　　this morning
keshigomu けしごむ＝消しゴム　　　1-2　 N　　eraser [rubber]
keshiki けしき＝景色　　　　　　　4-8　 N　　view; scenery
(o)keshoo (o) suru （お）けしょう（を）する＝(御) 化粧 (を) する
　　　　　　　　　　　　　　　　3-2　 V3　　(to) apply make-up
kesshite + Neg. けっして＋ Neg.　　2-4　 Adv　never
ki き＝木　　　　　　　　　　　　1-10 N　　tree
ki o tsukeru きをつける＝気をつける/きをつけます 2-3　V2　(to) be careful
kibishii きびしい＝厳しい　　　　　1-6　 A　　is strict
(〜ga) kieru (〜が) きえる＝消える/きえます
　　　　　　　　　　　　　　　　4-4　 V2　　(something) turns off [intransitive]
kifu (o) suru きふ (を) する＝寄付 (を) する　4-7　V3　(to) donate
kiiro きいろ＝黄色　　　　　　　　1-5　 N　　yellow
kiiroi きいろい＝黄色い　　　　　　1-6　 A　　is yellow
kikoemasen きこえません＝聞こえません　1-2　V2　cannot hear
kikoemasu きこえます＝聞こえます　1-2　V2　can hear
(something ga) kikoeru きこえる＝聞こえる/きこえます 2-3　V2　〜 can be heard
kiku きく＝聞く/ききます　　　　　1-4　 V1　　(to) listen, hear
(person ni) kiku きく＝聞く/ききます 2-3　V1　　(to) ask someone
(〜ga) kimaru (〜が) きまる＝決まる/きまります
　　　　　　　　　　　　　　　　4-2　 V1　　(to) be decided [intransitive]
(〜o) kimeru (〜を) きめる＝決める/きめます　4-2　V2　(to) decide [transitive]
kimochi ga ii きもちがいい＝気持ちがいい 2-14 A　is pleasant; comfortable
kimochi ga warui きもちがわるい＝気持ちが悪い
　　　　　　　　　　　　　　　　2-14　 A　　is unpleasant; uncomfortable
kin きん＝金　　　　　　　　　　　2-15 N　　gold
kinchoo (o) suru きんちょう (を) する＝緊張 (を) する　4-8　V3　(to) become nervous
kinen きんえん＝禁煙　　　　　　　4-8　 N　　no smoking
kinensha きんえんしゃ＝禁煙車　　 4-8　 N　　non-smoking car
kiniro きんいろ＝金色　　　　　　　1-5　 N　　gold (color)
kinjo no hito きんじょのひと＝近所の人　4-3　N　neighbor
kinniku きんにく＝筋肉　　　　　　4-7　 N　　muscles
(O)kinodoku ni. (お) きのどくに。＝(御) 気の毒に。
　　　　　　　　　　　　　　　　2-6　 Exp　I am sorry. [sympathy, formal]
kinoo きのう＝昨日　　　　　　　　1-4　 N　　yesterday
kinyoobi きんようび＝金曜日　　　　1-7　 N　　Friday
kippu きっぷ＝切符　　　　　　　　1-15 N　　ticket
kirai きらい＝嫌い　　　　　　　　1-5　 Na　dislike
kirei きれい　　　　　　　　　　　1-6　 Na　pretty; clean; neat; nice
kirei ni suru きれいにする　　　　　2-14 V3　(to) make clean; to clean
kirisutokyoo キリストきょう＝キリスト教 2-7　N　Christianity
Kiritsu. きりつ。＝起立。　　　　　1-1　 Exp　Stand.
kiru きる＝切る/きります　　　　　2-14 V1　(to) cut; slice

kiru きる＝着る/きます	2-3	V2	(to) wear [above the waist or on the entire body]
kisetsu きせつ＝季節	3-8	N	season
kisoku きそく＝規則	2-3	N	rule; regulation
kissaten きっさてん＝喫茶店	1-13	N	coffee shop
kita きた＝北	2-1	N	north
kitaguchi きたぐち＝北口	3-9	N	north entrance/exit
kitanai きたない	1-6	A	dirty; messy
kitte きって＝切手	3-3	N	stamp
kitto きっと	4-8	Adv	surely; most certainly
ko こな＝粉	4-4	N	powder
- ko - こ＝- 個	2-5	Nd	[general counter, informal]
kochira こちら	1-3	N	this one [polite equiv. of これ to introduce a person]
kochira こちら	2-5	N	here [polite equiv. of ここ]
kochira こちら	2-9	N	this one [polite equiv. of これ]
Kochirakoso. こちらこそ。	3-1	Exp	(It is) I, (not you.) [emphasis]
kodama こだま	4-8	N	Echo [A *shinkansen* that stops at most of the *shinkansen* stations.]
kodomo こども＝子供	1-10	N	child
koe こえ＝声	1-6	N	voice
(〜ni) koi (o) suru (〜 に) こい (を) する＝恋 (を) する			
	4-7	V3	(to) fall in love (with person)
koko ここ	1-2	N	here
kokonoka ここのか＝九日	1-11	N	the ninth day of the month
kokonotsu ここのつ＝九つ	1-2	N	nine [general counter]
kokoro こころ＝心	1-6	N	heart
komaasharu コマーシャル	3-6	N	commercial
komaru こまる＝困る/こまります	3-3	V1	be troubled
komori (o) suru こもり (を) する＝子守り (を) する	4-2	V3	(to) babysit
komu こむ＝込む/こみます	2-13	V1	(to) get crowded
komugiko こむぎこ＝小麦粉	4-3	N	(wheat) flour
konban こんばん＝今晩	1-7	N	tonight
Konban wa. こんばんは。＝今晩は。	1-7	Exp	Good evening.
konbini コンビニ	2-13	N	convenience store
konde iru こんでいる＝込んでいる/こんでいます	2-13	V1	is crowded
kongakki こんがっき＝今学期	3-2	N	this semester
kongetsu こんげつ＝今月	1-12	N	this month
konkuuru コンクール	2-15	N	competition [music]
Konnichi wa. こんにちは。	1-1	Exp	Hello; Hi.
kono 〜 この 〜	1-2	PN	this 〜
kono naka de このなかで＝この中で	2-9	PN+N+P	among these
konpyuutaa コンピューター	1-4	N	computer

konsaato コンサート	1-15	N	concert
konshuu こんしゅう＝今週	1-11	N	this week
Koobe こうべ＝神戸	2-1	N	Kobe
koocha こうちゃ＝紅茶	4-1	N	black tea
kooen こうえん＝公園	2-2	N	park
koofuku こうふく＝幸福	4-7	Na	happy; fortunate
koogai こうがい＝公害	4-9	N	pollution
koogeki (o) suru こうげき (を) する＝攻撃 (を) する	4-3	V3	(to) attack
koohii コーヒー	1-4	N	coffee
kookoo こうこう＝高校	1-3	N	high school
kookoo ichinensei こうこういちねんせい＝高校一年生	1-3	N	sophomore; tenth grader
kookoo ninensei こうこうにねんせい＝高校二年生	1-3	N	junior; eleventh grader
kookoo sannensei こうこうさんねんせい＝高校三年生	1-3	N	senior; twelfth grader
kookoosei こうこうせい＝高校生	1-3	N	high school student
kookyo こうきょ＝皇居	4-8	N	Imperial Palace
koora コーラ	1-4	N	cola (drink)
kooritsu こうりつ＝公立	3-2	N	public
koosaten こうさてん＝交差点	2-13	N	intersection
kooshuudenwa こうしゅうでんわ＝公衆電話	2-13	N	public phone
kootsuujiko こうつうじこ＝交通事故	2-4	N	traffic accident
kooyoo こうよう＝紅葉	4-6	N	autumn leaves
koppu コップ	1-14	N	cup
kore これ	1-1	N	this one
Kore wa sukoshi desu ga. これはすこしですが ...＝これは少しですが...	4-1	Exp	This is a small gift. [Used when handing someone a gift.]
korekara これから	1-14	SI	from now on
korera これら	4-6	N	these [plural of これ]
(time) koro -ころ	1-7	Nd	about (time)
korosu ころす＝殺す/ころします	4-4	V1	(to) kill
koshoo こしょう＝胡椒	2-14	N	pepper
kotae こたえ＝答え	2-2	N	answer
kotaeru こたえる＝答える/こたえます	2-2	V2	(to) answer
koto こと＝事	1-5	N	thing [intangible]
(Dic./Nai) koto (Dic./Nai) こと	4-9	Nd	[Used in giving instructions, directions, commands or resolutions.]
(Dic./Nai form) koto ni kimaru ～ことにきまる＝決まる/きまります	4-2	N+P+V1	It will be decided that ～
(Dic./Nai form) koto ni kimeru ～ことにきめる＝決める/きめます	4-2	N+P+V2	decide to do ～
(Dic./Nai form) koto ni naru ～ことになる	4-2	N+P+V2	It will be decided that ～
(Dic./Nai form) koto ni suru ～ことにする	4-2	N+P+V3	decide to do ～
kotoba ことば＝言葉	2-15	N	words; language
kotoshi ことし＝今年	1-15	N	this year

kotowaza ことわざ＝諺	3-1	N	proverb
kowai こわい＝恐い	2-4	A	is scary
(〜ga) kowareru (〜が) こわれる＝壊れる/こわれます			
	3-7	V2	(something) breaks [intransitive]
(〜o) kowasu (〜を) こわす＝壊す/こわします			
	3-7	V1	(to) break(something) [transitive]
(o)kozukai (お) こづかい＝(お) 小遣い	3-2	N	allowance
ku く＝九	1-1	N	nine
kubi くび＝首	1-6	N	neck
kuchi くち＝口	1-6	N	mouth
kuchibeni くちべに＝口紅	4-6	N	lipstick
kudamono くだもの＝果物	2-14	N	fruit
(〜o) kudasai. (〜を) ください。＝下さい	1-2	Exp	please give me 〜.
(-te) kudasaimasenka. (-て) くださいませんか。	4-1	E	Would/Won't you do 〜?
(-te) kudasaimasu (〜て) くださいます＝下さいます	3-3	E	(superior) do 〜 for me
kugatsu くがつ＝九月	1-3	N	September
kumo くも＝雲	2-11	N	cloud
kumori くもり＝曇り	2-7	N	cloudy (weather)
kumori ichiji hare くもりいちじはれ＝曇り一時晴れ			
	4-8	N	cloudy and occasionally clear
kun(yomi) くん (よみ)＝訓 (読み)	3-4	N	Japanese reading (of a *kanji*)
kuni くに＝国	2-9	N	country; nation
kuraberu くらべる＝比べる/くらべます	2-9	V2	(to) compare
kurai くらい＝暗い	2-11	A	is dark
〜kurai 〜くらい	1-13	Nd	about 〜 [not for time]
kurasu クラス	1-11	N	class; instruction
kurejitto kaado クレジットカード	2-9	N	credit card
kureru くれる/くれます	1-15	V2	(to) give (to me or to my family)
kurikaesu くりかえす＝繰り返す/くりかえします	3-9	V1	(to) repeat
kurisumasu クリスマス	2-7	N	Christmas
kurisumasukaado クリスマスカード	2-7	N	Christmas card
kurisumasutsurii クリスマスツリー	2-7	N	Christmas tree
kuro くろ＝黒	1-5	N	black
kuroi くろい＝黒い	1-6	A	is black
kuroo (o) suru くろう (を) する＝苦労 (を) する			
	4-2	V3	(to) suffer; have a hard time; struggle
kuru くる＝来る/きます	1-7	V3	(to) come
kuruma くるま＝車	1-7	N	car; vehicle
kurumaisu くるまいす＝車いす	4-9	N	wheelchair
kurushii くるしい＝苦しい	4-2	A	painful; have difficulty; distressing; hard; tough; poor
kusa くさ＝草	3-2	N	grass
kusai くさい＝臭い	3-8	A	(is) smelly

kusuri くすり=薬	1-12	N	medicine
kutsu くつ=靴	1-13	N	shoes
kutsushita くつした=靴下	2-3	N	socks
kuuki くうき=空気	4-9	N	air
kuukoo くうこう=空港	2-13	N	airport
kyaku きゃく=客	3-7	N	customer; guest
kyakuma きゃくま=客間	3-7	N	room where guests are received
kyandii キャンディ	2-5	N	candy
kyanpu キャンプ	1-7	N	camp
kyoku きょく=曲	3-6	N	musical piece; song
kyonen きょねん=去年	1-15	N	last year
kyoo きょう=今日	1-4	N	today
kyoodai きょうだい=兄弟	1-3	N	(my) sibling(s)
kyoodootoire きょうどうトイレ=共同トイレ	4-3	N	community restroom
(danjo) kyoogaku (だんじょ) きょうがく＝(男女) 共学	3-2	N	co-educational
kyooiku きょういく=教育	3-2	N	education
kyookai きょうかい=教会	2-7	N	church
kyookasho きょうかしょ=教科書	1-2	N	textbook
kyoomi きょうみ=興味	3-4	N	(personal) interest
kyooryoku (o) suru きょうりょく (を) する=協力 (を) する	4-7	V3	(to) cooperate
kyooryokuteki きょうりょくてき=協力的	4-7	Na	cooperative
kyooshitsu きょうしつ=教室	1-10	N	classroom
Kyooto きょうと＝京都	2-1	N	Kyoto
kyuu ni きゅうに=急に	2-4	Adv	suddenly
kyuu きゅう=九	1-1	N	nine
kyuu-juu きゅうじゅう=九十	1-1	N	ninety
kyuukyuusha きゅうきゅうしゃ=救急車	2-4	N	ambulance
kyuuryoo きゅうりょう=給料	3-6	N	salary; pay
Kyuushuu きゅうしゅう=九州	2-1	N	Kyushu

<M>

maamaa まあまあ	1-5	Adv	so, so
machi まち=町	2-13	N	town
machigaeru まちがえる=間違える/まちがえます	2-6	V2	(to) make a mistake
mada まだ + Aff.	2-2	Adv	still
mada まだ + Neg.	1-14	Adv	(not) yet
Mada desu. まだです。	1-14	Exp	Not yet.
〜made 〜まで	1-11	P	to 〜; until 〜
(time) made ni までに	2-10	P	by (a certain time)
mado まど=窓	1-10	N	window
mae まえ= 前	1-3	N	before
mae まえ= 前	2-2	N	front
〜mae 〜まえ= 〜前	1-7	Nd	before 〜
(Dic. form) mae ni (Dic. form) まえに=-前に	3-6	N+P	Before 〜

(～no) mae ni (～の) まえに＝(～の) 前に 1-12 P+N+P before ～

(place de/o) magaru まがる＝曲がる/まがります 2-4 V1 (to) turn at/along (place)

mago まご＝孫	4-2	N	own grandchild(ren)
- mai - まい＝- 枚	1-2	Nd	[counter for flat objects]
maigakki　まいがっき＝毎学期	3-2	N	every semester

maigo ni naru まいごになる＝迷子になる/なります 3-9 V1 (to) get lost

mainen まいねん＝毎年	1-15	N	every year
mainichi まいにち＝毎日	1-4	N	everyday
mairu まいる＝参る/まいります	4-1	V1	(to) come; go [humble equiv. of 来る, 行く]
maishuu まいしゅう＝毎週	1-11	N	every week
maitoshi まいとし＝毎年	1-15	N	every year
maitsuki まいつき＝毎月	1-12	N	every month
majime　まじめ＝真面目	3-3	Na	is serious
makeru まける＝負ける/まけます	1-12	V2	(to) lose
makka まっか＝真っ赤	4-4	N	bright red
makkura まっくら＝真っ暗	4-4	N	pitch dark
makkuro まっくろ＝真っ黒	4-4	N	pitch black
～mama ～まま	4-9	Nd	as it is; unchanged
mamoru まもる＝守る/まもります	4-3	V1	(to) protect; follow (the rules)
(ichi)man (いち) まん＝(一) 万	1-13	N	ten thousand
manga まんが＝漫画	3-4	N	comics
mannaka まんなか＝真ん中	4-4	N	center; middle
maru まる＝丸	3-8	N	circle
maru (o) suru まる (を) する＝丸 (を) する	3-8	V3	(to) circle
marui まるい＝丸い	3-8	A	is round
～masen ka ～ませんか	1-7	Dv	won't you do ～? [invitation]
～mashoo ～ましょう	1-7	Dv	let's do ～ [suggestion]
masshiro まっしろ＝真っ白	4-4	N	pure white
massugu まっすぐ	2-13	Adv	straight
mata また＝又	1-10	Adv	again

(Ja) mata ato de. (じゃ) またあとで。＝(じゃ) また後で。

1-14 Exp (Well,) see you later.

Mata doozo. またどうぞ。 2-9 Exp Please come again.

Mata irashite kudasai. また、いらしてください。＝また、いらして下さい。

4-1 Exp Please come again. [More polite than また、来て下さい。]

matcha まっちゃ＝抹茶	4-6	N	powdered green tea
matsu まつ＝松	4-7	N	pine tree
matsu まつ＝待つ/まちます	1-13	V1	(to) wait
mawasu まわす＝回す/まわします	4-6	V1	(to) turn (something) around; circulate [transitive]
mayaku　まやく＝麻薬	3-2	N	drugs

mazu まず	2-14	SI	first of all
mazui まずい	1-13	A	is unappetizing; is tasteless
mazushii まずしい＝貧しい	4-3	A	be poor [more formal than びんぼう]
mazushisa まずしさ＝貧しさ	4-3	N	poverty
me め＝目	1-6	N	eye
me ga fujiyuu na hito めがふじゆうなひと＝目が不自由な人	4-9	N	a blind person
mechakucha めちゃくちゃ	3-4	Na	messy; confusing; incorrect
megane めがね＝眼鏡	2-3	N	eyeglasses
meibutsu めいぶつ＝名物	4-8	N	well-known product (of a given area)
Meijijidai めいじじだい＝明治時代	4-2	N	Meiji Period (1868 - 1912)
meirei (o) suru めいれい (を) する＝命令 (を) る	4-3	V3	(to) command; order
menyuu メニュー	2-5	N	menu
meshiagaru めしあがる＝召し上がる/めしあがります	4-1	V1	(to) eat; drink [honorific equiv. of 食べる, 飲む]
meshita no hito めしたのひと＝目下の人	4-1	N	person of inferior status [lit., a person below your eye level]
meue no hito めうえのひと＝目上の人	4-1	N	someone whom you respect; a superior [lit., a person above your eye level]
mezurashii めずらしい＝珍しい	3-8	A	is rare; unusual
michi みち＝道	2-4	N	street; road
midori みどり＝緑	1-5	N	green
midori no madoguchi みどりのまどぐち＝みどりの窓口	4-8	N	JR ticket window
miemasen みえません＝見えません	2-1	V2	cannot see
miemasu みえます＝見えます	2-1	V2	can see
(something ga) mieru みえる＝見える/みえます	2-3	V2	～ can be seen
(ha o) migaku　(はを) みがく＝歯を磨く/みがきます	3-3	V1	(to) brush teeth
migi みぎ＝右	2-2	N	right side
mijikai みじかい＝短い	1-6	A	is short [not for height]
mikata みかた＝味方	4-3	N	ally; friend; supporter
mikka みっか＝三日	1-11	N	the third day of the month
mimi みみ＝耳	1-6	N	ear
minami みなみ＝南	2-1	N	south
minamiguchi みなみぐち＝南口	3-9	N	south entrance/exit
minasan みなさん＝皆さん	1-15	N	everyone [polite]
minato みなと＝港	4-3	N	port; harbor
minna みんな＝皆	1-15	N	everyone
(Verb TE) miru みる/みます	2-5	Dv	try doing ～
miru みる＝見る/みます	1-4	V2	(to) watch; look; see
miruku ミルク	1-4	N	(cow's) milk
(o)mise (お) みせ＝(御) 店	1-13	N	store
miseru みせる＝見せる/みせます	1-13	V2	(to) show
Misete kudasai. みせてください。＝見せて下さい。	1-2	Exp	Please show (it) to me.
(o)misoshiru (お) みそしる＝(御) 味噌汁	2-5	N	soup flavored with *miso*

~mitai (da) 〜みたい (だ)　　　　　　　4-8　A　seems 〜 [informal equiv. of 〜よう (だ)]

Mite kudasai. みてください。＝見て下さい。1-2 Exp　Please look.

(〜ga) mitsukaru みつかる＝見つかる/みつかります　3-4　V1　(something) is found

(〜o) mitsukeru みつける＝見つける/みつけます　3-4　V2　(to) find (something)

mittsu みっつ＝三つ　　　　　　　　　1-2　N　three [general counter]

(o)miyage (お) みやげ＝(御) 土産　　　　2-9　N　souvenir gift

(o)mizu (お) みず＝(御) 水　　　　　　1-4　N　water

〜mo 〜も (+ Aff.)　　　　　　　　　1-3　P　too; also

〜mo 〜も (+ Neg.)　　　　　　　　　1-3　P　either

(counter) mo (counter) も　　　　　　2-6　P　as many/long as 〜

mochiron もちろん　　　　　　　　　2-6　SI　of course

moenai gomi もえないゴミ＝燃えないゴミ 4-9　N　inflammable garbage

(〜ga) moeru (〜が) もえる＝燃える／もえます　4-9 V2 (something) burns [intransitive]

moeru gomi もえるゴミ＝燃えるゴミ　4-9　N　flammable garbage

mokuyoobi もくようび＝木曜日　　　　1-7　N　Thursday

momiji もみじ＝紅葉　　　　　　　　4-6　N　maple leaves

mon もん＝門　　　　　　　　　　　　2-3　N　gate

mondai もんだい＝問題　　　　　　　2-6　N　problem

mono もの＝物　　　　　　　　　　　1-5　N　thing [tangible]

moo もう＋ Aff.　　　　　　　　　　1-14　Exp　already

moo もう＋ Neg.　　　　　　　　　　2-2　Adv　(not) any more

moo (ippai) もう (いっぱい)＝もう (一杯)　1-14 Adv　(one) more (cup)

moo ichido もういちど＝もう一度　　1-1　Adv　one more time

moo sugu もうすぐ　　　　　　　　　1-15 Adv　very soon

mookeru もうける＝儲ける/もうけます　4-2　V2　(to) earn/make (money)

Mooshiwake gozaimasen.　　　　　　4-1　Exp　I am sorry. [polite}

(〜to) moosu (〜と) もうす＝申す/もうします

　　　　　　　　　　　　　　　　　4-1　V1　(to) ay 〜 [humble equiv. of 言う]

morau もらう/もらいます　　　　　　1-15 V1　(to) receive; get from

moshi もし　　　　　　　　　　　　　3-7　Adv　If

Moshi moshi. もしもし。　　　　　　2-6　Exp　Hello. [on the phone]

motsu もつ＝持つ/もちます　　　　　2-2　V1　(to) have; hold; carry

mottainai もったいない　　　　　　　4-9　Exp　wasteful; too good

motte iku もっていく＝持って行く/もっていきます　2-7　V1　(to) take (thing)

motte kaeru もってかえる＝持って帰る/もってかえります

　　　　　　　　　　　　　　　　　2-7　V1　(to) take/bring (thing) back home

motte kuru もってくる＝持って来る/もってきます　2-7　V3　(to) bring (thing)

motto もっと　　　　　　　　　　　　2-9　Adv　more

mottomo もっとも＝最も　　　　　　　4-6　Adv　the most

muika むいか＝六日　　　　　　　　　1-11 N　the sixth day of the month

mujitsu むじつ＝無実　　　　　　　　4-4　Na　innocent

(person o) mukae ni iku むかえにいく＝迎えに行く/むかえにいきます

　　　　　　　　　　　　　　　　　2-10 V1　(to) go to pick up (person)

(person o) mukae ni kaeru むかえにかえる＝迎えに帰る/むかえにかえります

2-10 V1 (to) return to pick up (person)

(person o) mukae ni kuru むかえにくる＝迎えに来る/むかえにきます

2-10 V3 (to) come to pick up (someone)

mukaigawa むかいがわ＝向かい側 3-9 N other side (of)

mukashibanashi むかしばなし＝昔話 2-11 N folk tale

mukashimukashi むかしむかし＝昔々 2-11 N long, long ago

mukoo むこう＝向こう 2-13 N other side; beyond

murasaki むらさき＝紫 1-5 N purple

muryoo むりょう＝無料 4-9 N free of charge [formal]

musekinin むせきにん＝無責任 4-2 Na irresponsible

mushiatsui むしあつい＝蒸し暑い 1-1 A is hot and humid

(o)musubi (お) むすび 1-14 N riceball

musuko むすこ＝息子 2-11 N (own) son

musukosan むすこさん＝息子さん 2-11 N (someone else's) son

musume むすめ＝娘 2-11 N (own) daughter; young lady

musumesan むすめさん＝娘さん 2-11 N (someone else's) daughter; young lady [polite]

muttsu むっつ＝六つ 1-2 N six [general counter]

muzukashii むずかしい＝難しい 1-11 A is difficult

<N>

(sentence) n dattte. (sentence) んだって。 4-8 SE I heard that 〜. [informal]

nabe なべ＝鍋 2-14 N pot; pan

〜nado 〜など 1-15 Nd 〜 etc.

nagai ながい＝長い 1-6 A (is) long

(V stem form) nagara 〜ながら 3-6 Rc While 〜 [Describing a person's simultaneous or concurrent actions]

Nagoya なごや＝名古屋 2-1 N Nagoya

naguru なぐる＝殴る/なぐります 4-2 V1 (to) hit (someone); to beat (someone)

Naha なは＝那覇 2-1 N Naha [a city in Okinawa]

〜naide 〜ないで 4-7 E Without doing 〜

naifu ナイフ 1-14 N knife

naka なか＝中 2-2 N inside

(〜to) naka ga ii (〜と) なかがいい＝仲がいい 4-7 A be on good terms with 〜

(〜to) naka ga warui (〜と) なかがわるい＝仲が悪い 4-7 A be on bad terms with 〜

nakanaka + Neg. なかなか+ Neg. 3-4 Adv (not) easily 〜

-nakereba narimasen -なければなりません 2-5 Dv have to (do); should (do)

naku なく＝泣く/なきます 2-15 V1 (to) cry

-nakucha(ikenai/naranai) -なくちゃ (いけない/ならない)

4-9 Dv have to do [informal use of -なければならない]

nakunaru なくなる＝亡くなる/なくなります

3-6 V1 (to) pass away; die [polite form of しぬ]

-nakutemo iidesu -なくてもいいです 2-5 Dv do not have to (do); no need to (do)

-nakya(ikenai/naranai) -なきゃ (いけない/ならない)

	4-9	Dv	have to do [informal use of -なければならない]
nama tamago なまたまご＝生卵	2-14	N	raw egg
namae なまえ＝名前	1-3	N	name
(o)namae おなまえ＝御名前	1-3	N	(someone's) name [polite]
namakemono なまけもの＝怠け者	4-7	N	lazy person
namida o nagasu なみだをながす＝涙を流す	4-7	V1	(to) cry [lit., to shed tears]
nan なん＝何	1-1	Ni	what?
nan-bai なんばい＝何杯	1-14	Ni	how many cups?
nan-gatsu なんがつ＝何月	1-3	Ni	what month?
nan-nensei なんねんせい＝何年生	1-3	N	what grade?
nan-nichi なんにち＝何日	1-11	Ni	(the) what day of the month?
nan-nin なんにん＝何人	1-3	Ni	how many people?
nan-sai なんさい＝何歳, 何才	1-3	Ni	how old?
nan-satsu なんさつ＝何冊	1-15	Ni	how many [bound objects]?
nan-yoobi なんようび＝何曜日	1-7	Ni	what day of the week?
nana なな＝七	1-1	N	seven
nana-juu ななじゅう＝七十	1-1	N	seventy
nanatsu ななつ＝七つ	1-2	N	seven [general counter]
nanbiki なんびき＝何匹	1-10	Ni	how many [small animals]?
nanbon なんぼん＝何本	1-10	Ni	how many [long cylindrical objects]?
nandai なんだい＝何台	1-10	Ni	how many [mechanized goods]?
nandemo なんでも＝何でも	3-1	Ni+P	anything
nandomo なんども＝何度も	2-6	Adv	many times
nani なに＝何	1-1	Ni	what?
Nani o sashiagemashoo ka. なにをさしあげましょうか。＝何を差し上げましょうか。			
	2-9	Exp	May I help you?
nani-jin なにじん＝何人	1-3	Ni	what nationality?
nanigo なにご＝何語	1-4	Ni	what language?
naniiro なにいろ＝何色	1-5	N	what color?
nanika なにか＝何か	2-15	N	something
nanika ～ mono なにか～もの＝何か～物	4-6	N	something ～
nanimo なにも＝何も＋ Neg.	1-4	Ni+P	(not) anything
nanji なんじ＝何時	1-7	Ni	what time?
～nanka ～なんか	4-9	Nd	and so on; and the like; for example; things like ～ [informal use of など]
nanninmo なんにんも＝何人も	4-3	N	several people
～nano? ～なの？	3-1	SP	[female sentence ending particle]
nanoka なのか＝七日	1-11	N	the seventh day of the month
nanwa なんわ＝何羽	1-10	Ni	how many [birds]?
naosu なおす＝直す/なおします	3-7	V1	(to) fix
napukin ナプキン	1-14	N	napkin
Nara なら＝奈良	2-1	N	Nara

(〜ga) narabu (〜が) ならぶ＝並ぶ/ならびます	4-8	V1	(someone/something) lines up [Intransitive]
narau ならう＝習う/ならいます	2-2	V1	(to) learn
nareetaa ナレーター	2-11	N	narrator
narimasen なりません	2-5	V1	it won't do
(〜ni) naru なる/なります	2-12	V1	(to) become 〜
Naruhodo. なるほど。	2-11	Exp	Indeed! I see!
(V stem) nasai. 〜なさい。	4-3	E	Do 〜. [polite command]
nasaru なさる/なさいます	4-1	V1	(to) do [honorific equiv. of する]
natsu なつ＝夏	1-12	N	summer
natsukashii なつかしい＝懐かしい	3-6	A	is nostalgic
nattoo なっとう＝納豆	3-8	N	fermented soybeans
nayami なやみ＝悩み	4-7	N	trouble; worry [personal]
nayamu なやむ＝悩む/なやみます	4-7	V1	(to) be troubled; be worried [personal]
naze なぜ	1-11	Ni	why?
Nazenara なぜなら	4-2	SI	That's because
(sentence) n datte. (sentence) んだって。	4-8		I heard that 〜. [informal]
(sentence) ne. (sentence) ね。	1-6	SP	isn't it? [sentence ending particle]
(o)nedan (お) ねだん＝(御) 値段	2-9	N	price
nekkuresu ネックレス	2-3	N	necklace
neko ねこ＝猫	1-10	N	cat
nemui ねむい＝眠い	1-12	A	is sleepy
- nen - ねん＝ - 年	1-15	Nd	- year
- nen(kan) - ねんかん＝ - 年間	2-6	Nd	- year(s)
- nendai - ねんだい＝- 年代	4-2	N	decade [1970 年代 means 1970's.]
nengajoo ねんがじょう＝年賀状	2--7	N	New Year's card
neru ねる＝寝る/ねます	1-7	V2	(to) sleep; go to bed
netsu ねつ＝熱	1-12	N	fever
nezumi ねずみ＝鼠	1-10	N	mouse
〜 ni 〜 に	2-6	P	per 〜
〜 ni 〜 〜に〜	2-5	P	〜 and 〜 (as a set)
ni に＝ニ	1-1	N	two
(place) ni に (+ direction verb)	1-7	P	to (place)
(place) ni に (+ existence verb)	1-10	P	in; at (place)
(specific time) ni に	1-7	P	at (specific time)
(activity) ni に	1-7	P	for (activity)
〜ni chigainai 〜にちがいない	4-8	E	must be 〜; without doubt
〜ni tsuite 〜について	2-2	P+V	about 〜
〜ni yoruto 〜によると	3-6	P+V+P	according to 〜
ni-juu にじゅう＝二十	1-1	N	twenty
(〜)ni yotte 〜によって	4-6	P+V	by 〜 [formal equiv. of 〜に]
(〜)ni yotte 〜によって	4-8	P+V	depending on 〜
- nichi - にち＝ - 日	1-11	Nd	day of the month

- nichi(kan) - にち (かん) = - 日 (間)	2-6	Nd	- day(s)
nichibei にちべい = 日米	4-3	N	Japan-U.S.
nichiyoobi にちようび = 日曜日	1-7	N	Sunday
Nido aru koto wa sando aru. にどあることはさんどある。 = 二度あることは三度ある。			
	3-2	Prov	If something happens twice, it will happen three times.
nigai にがい = 苦い	3-8	A	is bitter
nigate にがて = 苦手	1-5	Na	be weak in
nigatsu にがつ = 二月	1-3	N	February
nigeru にげる = 逃げる/にげます	4-4	V2	(to) escape; run away
(o)nigiri (お) にぎり	1-14	N	riceball
nigirizushi にぎりずし = にぎり寿司	2-5	N	*sushi* rice shaped in bite-sized rectangles topped with fish, roe, shellfish, vegetables or egg
nigiyaka にぎやか = 賑やか	3-6	Na	lively; bustling
nihon にほん = 日本	1-3	N	Japan
(〜wa) nihongo de nan to iimasu ka. (〜は) にほんごでなんといいますか。			
= (〜は) 日本語で何と言いますか。	1-1	Exp	How do you say 〜 in Japanese?
nihongo にほんご = 日本語	1-4	N	Japanese language
nihongun にほんぐん = 日本軍	4-3	N	Japanese military
nihonjin にほんじん = 日本人	1-3	N	Japanese citizen
nijuu-yokka にじゅうよっか = 二十四日	1-11	N	the twenty-fourth day of the month
nikaidate にかいだて = 二階建て	3-7	N	two story house
nikkei(jin) にっけい (じん) = 日系 (人)	4-2	N	person of Japanese descent
nikki にっき = 日記	4-8	N	a diary; journal
nikoniko ニコニコ	2-15	Adv	smilingly [onomatopoetic]
(V stem) nikui (V stem) にくい	3-4	A	is hard to do 〜
nikuudon にくうどん = 肉うどん	2-5	N	*udon* topped with beef
nimono にもの = 煮物	3-11	N	boiled (in broth) foods
nimotsu にもつ = 荷物	4-8	N	baggage; bags
- nin - にん = - 人	1-3	Nd	[counter for people]
ninjin にんじん = 人参	3-1	N	carrot
ninki ga aru にんきがある = 人気がある/あります	3-6	V1	(to) be popular
ninshin (o) suru にんしん (を) する = 妊娠 (を) する	4-2	V3	(to) get pregnant
nioi におい = 臭い	2-7	N	smell; fragrance
niru にる = 煮る/にます	3-8	V2	(to) boil (in broth); simmer
nisei にせい = 二世	4-2	N	second generation
nishi にし = 西	2-1	N	west
nishiguchi にしぐち = 西口	3-9	N	west entrance/exit
nishikaigan にしかいがん = 西海岸	4-3	N	west coast
nitteihyoo にっていひょう = 日程表	4-8	N	itinerary; daily schedule
niwa にわ = 庭	1-10	N	garden; yard
no の	1-3	P	[possessive and descriptive particle]

JE

〜 no? 〜の？	3-1	SP	[female sentence ending particle]
noboru のぼる＝登る／のぼります	4-8	V1	(to) climb
〜 node 〜ので	3-3	R	since 〜; because 〜 [expected result] ; 〜, so
nodo のど＝喉	1-6	N	throat
Nodo ga karakara desu. のどがカラカラです。＝喉がカラカラです。			
	1-14	Exp	I am thirsty.
Nodo ga kawakimashita. のどがかわきました。＝喉が渇きました。			
	1-14	Exp	I got thirsty.
nohara のはら＝野原	4-7	N	field
nokori のこり＝残り	4-9	N	leftovers; remainder(s)
(〜ga) nokoru (〜が) のこる＝残る／のこります			
	4-9	V1	(something) remains [intransitive]
nomaseru のませる＝飲ませる／のませます	4-4	V1	(to) make someone drink [causative]; give someone a drink
nomimono のみもの＝飲み物	1-5	N	a drink
nomu のむ＝飲む／のみます	1-4	V1	(to) drink
(kusuri o) nomu のむ＝飲む／のみます	1-12	V1	(to) take (medicine)
〜noni 〜のに	3-3	Rc	in spite of 〜; although 〜 [reverse result]
noogyoo のうぎょう＝農業	4-3	N	agriculture; farming
nooto ノート	1-2	N	notebook
noriba のりば＝乗り場	3-9	N	place of embarkment; place one gets on a vehicle
(vehicle ni) noru のる＝乗る／のります	2-4	V1	(to) ride
nozomi のぞみ	4-8	N	Hope [A *shinkansen* that stops at only the largest *shinkansen* stations]
nryo (o) suru えんりょ (を) する＝遠慮 (を) する	3-8	V3	(to) hesitate; be reserved
nugu ぬぐ＝脱ぐ／ぬぎます	3-2	V1	(to) remove clothing [i.e., shoes, dress, hat]
(〜ga) nureru (〜が) ぬれる＝濡れる／ぬれます	4-8	V2	(someone/something) gets wet [intransitive]
nusumu ぬすむ＝盗む／ぬすみます	4-2	V1	to steal

<O>

(street) o 〜を	2-4	P	through 〜; along 〜
Oagari kudasai. おあがりください。＝お上がり下さい。	4-1	Exp	Please step up. [More polite than 上がって下さい。]
oba おば＝叔母	3-1	N	(one's own) aunt
obaasan おばあさん	1-3	N	grandmother; elderly woman
obasan おばさん	1-15	N	aunt; middle aged woman
oboeru おぼえる＝覚える／おぼえます	2-6	V2	(to) memorize
ocha おちゃ＝お茶	1-4	N	tea
Ochanomizu おちゃノみず＝御茶ノ水	3-9	N	Ochanomizu [a city in Tokyo]

(～ga) ochiru (～が) おちる＝落ちる/おちます

                         4-4 V2   (something) drops; falls [intransitive]

ochitsuku おちつく＝落ち着く/おちつきます   3-7 V1 (to) become calm

odori おどり＝踊り   3-6 N   dance

odoroku おどろく＝驚く/おどろきます 4-2 V1   (to) be surprised; be shocked

odoru おどる＝踊る/おどります   3-6 V1   (to) dance

Ohairi kudasai. おはいりください。＝お入り下さい。   4-1 Exp Please come in.

                         [More polite than 入って下さい]

Ohayoo. おはよう。   1-1 Exp Good morning. [informal]

Ohayoo gozaimasu. おはようございます。 1-1 Exp Good morning. [formal]

ohisama おひさま＝御日様   2-11 N   sun [polite]

Ohisashiburi desu. おひさしぶりです。＝お久しぶりです。

                         3-3 Exp   (I) have not seen you for a long time.

oishasan おいしゃさん＝御医者さん 1-3 N   (medical) doctor [polite form of いしゃ]

oishii おいしい＝美味しい   1-13 A   is delicious

Ojamashimashita. おじゃましました。＝御邪魔しました。

                         4-1 Exp Thank you for allowing me to trouble
                                    you. [Used when leaving after a visit.
                                    lit., I have committed a rudeness.]

Ojamashimasu. おじゃまします。＝御邪魔します。

                         4-1 Exp Excuse me. [lit., I will commit a
                                    rudeness by troubling you. Used after
                                    one enters the host's home.]

oji おじ＝叔父   3-1 N   (one's own) uncle

ojigi (o) suru おじぎ (を) する   4-6 V3   (to) bow

ojiisan おじいさん   1-3 N   grandfather; elderly man

ojisan おじさん   1-15 N   uncle; man

okaasan おかあさん＝お母さん   1-3 N   (someone's) mother

Okaerinasai. おかえりなさい。   3-1 Exp Welcome home. [Used by a family
  ＝お帰りなさい。   member who welcomes another
                                    family member home.]

Okagesama de. おかげさまで。＝御陰様で。   3-3 Exp Thanks to you . . .

Okawari おかわり＝お代わり   3-8 N   second serving

Okawari wa? おかわりは？＝御代わりは？ 3-8 Exp Will you have seconds?

Okinawa おきなわ＝沖縄   2-1 N   Okinawa

okiru おきる＝起きる/おきます   1-7 V2   (to) wake up; get up

(～ga) okiru (～が) おきる＝起きる/おきます

                         4-4 V2   (something) happens [intransitive]

okoru おこる＝怒る/おこります   2-15 V1 (to) become angry

(～o) okosu (～を) おこす＝起こす/おこします   4-4 V1   (to) cause [transitive]

(-te) oku (～て) おく/おきます   3-8 V1   (to) do (something in advance)

oku おく＝置く/おきます   2-5 V1   (to) put; leave

okuru おくる＝送る/おくります   2-7 V1   (to) send; mail

JE

okusan おくさん＝奥さん 3-6 N (someone else's) wife
okyakusama おきゃくさま＝御客様 4-1 N customer; guest [polite]
Omedetoo gozaimasu. おめでとうございます 1-15 Exp Congratulations.
omae おまえ 4-3 N you [used to an inferior by male]
omagosan おまごさん＝お孫さん 4-2 N other's grandchild(ren)
omamori おまもり＝御守り 4-8 N good-luck charm
omoi おもい＝重い 3-7 A is heavy
omoidasu おもいだす＝思い出す/おもいだします 3-4 V1 (to) recall
omoide おもいで＝思い出 4-8 N memories
omoshiroi おもしろい＝面白い 1-11 A is interesting; is funny
omote おもて＝表 4-4 N front (side)
(-oo to) omotte iru (-oo と) おもっている＝思っている
 3-8 V1+V1 (I am) thinking of doing
omou おもう＝思う/おもいます 2-11 V1 (to) think
on(yomi) おん (よみ)＝音 (読み) 3-4 N Chinese reading (of a *kanji*)
onaji おなじ＝同じ 2-9 N same
onaka おなか＝お腹 1-6 N stomach
Onaka ga ippai desu. おなかがいっぱいです＝お腹が一杯です 1-14 Exp (I am) full.
Onaka ga pekopeko desu. おなかがペコペコです。＝お腹がペコペコです。
 1-14 Exp I am hungry.
Onaka ga sukimashita. おなかがすきました。＝お腹が空きました。
 1-14 Exp I got hungry.
ondo おんど＝温度 2-7 N (weather) temperature
oneesan おねえさん＝お姉さん 1-3 N (someone's) older sister
Onegaishimasu. おねがいします。＝御願いします。 1-1 Exp Please. [request]
ongaku おんがく＝音楽 1-5 N music
oniisan おにいさん＝お兄さん 1-3 N (someone's) older brother
onna おんな＝女 1-10 N female
onna no hito おんなのひと＝女の人 1-10 N woman; lady
onna no ko おんなのこ＝女の子 1-10 N girl
onsen おんせん＝温泉 4-8 N hot spring
ooen (o) suru おうえん (を) する＝応援 (を) する 2-10 V3 (to) cheer
ooi おおい＝多い 1-11 A (are) many, much
ookii おおきい＝大きい 1-6 A (is) big
orenji (iro) オレンジいろ＝オレンジ色 1-5 N orange (color)
(kaidan o) oriru おりる＝下りる/おります 3-7 V2 (to) go down (stairs)
(vehicle kara/o) oriru おりる＝降りる 2-4 V2 (to) get off (vehicle)
oru おる/おります 4-1 V1 (to) be [humble equiv. of いる]
Osaka おおさか＝大阪 2-1 N Osaka
Osaki ni. おさきに。＝お先に。 3-1 Exp Excuse me for going/doing something first.
Osewa ni narimashita. おせわになりました。＝お世話になりました。
 3-3 Exp Thank you for your kind help.

oshaberi おしゃべり　　　　　　　　4-3　N　　chatting; a chatterbox
oshaberi (o) suru おしゃべり (を) する 4-3 V3　(to) chat
oshie おしえ＝教え　　　　　　　　4-6　N　　teaching
oshieru おしえる＝教える/おしえます 2-4　V2　(to) teach
oshimai おしまい　　　　　　　　　2-11 N　　the end
oshirase おしらせ＝お知らせ　　　　4-3　N　　announcement
Oshooban itashimasu. おしょうばんいたします。＝お相伴いたします。
　　　　　　　　　　　　　　　　　4-6　Exp　I will accompany you. {tea ceremony}
osoi おそい＝遅い　　　　　　　　1-7　A　　is late
osoku おそく＝遅く　　　　　　　 1-12 Adv late (+ verb)
Osoku narimashita. おそくなりました。＝遅くなりました。
　　　　　　　　　　　　　　　　　2-14 Exp　Sorry to be late.
ossharu おっしゃる/おっしゃいます　4-1　V1　(to) say [honorific equiv. of 言う]
osu おす＝押す/おします　　　　　4-4　V1　(to) push
Osuki desu ka. おすきですか。＝お好きですか。2-9　Exp　Do you like it? [polite]
otaku おたく＝お宅　　　　　　　　2-6　N　　(someone's) house; residence [polite]
Otemae choodai itashimasu. おてまえちょうだいいたします。
　＝お手前ちょうだいいたします。　4-6 Exp　I will receive your serving. [tea cerem.]
oto おと＝音　　　　　　　　　　　3-3　N　　sound
otoko おとこ＝男　　　　　　　　　1-10 N　　male
otoko no hito おとこのひと＝男の人　1-10 N　　man
otoko no ko おとこのこ＝男の子　　　1-10 N　　boy
otona おとな＝大人　　　　　　　　2-14 N　　adult
otonashii おとなしい　　　　　　　3-3　A　　is quiet (refers to people only)
otoosan おとうさん＝お父さん　　　　1-3　N　　(someone's) father
otooto おとうと＝弟　　　　　　　　1-3　N　　(own) younger brother
otootosan おとうとさん＝弟さん　　　1-3　N　　(someone's) younger brother
otoshidama おとしだま＝御年玉　　　2-7　N　　money received mainly by children
　　　　　　　　　　　　　　　　　　　　　　from adults at New Year's
(〜o) otosu (〜を) おとす＝落とす/おとします
　　　　　　　　　　　　　　　　　4-4　V1　(to) drop (something) [transitive]
ototoi おととい＝一昨日　　　　　　1-11 N　　the day before yesterday
Otsukaresama. おつかれさま。＝お疲れ様。4-9 Exp　Thank you very much (for your
　　　　　　　　　　　　　　　　　　　　　　hard work).
otsuri おつり＝お釣　　　　　　　　2-9　N　　change (from a larger unit of money)
owari ni おわりに＝終わりに　　　　2-14 Adv at the end
Owarimashoo. おわりましょう。＝終わりましょう。1-4　Exp　Let's finish.
(V stem) owaru (V stem) おわる＝終わる/おわります　3-4　V1　(to) finish doing 〜
(〜o) owaru おわる＝終わる/おわります 2-10　V1　(someone will) finish (something)
(〜ga) owaru おわる＝終わる＝おわります 2-10　V1　(something) finish; end
oyako donburi おやこどんぶり＝親子丼 2-5　N　　chicken and egg over a bowl of
　　　　　　　　　　　　　　　　　　　　　　steamed rice
oyakookoo おやこうこう＝親孝行　　4-2　Na　filial piety; devotion to parents

Oyasumi(nasai). お休み (なさい)。=おやすみ (なさい)。 3-1 Exp Good night.
oyasumi ni naru おやすみになる=お休みになる/おやすみになります
 4-1 V1 (to) sleep [honorific equiv. of 寝る]
oyatsu おやつ 4-7 N snacks
oyogu およぐ=泳ぐ/およぎます 1-15 V1 (to) wim
<P>
paama o kakeru パーマをかける/かけます 3-2 V2 (to) perm (one's hair)
- paasento - パーセント 2-5 Nd percent
paatii パーティー 1-7 N party
- pai - ぱい= - 杯 1-14 Nd cupful; glassful; bowlful; spoonful
- paku/- haku - ぱく/- はく =- 泊 4-8 Nd - night(s)
pan パン 1-4 N bread
panda パンダ 3-9 N panda
pantsu パンツ 1-13 N pants
pasupooto パスポート 2-3 N passport
patokaa パトカー 2-4 N patrol car
petto o kau ペットをかう=飼う/かいます 3-3 V1 (to) raise a pet
pettobotoru ペットボトル 4-9 N plastic bottle
piano ピアノ 1-5 N piano
piasu ピアス 2-3 N pierced earrings
pikatto hikaru ピカッとひかる=光る/ひかります 4-4 V1 (to) flash
pikunikku ピクニック 1-7 N picnic
pinku ピンク 1-5 N pink
piza ピザ 1-14 N pizza
- pon - ぽん= - 本 1-10 Nd [counter for long cylindrical objects]
posuto ポスト 3-9 N mail box
potetochippu ポテトチップ 2-4 N potato chips
puranteeshon プランテーション 4-2 N plantation
purasuchikku プラスチック 4-9 N plastic
purezento プレゼント 1-15 N present
puroyakyuu プロやきゅう=プロ野球 3-6 N professional baseball
puuru プール 1-10 N pool
<R>
raamen ラーメン 2-5 N Chinese noodle soup
raigakki　らいがっき=来学期き 3-2 N next semester
raigetsu らいげつ=来月 1-12 N next month
rainen らいねん=来年 1-15 N next year
rairupasu レールパス 4-8 N JR railpass (for foreigners)
raishuu らいしゅう=来週 1-11 N next week
raisukaree ライスカレー 2-5 N curry rice
rajio ラジオ 1-4 N radio
raku　らく=楽 3-3 NA is comfortable
〜rashii 〜らしい 3-8 Da It seems that 〜

Rei. れい。＝礼。	1-1	Exp	Bow.
(o)rei (お) れい＝(御) 礼	3-3	N	thanks; gratitude; appreciation
(o)reijoo (お) れいじょう＝(御) 礼状	3-3	N	thank you letter
reizooko れいぞうこ＝冷蔵庫	3-7	N	refrigerator
reji レジ	2-5	N	cash register
rekishi れきし＝歴史	3-1	N	history
renshuu (o) suru れんしゅう (を) する＝練習 (を) する	1-12	V3	(to) practice
repooto レポート	1-4	N	report; paper
resutoran レストラン	1-7	N	restaurant
rika りか＝理科	3-1	N	science
rikon (o) suru りこん (を) する＝離婚 (を) する	2-15	V3	(to) divorce
risaikuru リサイクル	4-9	N	recycling
rokkaa ロッカー	1-10	N	locker
roku ろく＝六	1-1	N	six
roku-juu ろくじゅう＝六十	1-1	N	sixty
rokugatsu ろくがつ＝六月	1-3	N	June
roojinhoomu ろうじんホーム＝老人ホーム	4-9	N	a care/nursing home for the elderly
rusu るす＝留守	2-6	N	is not at home
ryokan りょかん＝旅館	4-8	N	Japanese inn
ryokoo (o) suru りょこう (を) する＝旅行 (を) する	1-7	V3	(to) travel
ryokoo りょこう＝旅行	1-7	N	trip; traveling
ryoo りょう＝寮	2-2	N	dormitory
ryoohoo りょうほう＝両方	2-9	N	both
ryookin りょうきん＝料金	3-9	N	fare
ryoori (o) suru りょうり (を) する＝料理 (を) する	2-7	V3	(to) cook
ryooshin りょうしん＝両親	2-2	N	(own) parents
ryuugaku (o) suru りゅうがく (を) する＝留学 (を) する	3-2	V3	(to) study abroad

<S>

Saa . . . さあ. . .	2-9	SI	Well . . . [Used when one does not know or is unsure of an answer.]
sabetsu (o) suru さべつ (を) する＝差別 (を) する	4-3	V3	(to) discriminate
sabishii さびしい＝寂しい	3-6	A	is lonely
sadoo さどう＝茶道	4-6	N	tea ceremony
～sae ～さえ	4-3	Nd	even ～
sagasu さがす＝探す/さがします	3-4	V1	(to) look for; search for
- sai - さい＝- 才, - 歳	1-3	Nd	[counter for age]
saifu さいふ＝財布	2-5	N	wallet
saigo さいご＝最後	3-8	N	the last; final
saigo ni さいごに＝最後に	3-8	Adv	at last; finally
saikin さいきん＝最近	3-4	Adv	recently
saikon (o) suru さいこん (を) する＝再婚 (を) する	4-2	V3	(to) remarry
saikoo さいこう＝最高	3-8	N	the best

saikoo ni さいこうに＝最高に	3-8	Adv	the most
sainoo さいのう＝才能	4-7	N	ability; talent
saisho さいしょ＝最初	3-8	N	the first
saisho ni さいしょに＝最初に	3-8	Adv	first of all
saizu サイズ	1-14	N	size
sakana さかな＝魚	1-10	N	fish
(o)sake (お) さけ＝(御) 酒	2-14	N	rice wine; liquor in general
sakkaa サッカー	1-5	N	soccer
saku さく＝咲く/さきます	4-6	V1	(to) bloom
sakura さくら＝桜	4-6	N	cherry blossom
samui さむい＝寒い	1-1	A	is cold (temperature)
samurai さむらい＝侍	3-6	N	Japanese warrior
～san ～さん	1-1	Nd	Mr./Mrs./Ms.
san さん＝三	1-1	N	three
san-juu さんじゅう＝三十	1-1	N	thirty
sandoitchi サンドイッチ	1-14	N	sandwich
sangatsu さんがつ＝三月	1-3	N	March
sangurasu サングラス	2-3	N	sunglasses
sanjo さんじょ＝三女	4-2	N	a third daughter
(～ni) sanka (o) suru (～に) さんか (を) する＝参加 (を) する			
	4-9	V3	(to) participate (in ～)
sankaku さんかく＝三角	3-8	N	triangle
sannan さんなん＝三男	4-2	N	a third son
sanpo (o) suru さんぽ (を) する＝散歩 (を) する	2-15	V3	(to) take a walk
sansei (o) suru さんせい (を) する＝賛成 (を) する	4-4	V3	(to) agree
Sapporo さっぽろ＝札幌	2-1	N	Sapporo
(o)sara (お) さら＝(御) 皿	1-14	N	plate; dish
sarada サラダ	1-14	N	salad
sasaru ささる/ささります	4-4	V1	(to) stick; be stuck
(superior ni) sashiageru さしあげる＝差し上げる/さしあげます			
	2-9	V2	(to) give (to a superior)
satoo さとう＝砂糖	2-14	N	sugar
satookibi さとうきび	4-2	N	sugar cane
- satsu - さつ＝ - 冊	1-15	Nd	[counter for bound objects]
Sayoonara. さようなら。	1-1	Exp	Good-bye.
se(i) せ (い)＝背	1-6	N	height
seeru(chuu) セール (中)	2-9	N	(on) sale
seetaa セーター	2-3	N	sweater
- sei - せい＝- 世	4-2	Nd	(counter for) generation
seifuku せいふく＝制服	2-3	N	(school) uniform
seijitsu せいじつ＝誠実	4-7	Na	sincere
seikaku せいかく＝性格	3-3	N	personality
seikatsu せいかつ＝生活	3-3	N	life; living

- seiki - せいき =- 世紀	4-6	Nd	- century
seikoo せいこう＝成功	3-6	N	success
seikoo (o) suru せいこう (を) する＝成功 (を) する	3-6	V3	(to) succeed
seiseki せいせき＝成績	1-11	N	grade
seito せいと＝生徒	1-3	N	student [non-college]
seiyoo ryoori せいようりょうり＝西洋料理	3-8	N	Western-style cooking
seiyooteki せいようてき＝西洋的	3-7	Na	Western style
seiza (o) suru せいざ (を) する＝正座 (を) する	3-7	V3	(to) sit properly
sekai せかい＝世界	2-9	N	world
sekinin せきにん＝責任	4-2	N	responsibility
sekininkan ga aru せきにんかんがある＝責任感がある	4-2	V1	(to) be responsible
sekitei せきてい＝石庭	4-6	N	rock garden
semai せまい＝狭い	1-10	A	is narrow; small (room)
sen せん＝千	1-13	N	thousand
senbei せんべい＝煎餅	4-8	N	Japanese crackers
Sendai せんだい＝仙台	2-1	N	Sendai
sengakki せんがっき＝先学期	3-2	N	last semester
sengetsu せんげつ＝先月	1-12	N	last month
senkoo せんこう＝線香	4-2	N	incense stick
senkoo (o) suru せんこう (を) する＝専攻 (を) する	3-1	V3	(to) major (in)
sensei せんせい＝先生	1-1	N	teacher; Mr./Mrs./Ms./Dr.
senshu せんしゅ＝選手	2-10	N	(sports) player
senshuu せんしゅう＝先週	1-11	N	last week
sensoo せんそう＝戦争	4-2	N	war; warfare
sentaku (o) suru せんたく (を) する＝洗濯 (を) する	2-7	V3	(to) do laundry
- sento - セント	1-13	Nd	- cent(s)
senzo せんぞ＝先祖	4-2	N	ancestor
seou せおう＝背負う/せおいます	4-4	V1	(to) carry something on one's back
setsumei せつめい＝説明	3-9	N	an explanation
setsumei (o) suru せつめい (を) する＝説明 (を) する	3-9	V3	(to) explain
sewa o suru せわ (を) する＝世話 (を) する	3-3	V3	(to) take care of ～
shachoo しゃちょう＝社長	4-1	N	company president
shain しゃいん＝社員	4-1	N	company employee
shakai しゃかい＝社会	1-11	N	social studies; society
shakaifukushi しゃかいふくし＝社会福祉	4-9	N	social welfare
shashin しゃしん＝写真	1-2	N	photo
shatsu シャツ	1-13	N	shirt
shawaa o abiru シャワーをあびる/あびます	3-3	V2	(to) take a shower
～shi ～し、	3-4	Rc	besides; what's more
shi し＝詩	4-7	N	poem
shi し＝四	1-1	N	four
shi し＝市	2-9	N	city
shiai しあい＝試合	1-12	N	(sports) game

shiawase しあわせ＝幸せ	3-6	Na	happy (life)	
shibafu しばふ＝芝生	3-2	N	lawn	
shibaraku しばらく	4-8	Adv	for a while	
Shibuya しぶや＝渋谷	3-9	N	Shibuya [a city in Tokyo]	
shichi しち＝七	1-1	N	seven	
shichi-juu しちじゅう＝七十	1-1	N	seventy	
shichigatsu しちがつ＝七月	1-3	N	July	
shichoo しちょう＝市長	4-4	N	(city) mayor	
shigatsu しがつ＝四月	1-3	N	April	
(o)shigoto (お)しごと＝(お)仕事	1-3	N	job	
shiitoberuto o suru シートベルトをする	2-4	V3	(to) wear a seat belt	
shijin しじん＝詩人	4-7	N	poet	
shika しか＝鹿	4-8	N	deer	
～shika ～しか＋Neg.	3-1	P	only ～ [emphasis]	
shika しか＝鹿	3-10	N	deer	
shikaku しかく＝四角	3-8	N	square	
shikakui しかくい＝四角い	3-8	A	is square (shaped)	
shikaru しかる＝叱る/しかります	2-15	V1	(to) scold	
Shikashi しかし	2-15	SI	However [formal equivalent of でも]	
Shikata ga arimasen/nai. しかたがありません/ない。＝仕方がありません/ない。				
	2-6	Exp	It cannot be helped.	
shiken しけん＝試験	1-2	N	exam	
shiken o ukeru しけんをうける＝試験を受ける/うけます				
	3-3	V2	(to) take an exam	
Shikoku しこく＝四国	2-1	N	Shikoku	
shima しま＝島	2-9	N	island	
(～ga) shimaru (～が)しまる＝閉まる/しまります				
	4-4	V1	(something; someplace) closes [intransitive]	
(V TE) shimau しまう/しまいます	2-11	V1	(to) do ～ completely [regret, criticism]	
shimeru しめる＝閉める/しめます	1-13	V2	(to) close	
Shimete kudasai. しめてください。＝閉めて下さい。	1-1	Exp	Please close.	
Shinagawa しながわ＝品川	3-9	N	Shinagawa [a city in Tokyo]	
shinbun しんぶん＝新聞	1-4	N	newspaper	
shingoo しんごう＝信号	2-4	N	traffic lights	
shinisoo na kao しにそうなかお＝死にそうな顔				
	4-7	N	an expression of exhaustion (lit., a face that looks like one is about to die.)	
shinjiru しんじる＝信じる/しんじます	4-2	V2	(to) believe; to trust	
Shinjuku しんじゅく＝新宿	3-9	N	Shinjuku [a city in Tokyo]	
shinjuwan しんじゅわん＝真珠湾	4-3	N	Pearl Harbor	
shinkansen しんかんせん＝新幹線	3-9	N	bullet train	
shinpai (o) suru しんぱい(を)する＝心配(を)する	2-4	V3	(to) worry	
shinseki しんせき＝親戚	1-15	N	relatives	

shinsetsu しんせつ＝親切	3-3	Na	is kind
shinshitsu しんしつ＝寝室	3-7	N	bedroom
shintoo しんとう＝神道	4-6	N	Shintoism
shinu しぬ＝死ぬ/しにます	1-12	V1	(to) die
shio しお＝塩	2-14	N	salt
shiokarai しおからい＝塩辛い	2-14	A	is salty
shiraberu しらべる＝調べる/＝しらべます	3-4	V2	(to) check; investigate
shiraseru しらせる＝知らせる/しらせます	4-3	V2	(to) report; inform
shirimasen しりません＝知りません	1-2	V1	do not know
shiritsu しりつ＝私立	3-2	N	private
shiro しろ＝城	4-8	N	castle
shiro しろ＝白	1-5	N	white
shiroi しろい＝白い	1-6	A	is white
shita した＝下	2-2	N	under; below

(part of body o) shite iru (part of body を) している 3-5 V have (part of body)

shiteiseki していせき＝指定席	4-8	N	reserved seat
shitsumon しつもん＝質問	2-2	N	question

shitsumon (o) suru しつもん (を) する＝質問 (を) する 2-2 V3 (to) ask a question

Shitsurei shimashita. しつれいしました。＝失礼しました。
3-1 Exp (I am) sorry to have inconvenienced you, or for a rude act I have committed.

Shitsurei shimasu. しつれいします。＝失礼します。
3-1 Exp Excuse me, I must be going now. [Used when one must leave a place. lit., I will be rude]

shitte iru しっている＝知っている	2-2	V1	(to) know
shizen しぜん＝自然	3-8	N	nature
shizuka しずか＝静か	1-6	Na	quiet

shizuka ni suru しずかにする＝静かにする 1-13 V3 quiet down

Shizuka ni shite kudasai. しずかにしてください＝静かにして下さい
1-2 Exp Please be quiet.

sho しょ＝書	4-6	N	calligraphy piece
shodoo しょどう＝書道	4-6	N	calligraphy
shokuji しょくじ＝食事	1-7	N	meal; dining

shokuji (o) suru しょくじ (を) する＝食事 (を) する 1-7 V3 (to) dine; have a meal

shokyuu しょきゅう＝初級	3-4	N	beginner level
shoo しょう＝賞	4-9	N	award; prize
shoogakukin しょうがくきん＝奨学金	4-9	N	scholarship
(o)shoogatsu (お) しょうがつ＝(御) 正月	2-7	N	New Year
shooji しょうじ＝障子	3-7	N	*shoji* (rice paper) door
shoojiki しょうじき＝正直	4-7	Na	honest

shookai (o) suru しょうかい (を) する＝紹介 (を) する 2-2 V3 (to) introduce

shoomeisho しょうめいしょ＝証明書	2-3	N	I. D.
shoorai しょうらい＝将来	2-14	N	future
Shooshoo omachi kudasai. しょうしょうおまちください。＝少々お待ち下さい。	4-1	Exp	Just a minute please. [More polite than ちょっと待って下さい]
shootesuto しょうテスト＝小テスト	1-2	N	quiz
shooshuu (o) suru しょうしゅう (を) する＝召集 (を) する	4-3	V3	(to) draft (for military service)
shootopantsu ショートパンツ	2-3	N	shorts
shootsu ショーツ	2-3	N	shorts
shufu しゅふ＝主婦	1-3	N	housewife
shujin しゅじん＝主人	3-6	N	(own) husband
shukudai しゅくだい＝宿題	1-2	N	homework
shumi しゅみ＝趣味	1-5	N	hobby
shuppatsu (o) suru しゅっぱつ (を) する＝出発 (を) する	4-8	V3	vdepart
shuppatsu jikan しゅっぱつじかん＝出発時間	4-8	N	departure time
(go)shusshin (ご) しゅっしん＝(御) 出身	4-1	N	place of origin
shuu しゅう＝州	2-9	N	state
- shuukan - しゅうかん＝- 週間	2-6	Nd	- week(s)
shuukyoo しゅうきょう＝宗教	4-6	N	religion
shuumatsu しゅうまつ＝週末	1-11	N	weekend
shuuyoojo しゅうようじょ＝収容所	4-3	N	internment camp; concentration camp
soba そば＝傍	2-2	N	by; nearby
sobo そぼ＝祖母	3-1	N	(one's own) grandmother
sochira そちら	2-5	N	there [polite equiv. of そこ]
sochira そちら	2-9	N	that one [polite equiv. of それ]
sodateru そだてる＝育てる/そだてます	4-2	V2	(to) raise (a person/pet)
sofu そふ＝祖父	3-1	N	(one's own) grandfather
sokkusu ソックス	2-3	N	socks
soko そこ	1-2	N	there
sonchoo そんちょう＝村長	4-3	N	village chief
sonkei suru そんけいする＝尊敬する	3-3	V3	(to) respect
sonkeigo そんけいご＝尊敬語	4-1	N	respect language
sono koro そのころ＝その頃	2-10	PN+N	around that time
sono toki そのとき＝その時	2-15	N	at that time
sono 〜 その 〜	1-2	PN	that 〜
〜soo da 〜そうだ	3-6	Nd+ C	I heard that 〜
(V stem) soo desu -そうです	2-5	SI	looks 〜
Soo desu ka. そうですか。	1-3	Exp	Is that so?
Soo desu. そうです。	1-1	Exp	It is.
Soo desu nee . . . そうですねえ...	1-5	Exp	Let me see . . .
Soo dewa arimasen. そうではありません。	1-1	Exp	It is not so. [formal]
Soo ja arimasen. そうじゃありません。	1-1	Exp	It is not so. [informal]

Soobusen そうぶせん＝総武線　　　　3-9　N　　Sobu Line [yellow colored train line in Tokyo]

soodan (o) suru　そうだん (を) する＝相談 (を) する　3-3　V3　(to) consult

sooji (o) suru そうじ (を) する＝掃除 (を) する 2-7 V3　(to) clean up

(o) sooshiki (お) そうしき＝(御) 葬式　4-2　N　　funeral

sora そら＝空　　　　　　　　　　4-4　N　　sky

sore それ　　　　　　　　　　　　1-1　N　　that one

Sore wa ii kangae desu. それはいいかんがえです。＝それはいい考えです。

　　　　　　　　　　　　　　　　2-10　Exp　That is a good idea.

Soredake desu. それだけです。　　　2-5　Exp　That's all.

Sorekara それから　　　　　　　　1-7　SI　　And then

Soreni それに　　　　　　　　　　1-11　SI　Moreover; Besides

Soretomo それとも　　　　　　　　1-6　SI　　(Question 1). Or (Question 2)

Sorosoro shitsureishimasu. そろそろしつれいします。＝そろそろ失礼します。

　　　　　　　　　　　　　　　　4-1　Exp　It's almost time (for me) to leave.

Soshite そして　　　　　　　　　　1-3　SI And [Used at the beginning of a sentence.]

soto そと＝外　　　　　　　　　　1-10　N　outside

(school o) sotsugyo suru　そつぎょうする＝卒業する 3-1 V3 (to) graduate (from school)

sotsugyooshiki　そつぎょうしき＝卒業式 3-2　N　graduation ceremony

su す＝酢　　　　　　　　　　　　2-14　N　vinegar

subarashii すばらしい＝素晴らしい　1-13　A　　is wonderful

subete すべて　　　　　　　　　　4-6　N　　all [formal equivalent of ぜんぶ]

suekko すえっこ＝末っ子　　　　　4-2　N　　youngest child (in a family)

〜sugi 〜すぎ＝ 〜過ぎ　　　　　　1-7　Nd　after 〜

(V stem) sugiru すぎる＝過ぎる/すぎます 2-14　V2　too 〜

sugoi すごい＝凄い　　　　　　　　1-13　A　　is terrible; terrific

suiei すいえい＝水泳　　　　　　　1-5　N　　swimming

suisen (o) suru すいせん (を) する＝推薦 (を) する 4-9　V3　(to) recommend

suisenjoo すいせんじょう＝推薦状　4-9　N　　recommendation

suite iru すいている/すいています　2-13　V1　is not crowded; is empty

suiyoobi すいようび＝水曜日　　　　1-7　N　　Wednesday

sukaato スカート　　　　　　　　　2-3　N　　skirt

suki すき＝好き　　　　　　　　　1-5　Na　like

sukiyaki すきやき＝鋤焼き　　　　　2-14 N　*sukiyaki*

sukoa スコア　　　　　　　　　　　2-10 N　score

sukoshi すこし＝少し　　　　　　　1-10　Adv a few; a little [formal]

suku すく/すきます　　　　　　　　2-13 V1　(to) get empty; be empty

sukunai すくない＝少ない　　　　　1-11　A　is few; little

sukunakutomo すくなくとも＝少なくとも　4-6　Adv　at least

sukuurubasu スクールバス　　　　　2-4　N　　school bus

Sumimasen. すみません。　　　　　1-1　Exp　Excuse me.

Sumimasen. すみません。　　　　　1-13 Exp　Excuse me. [to get attention]

(place ni) sumu すむ＝住む/すみます 2-2　V1　live (in 〜)

sunakkubaa スナックバー	1-4	N	snack bar
sunomono すのもの＝酢の物	3-8	N	vinegared vegetables
supein スペイン	1-3	N	Spain
supeingo スペインご＝スペイン語	1-4	N	Spanish language
supiido o dasu スピードをだす＝出す/だします	2-4	V1	(to) speed
supootsu スポーツ	1-5	N	sports
suppai すっぱい＝酸っぱい	2-14	A	is sour
supuun スプーン	1-14	N	spoon
suru する/します	1-4	V3	(to) do
(accessories o) suru する/します	2-3	V3	(to) wear [accessories]
(something ni) suru する/します	2-5	V3	(to) decide on ～
Suruto すると	2-13	SI	Thereupon
sushiya すしや＝寿司屋	1-13	N	sushi shop/bar
(gomi o) suteru (ごみを) すてる/すてます	2-3	V2	(to) litter; throw away (garbage)
Sutoresu ga ippai desu. ストレスがいっぱいです。	2-6	Exp	is very stressed
sutoroo ストロー	1-14	N	straw
(tabako o) suu (たばこを) すう/すいます	2-3	V1	(to) smoke (cigarettes)
suugaku すうがく＝数学	1-11	N	math
suupaa スーパー	1-13	N	supermarket
suwaru すわる＝座る/すわります	1-13	V1	(to) sit
Suwatte kudasai. すわってください。＝座って下さい。	1-2	Exp	Please sit.
suzushii すずしい＝涼しい	1-1	A	is cool [temperature]

<T>

tabako たばこ	2-3	N	tobacco; cigarettes
tabemono たべもの＝食べ物	1-5	N	food
taberu たべる＝食べる/たべます	1-4	V2	(to) eat
tabeyoo たべよう＝食べよう	3-1	V2	let's eat [informal form of 食べましょう]
tabun たぶん＝多分	2-7	Adv	probably
～tachi ～たち＝～達	1-12	Nd	[suffix for animate plurals]
tada ただ	4-9	N	free of charge [informal]
Tadaima. ただいま。	3-1	Exp	(I'm) home. [Used by a family member who has come home.]
tadashii ただしい＝正しい	2-2	A	is correct
～ tai ～　～たい～＝～対 ～	2-10	PN	～ to ～; ～ vs. ～
(V stem) tai (V stem) たい	1-12	Da	want (to do)
taihen たいへん＝大変	1-11	Na	hard; difficult
taiho (o) suru たいほ (を) する＝逮捕 (を) する	4-3	V3	(to) arrest
taiiku たいいく＝体育	1-11	N	P.E.
taiikukan たいいくかん＝体育館	2-10	N	gym
taiken (o) suru たいけん (を) する＝体験 (を) する	4-3	V3	(to) experience (personally)
taipu (o) suru タイプ (を) する	1-4	V3	(to) type
(～o) taisetsu ni suru (～を) たいせつにする＝(～を) 大切にする	4-6	V3	(to) value; take good care of ～

taishoku (o) suru たいしょく（を）する＝退職（を）する

　　　　　　　　　　　　　　4-2　V3　(to) retire (from a job)

taitei たいてい＝大抵　　　　1-4　Adv　usually

takai たかい＝高い　　　　　1-6　A　is tall

takai たかい＝高い　　　　　1-13　A　is expensive

takenoko たけのこ＝竹の子　3-8　N　bamboo shoot

takusan たくさん＝沢山　　　1-10　Adv　a lot; many

takushii タクシー　　　　　1-7　N　taxi

takuwan たくわん＝沢庵　　　3-8　N　pickled turnip

tama ni たまに　　　　　　2-15　Adv　occasionally; once in a while

tamago たまご＝卵　　　　　2-14　N　egg

(〜no) tame (ni)（〜の）ため（に）4-2　N　for the sake of 〜

(Dic./NAI form) tame (ni) ため（に）4-2　N　in order to do/not to do 〜

(o)tanjoobi （お）たんじょうび＝(御) 誕生日　1-11　N　birthday

tanoshii たのしい＝楽しい　1-11　A　is fun; enjoyable

tanoshimi たのしみ＝楽しみ　4-9　N　enjoyment

(〜o) tanoshimi ni shite imasu （〜を）たのしみにしています。

　＝(〜を) 楽しみにしています。　1-15　Exp　I am looking forward to (something).

tanoshimu たのしむ＝楽しむ／たのしみます 3-6　V1　(to) enjoy

tasukeru たすける＝助ける／たすけます 2-15　V2　(to) rescue; (to) help

tatakau たたかう＝戦う／たたかいます 4-2　V1　(to) fight a battle; battle

(doramu o) tataku （ドラムを）たたく／たたきます 3-5　V1　(to) beat (a drum)

tatami たたみ＝畳　　　　　3-7　N　straw mat

tatemono たてもの＝建物　　1-10　N　building

tateru たてる＝建てる／たてます 3-7　V1　(to) build

tatoeba たとえば＝例えば　3-4　SI　For example

tatsu たつ＝立つ／たちます　1-13　V1　(to) stand

Tatte kudasai. たってください。＝立って下さい。1-2　Exp　Please stand.

〜te (kara) 〜て（から）、　3-4　V+P　After 〜

te て＝手　　　　　　　　　1-6　N　hand

(o)tearai （お）てあらい＝(御) 手洗い　1-10　N　bathroom; restroom

teeburu テーブル　　　　　1-2　N　table

teepu テープ　　　　　　　1-4　N　tape

tegami てがみ＝手紙　　　　1-4　N　letter

teien ていえん＝庭園　　　4-6　N　garden [formal]

teinei ていねい＝丁寧　　　4-1　Na　polite

teineigo ていねいご＝丁寧語　4-1　N　polite language

teki てき＝敵　　　　　　　4-3　N　enemy

tekikokujin てきこくじん＝敵国人　4-3　N　a citizen of a hostile (an enemy) country

tekisuto テキスト　　　　　1-2　N　textbook

tekitoo てきとう＝適当　　　4-6　Na　proper; appropriate

〜tekure 〜てくれ　　　　3-1　E　[male informal form of 〜て下さい]

temae てまえ＝手前　　　　3-9　N　this side (of)

49

- ten - てん＝ - 点	2-10	Nd	- point(s)
tengoku てんごく＝天国	4-3	N	heaven
tenin てんいん＝店員	4-1	N	store clerk
tenisu テニス	1-5	N	tennis
(o)tenki (お) てんき＝(お) 天気	1-1	N	weather
tenkiyohoo てんきよほう＝天気予報	3-6	N	weather forecast
tennoo てんのう＝天皇	3-9	N	Emperor
(o)tera (お) てら＝(御) 寺	2-7	N	temple (Buddhist)
terebi テレビ	1-4	N	TV
terebigeemu テレビゲーム	1-5	N	video game
tetsudau てつだう＝手伝う/てつだいます	2-7	V3	(to) help
tiishatsu T シャツ	2-3	N	T-shirt
tisshu ティッシュ	1-2	N	tissue
to と	1-3	P	and [used between two nouns]
to と＝戸	1-10	N	door
(quotation) to と	2-11	P	[quotation particle]
to (issho ni) と (いっしょに)	1-4	P	with (person)
～to ii(desu) ～ といい (です)。	4-9	Exp	I hope/wish that ～
(N1) to iu (N2) N1 という N2	3-2	P+V	N2 called N1
(～) to wakatta ～とわかった＝～と分かった	4-7	P	understand that ～
tobu とぶ＝飛ぶ/とびます	4-4	V1	(to) fly
tochuu とちゅう＝途中	4-4	N	on the way
(o)toire (お) トイレ	1-10	N	bathroom; restroom
(N1) toka (N2) N1 とか N2	3-2	P	(N1) and (N2) (among others)
tokai とかい＝都会	4-4	N	(large) city; metropolis
tokei とけい＝時計	1-13	N	watch, clock
～toki ～とき＝～時	2-15	N	time; when ～
tokidoki ときどき＝時々	1-4	Adv	sometimes
tokoro ところ	3-2	N	point
tokoro ところ＝所	2-2	N	place
Tokorode ところで	2-3	SI	By the way
toku ni とくに＝特に	2-2	Adv	especially
tokubetsu　とくべつ＝特別	3-3	Na	special
tokui とくい＝得意	1-5	Na	be strong in; can do well
Tokyo とうきょう＝東京	2-1	N	Tokyo
Tomare. とまれ。＝止まれ。	4-3	V1	Stop. [command form]
tomaru とまる＝泊まる/とまります	4-8	V1	(to) stay overnight
(place de/ni) tomaru とまる＝止まる/とまります	2-4	V1	(to) stop
(place ni) tomaru とまる＝泊まる/とまります	3-10	V1	(to) stay overnight
tomodachi ともだち＝友達	1-4	N	friend
tonari となり＝隣	2-2	N	next to
Tondemogozaimasen. とんでもございません。	4-1	Exp	Don't mention it. [Politely denies what the other person says.]

Tondemonai. とんでもない。		2-11 Exp	How ridiculous! That's impossible!
tonkatsu とんかつ＝豚カツ		2-5 N	pork cutlet
too とお＝十		1-2 N	ten [general counter]
toochaku (o) suru とうちゃく（を）する＝到着（を）する		4-8 V3	(to) arrive
toochakujikan とうちゃくじかん＝到着時間		4-8 N	arrival time
toogei とうげい＝陶芸		4-6 N	ceramics
tooi とおい＝遠い		1-10 A	is far
tooka とおか＝十日		1-11 N	the tenth day of the month
tooku とおく＝遠く		2-2 N	far away
Tookyooeki とうきょうえき＝東京駅		3-9 N	Tokyo Station [a station in Tokyo]
toori とおり＝通り		2-13 N	street; avenue
tootoo とうとう		2-11 Adv	finally; at last [after much effort]
tooyooteki とうようてき＝東洋的		3-7 Na	Eastern style
toraberaazu chekku トラベラーズチェック		2-9 N	traveler's checks
toranpu トランプ		1-5 N	(playing) cards
toree トレー		4-9 N	tray
tori とり＝鳥		1-10 N	bird
(thing o) tori ni iku とりにいく＝取りに行く／とりにいきます			
		2-10 V1	(to) go to pick up (thing)
(thing o) tori ni kaeru とりにかえる＝取りに帰る／とりにかえります			
		2-10 V1	(to) return to pick up (thing)
(thing o) tori ni kuru とりにくる＝取りに来る／とりにきます			
		2-10 V3	(to) come to pick up (thing)
toriniku とりにく＝鳥肉		2-14 N	chicken (meat)
toru とる＝取る／とります		1-15 V1	(to) take; get
toshi o totte iru としをとっている＝年を取っている			
		1-6 V1	is old (person's, animal's age)
～toshite ～として		3-2 P+V	as ～; for ～
(o)toshiyori （お）としより＝（お）年寄り		4-9 N	old person(s); senior citizen(s)
toshokan としょかん＝図書館		1-4 N	library
totemo とても		1-5 Adv	very
totsuzen とつぜん＝突然		4-3 Adv	suddenly; unexpectedly
(～o) totte kudasai. (～を) とってください。＝取って下さい。			
		3-8 Exp	Excuse me. Please pass me ～.
tsugi つぎ＝次		1-11 N	next
tsugi ni つぎに＝次に		2-14 Adv	next
tsuitachi ついたち＝一日		1-11 N	the first day of the month
tsukaremashita つかれました＝疲れました		1-12 V2	(got) tired
tsukarete imasu つかれています＝疲れています		1-12 V2	is tired
tsukau つかう＝使う／つかいます		3-1 V1	(to) use
tsukemono つけもの＝漬け物		3-8 N	pickled vegetable
tsukeru つける／つけます		4-4 V2	(to) apply (the medicine)
(object o thing ni) tsukeru つける／つけます		2-14 V2	(to) dip (object in thing)

tsukiatari つきあたり＝突き当たり　3-9　N　end (of a street)

(〜to) tsukiau （〜と）つきあう/つきあいます 3-5　V1　(to) associate with 〜

(〜ga) tsuku　（〜が）つく/つきます　4-4　V1 (something) turns on [intransitive verb]

(place ni) tsuku つく＝着く/つきます 2-4　V1　(to) arrive (at a place)

tsukue つくえ＝机　　　　　　　1-10　N　desk

(〜no) tsukurikata つくりかた＝作り方　2-14 N　how to make 〜

tsukuru つくる＝作る/つくります　1-15 V1　(to) make

tsumaranai つまらない　　　　　1-11　A　is boring, uninteresting

tsumetai つめたい＝冷たい　　　1-14　A　cold (to the touch)

(Dic./NAI) tsumori desu つもりです 2-6　Nd　plan to do/do not plan to do

tsurai つらい＝辛い　　　　　　3-3　A　is hard; bitter; painful

tsurete iku つれていく＝連れて行く/つれていきます 2-7　V1　(to) take (animate)

tsurete kaeru つれてかえる＝連れて帰る/つれてかえります

　　　　　　　　　　　　　　　2-7　V1　(to) take/bring (animate) back home

tsurete kuru つれてくる＝連れて来る/つれてきます 2-7　V3 (to) bring (animate)

tsuru つる＝鶴　　　　　　　　4-4　N　crane (bird)

(place ni) tsutomeru つとめる＝勤める/つとめます 2-2　V2　(to) be employed (at 〜)

tsuuyaku (o) suru つうやく（を）する＝通訳（を）する 4-3　V3　(to) interpret

tsuyoi つよい＝強い　　　　　　1-12　A　is strong

(V stem) tsuzukeru (V Stem) つづける＝続ける/つづけます

　　　　　　　　　　　　　　　3-4　V2　(to) continue/keep doing 〜

(〜ga) tsuzuku （〜が）つづく＝続く/つづきます

　　　　　　　　　　　　　　　4-6　V1　(something) continues [intransitive]

〜tte 〜って　　　　　　　　　3-1　P　[informal form of quotaion particle と]

(topic) tte (topic) って　　　　4-6 P　[A topic particle used for conversation only.]

<U>

uchi うち　　　　　　　　　　1-4　N　house

uchi うち＝内　　　　　　　　3-7　N　inside

(〜no) uchi （〜の）うち　　　4-4　P+N among 〜

udon うどん　　　　　　　　　2-5　N　thick white noodles in broth

ue うえ＝上　　　　　　　　　2-2　N　on; top

Ueno うえの＝上野　　　　　　3-9　N　Ueno [city in Tokyo]

(thing ga) ugoku うごく＝動く/うごきます 2-11 V1　(thing) moves

ukagau うかがう＝伺う/いかがいます 2-13 V1　(to) ask [polite equiv. of 聞く]

uketoru うけとる＝受け取る/うけとります 3-3　V1　(to) receive

(place de) umareru うまれる＝生まれる/うまれます 2-2　V2　be born (in 〜)

umi うみ＝海　　　　　　　　　1-7　N　beach; ocean; sea

Un うん　　　　　　　　　　　2-4　SI　Yes [informal]

un ga ii うんがいい＝運がいい　4-2　A　lucky

un ga warui うんがわるい＝運が悪い 4-2　A　unlucky

undoo (o) suru うんどう（を）する＝運動（を）する 2-10 V3　(to) exercise

undoo うんどう＝運動　　　　　2-10 N　sports

undoogutsu うんどうぐつ＝運動靴 2-10 N　sports shoes

undoojoo うんどうじょう＝運動場	2-10	N	athletic field
unten (o) suru うんてん (を) する＝運転 (を) する	2-3	V3	(to) drive
untenmenkyo うんてんめんきょ＝運転免許	2-3	N	driver's license
untenshu うんてんしゅ＝運転手	2-4	N	driver
unwaruku うんわるく＝運悪く	4-2	Adv	unluckily; unfortunately
unyoku うんよく＝運良く	4-2	Adv	luckily; fortunately
ura うら＝裏	4-4	N	back (side)
urayamashii うらやましい＝羨ましい	3-6	A	envious
ureshii うれしい＝嬉しい	1-11	A	is glad; happy
uru うる＝売る/うります	2-9	V1	(to) sell
urusai うるさい	1-6	A	is noisy
ushiro うしろ＝後ろ	2-2	N	back; behind
uso うそ＝嘘	2-10	N	(a) lie
Uso deshoo. うそでしょう。	2-10	Exp	Are you kidding? Are you serious?
usotsuki うそつき	4-7	N	liar
usui うすい＝薄い	2-14	A	is thin (object)
usuku うすく＝薄く	2-14	Adv	thin
uta うた＝歌	1-5	N	song; singing
utau うたう＝歌う/うたいます	1-15	V1	(to) sing
utsukushii うつくしい＝美しい	1-10	A	is beautiful
Uun う～ん	2-5	SI	Yummm . . .
Uun ううん	2-4	SI	No [informal]
uwasa うわさ	3-6	N	rumor

<W>

wa は	1-1	P	[particle marking the topic of the sentence]
- wa - わ=- 羽	1-10	Nd	[counter for birds]
wa-kei-sei-jaku わけいせいじゃく＝和敬清寂	4-6	N	harmony, respect, purity and tranquility (tea ceremony)
Waa わあ	1-13	SI	Wow!
waakushiito ワークシート	1-2	N	worksheet
waeijiten わえいじてん＝和英辞典	3-4	N	Japanese-English dictionary
wagamama わがまま	4-7	Na	selfish; self-centered
wagashi わがし＝和菓子	4-6	N	Japanese sweets
wakai わかい＝若い	1-6	A	is young
wakareru わかれる＝別れる/わかれます	3-5	V2	(to) separate [intransitive]
wakaru わかる＝分かる/わかります	1-2	V1	(to) understand
(～o) wakeru わける＝分ける/わけます	4-9	V2	(to) divide; sort; share [transitive]
wanpiisu ワンピース	2-3	N	dress
warau わらう＝笑う/わらいます	2-15	V1	(to) smile; laugh
warui わるい＝悪い	1-6	A	is bad
washitsu わしつ＝和室	3-7	N	Japanese-style room
washoku わしょく＝和食	3-8	N	Japanese meal
wasureru わすれる＝忘れる/わすれます	1-14	V2	(to) forget

JE

(place o) wataru わたる＝渡る/わたります 2-13 V1 (to) cross; go over
watashi わたし＝私   1-1 N   I (used by anyone informally)
watashino わたしの＝私の   1-2 N   mine
watashitachi わたしたち＝私達   1-12 N   we
watasu わたす＝渡す/わたします   4-1 V1   (to) hand over; pass (to)
weitaa ウェイター   2-5 N   waiter
weitoresu ウェイトレス   2-5 N   waitress
wookuman ウォークマン   1-4 N   walkman
<Y>
(N1) ya や (N2)   1-15 P   (N1) and (N2), etc.
yahari やはり   4-8 SI   just as I thought; Indeed!
yakedo (o) suru やけど (を) する＝火傷 (を) する 4-4 V3 (to) get burned
yakiniku やきにく＝焼肉   2-5 N   meat grilled on fire
yakitori やきとり＝焼き鳥   2-5 N   grilled skewered chicken
yakizakana やきざかな＝焼魚   3-8 N   grilled fish
yaku やく＝焼く/やきます   3-8 V1   (to) grill; roast; bake; toast; fry
yaku やく＝訳   3-4 N   translation
(〜no) yaku ni tatsu やくにたつ＝役に立つ/たちます 4-9 V1 (to) be useful to 〜
yakusoku (o) suru やくそく (を) する＝約束 (を) する 3-9 V3 (to) make a promise
yakusoku やくそく＝約束   3-9 N   (a) promise
yakusu やくす＝訳す/やくします   3-4 V1   (to) translate
yakyuu やきゅう＝野球   1-5 N   baseball
yama やま＝山   1-7 N   mountain
Yamanotesen やまのてせん＝山手線 3-9 N   Yamanote Line [green colored train
                                            line in Tokyo]
yameru やめる＝辞める/やめます   3-2 V2   (to) quit; discontinue
(〜ga) yamu (〜が) やむ＝止む/やみます 4-3 V1 (something) stops [intransitive]
yane やね＝屋根   4-4 N   roof
yappari やっぱり   4-8 SI   just as I thought; Indeed!
yaru やる/やります   1-15 V2   (to) give (to inferior)
yaru やる/やります   3-2 V1   (to) do [informal form of する]
yasai やさい＝野菜   2-14 N   vegetable
yasashii やさしい＝易しい   1-11 A   is easy
yasashii やさしい＝優しい   1-6 A   is nice, kind
yasete iru やせている＝痩せている/やせています 1-6 V2 is thin
(V stem) yasui (V stem) やすい   3-4 A   is easy to do 〜
yasui やすい＝安い   1-13 A   is cheap
(o)yasumi (お) やすみ＝(お) 休み 1-7 N   day off; vacation
(o)yasumi (お) やすみです＝(お) 休みです 1-1 Exp is absent
yasumijikan やすみじかん＝休み時間 1-11 N   (a) break
(〜o) yasumu やすむ＝休む/やすみます 1-12 V1 (to) be absent (from 〜)
yasumu やすむ＝休む/やすみます   1-12 V1   (to) rest
Yattaa. やったあ。   2-10 Exp We did it!

yatto やっと	4-3	Adv	at last; finally
yattsu やっつ＝八つ	1-2	N	eight [general counter]
yawarakai やわらかい＝柔らかい	3-8	A	is soft; tender
(sentence) yo (sentence) よ	1-6	SP	you know [sentence ending particle]
yobu よぶ＝呼ぶ/よびます	4-1	V1	(to) call for
yoi よい＝良い	1-6	A	is good
Yoi shuumatsu o. よいしゅうまつを。＝良い週末を。	4-0	Exp	Have a nice weekend.
yojoohan よじょうはん＝四畳半	3-7	N	4 1/2-mat room
Yokatta desu nee. よかったですねえ。＝良かったですねえ。	1-11	Exp	How nice! [on a past event]
yokka よっか＝四日	1-11	N	(the) fourth day of the month
yoku よく	1-4	Adv	well; often
yoku よく＝欲	4-7	N	greed
Yoku dekimashita. よくできました。＝良く出来ました。	1-2	Exp	Well done.
yokubari よくばり＝欲張り	4-7	Na	greedy (person)
yomu よむ＝読む/よみます	1-4	V1	(to) read
yon よん＝四	1-1	N	four
yon-juu よんじゅう＝四十	1-1	N	forty
yonbun no ichi よんぶんのいち＝四分の一	4-2	N	1/4
Yonde kudasai. よんでください。＝読んで下さい。	1-2	Exp	Please read.
(～no) yoo da. ～のようだ。	4-3	P+Na+C	It is like ～.
～yoo na ki ga suru ～ようなきがする＝～ような気がする	4-6	Na+P+V3	feel like ～
(N1 no) yoo na N2 (N1 の) ような N2	3-5	P+Nd+C	N2 like N1
(～no) yoo ni ～のように	4-3	P+Na+P	like ～
～yoo ni iu ～ようにいう＝～ように言う	4-8	Na+P+V1	say that ～
(Dic./NAI) yoo ni naru (Dic./NAI) ようになる	4-4	Na+P+V1	come to do/come not to do ～
(Dic./NAI) yoo ni suru (Dic./NAI) ようにする	4-3	Na+P+V3	make an effort to do/not to do ～
yoochien ようちえん＝幼稚園	3-1	N	kindergarten
yooka ようか＝八日	1-11	N	the eighth day of the month
yooshitsu ようしつ＝洋室	3-7	N	Western-style room
yooshoku ようしょく＝洋食	3-8	N	Western style meal
～yori ～より	2-9	P	more than ～
yorokobu よろこぶ＝喜ぶ/よろこびます	4-3	V1	(to) be glad; be pleased
yoroshii よろしい	4-1	A	is good [polite equiv. of いい]
yoru よる＝夜	1-4	N	night
(place ni) yoru よる＝寄る/よります	2-10	V1	(to) stop by; drop by (a place)
yottsu よっつ＝四つ	1-2	N	four [general counter]
yowai よわい＝弱い	1-12	A	is weak
yoyaku (o) suru よやく (を) する＝予約 (を) する	2-5	V3	(to) make a reservation
yubi ゆび＝指	1-6	N	finger; toe

yubiwa ゆびわ＝指輪	2-3	N	ring
yuka ゆか＝床	2-4	N	floor
yukata ゆかた＝浴衣	4-8	N	summer cotton *kimono*
yuki ゆき＝雪	2-7	N	snow
yukkuri ゆっくり	1-1	Adv	slowly
yume ゆめ＝夢	3-3	N	dream
yunifoomu ユニフォーム	2-10	N	(sports) uniform
yutaka ゆたか＝豊か	4-9	Na	abundant; rich (life)
yuube ゆうべ	1-12	N	last night
yuubinkyoku ゆうびんきょく＝郵便局	2-13	N	post office
yuugata ゆうがた＝夕方	1-4	N	late afternoon; early evening
yuuki ゆうき＝勇気	4-8	N	courage
yuumei ゆうめい＝有名	1-10	Na	famous
yuuryoo ゆうりょう＝有料	4-9	N	a charge
yuushoku ゆうしょく＝夕食	3-1	N	dinner; supper
yuushoo (o) suru ゆうしょう (を) する＝優勝 (を) する			
	2-10	V3	(to) win a championship

<Z>

zabuton ざぶとん＝座布団	3-7	N	floor cushion
zairyoo ざいりょう＝材料	3-8	N	ingredients
Zannen deshita nee. ざんねんでしたねえ。＝残念でしたねえ。			
	1-11	Exp	How disappointing! [on a past event]
Zannen desu ga . . . ざんねんですが 残念ですが . . .	2-6	Exp	Sorry, but . . .
Zannen desu nee. ざんねんですねえ。＝残念ですねえ。			
	1-11	Exp	How disappointing! [on a future event]
zarusoba ざるそば	2-5	N	buckwheat noodle dish
zasshi ざっし＝雑誌	1-4	N	magazine
zazen ざぜん＝座禅	4-6	N	seated Zen meditation
zehi ぜひ＝是非	2-7	Adv	by all means; definitely
zeikin ぜいきん＝税金	2-9	N	tax
zeitaku ぜいたく＝贅沢	4-7	Na	luxurious; extravagant
zen ぜん＝禅	4-6	N	Zen (Buddhism)
zenbu ぜんぶ＝全部	1-14	N	everything
zenbu de ぜんぶで＝全部で	1-14	N	for everything
zenzen (+ Neg.) ぜんぜん＝全然	1-5	Adv	(not) at all
zettai ni ぜったいに＝絶対に	2-3	Adv	absolutely
zubon ズボン	2-3	N	pants
zuibun ずいぶん＝随分	3-3	Adv	quite; fairly
～zuni ～ずに	4-7	E	Without doing ～
(counter) zutsu (counter) ずつ	4-4	Nd	～ each
zutto ずっと	2-15	Adv	throughout; all the time

English	Volume-Lesson #	Word type	Japanese
1/4	4-2	N	よんぶんのいち＝四分の一
<A>			
ability; power	2-11	N	ちから＝力
ability; talent	4-7	N	さいのう＝才能
(be) able to do ～	2-6	V2	(～が) できる＝出来る [できます]
about (time)	1-7	Nd	～ころ; ～ごろ
about how long/far/often?	2-6	Ni	どのぐらい
about ～ [Not used for time]	1-13	Nd	～くらい; ～ぐらい
about ～ [topic]	2-2	P+V	～について
(be) absent (from ～)	1-12	V2	(～を) やすむ＝休む [やすみます]
(He/She is) absent.	1-4	Exp	(お) やすみです。＝(お) 休みです。
absolutely	2-3	Adv	ぜったいに＝絶対に
abundant	4-9	Na	ゆたか＝豊か
(be) accepted (by school)	4-9	V3	(school に) ごうかく (を) する＝合格 (を) する [-します]
(I will) accompany you.	4-6	Exp	おしょうばんいたします。＝お相伴いたします。[tea ceremony]
according to ～	3-6	P+V+P	～によると
accounting	4-3	N	かいけいがく＝会計学
actor	3-6	N	はいゆう＝俳優
actress	3-6	N	じょゆう＝女優
address	1-15	N	じゅうしょ＝住所
adult	2-14	N	おとな＝大人
advanced level	3-4	N	じょうきゅう＝上級
affection	2-15	N	あい＝愛
after (an event)	1-12	P+N+P	～のあとで＝ ～の後で
after (time)	1-7	Nd	～すぎ＝ ～過ぎ
After ～	3-4	V+P	-て (から)、
After (sentence)	3-6	N+P	(TA form) あとで＝-後で
after school	3-2	N	ほうかご＝放課後
again	1-10	Adv	また＝又
(to) agree	4-4	V3	さんせい (を) する＝賛成 (を) する [-します]
agriculture	4-3	N	のうぎょう＝農業
air	4-9	N	くうき＝空気
airplane	7-4	N	ひこうき＝飛行機
airport	2-13	N	くうこう＝空港
Akihabara [a city in Tokyo]	3-9	N	あきはばら＝秋葉原
all [formal equivalent of ぜんぶ]	4-6	N	すべて
all right	1-12	Na	だいじょうぶ＝大丈夫
all the time	2-15	Adv	ずっと

allowance	3-2	N	(お) こづかい＝(お) 小遣い
ally	4-3	N	みかた＝味方
almost; mostly	3-2	Adv	ほとんど
(It's) almost time (for me) to leave.	4-1	Exp	そろそろしつれいします。＝そろそろ 失礼します。
alone; lonely	4-7	N	ひとりぼっち＝独りぼっち
along (street)	2-4	P	(street) を
already	1-14	Exp	もう (+aff.)
(a Buddhist family) altar	4-2	N	ぶつだん＝仏壇
[alternative]	2-9	N	(〜の) ほう＝方
Although 〜	2-6	Pc	〜けど; 〜けれど
always	1-4	Adv	いつも
a.m.	1-7	N	ごぜん＝午前
ambulance	2-4	N	きゅうきゅうしゃ＝救急車
American military	4-3	N	べいぐん＝米軍
among 〜	2-9	P	(〜のなか＝〜の中) で
among 〜	4-4	P+N	〜のうち
among these	2-9	PN+N+P	このなかで＝この中で
amount	3-4	N	かず＝数
amuse [not used for sports & music]	1-15	V1	あそぶ＝遊ぶ [あそびます]
ancestor	4-2	N	せんぞ＝先祖
(N1) and (N2) (among others)	3-2	P	N1 とか N2 (とか) [informal]
(N1) and (N2), etc.	1-15	P	N1 や N2 など
and [used between two nouns]	1-3	P	(N1) と (N2)
And [used only at the beginning of a sentence]	1-3	SI	そして
And then	1-7	SI	それから
(to become) angry	2-15	V1	おこる＝怒る [おこります]
announcement	4-3	N	おしらせ＝お知らせ
answer	2-2	N	こたえ＝答え
(to) answer	2-2	V2	こたえる＝答える [こたえます]
(not) any more	2-2	Adv	もう+ Neg.
(Is) anyone home? (when visiting someone's home); Excuse me. (at the store)	3-8	Exp	ごめんください。
anyplace	3-1	Ni+P	どこでも
Anything else?	2-5	Exp	ほかになにか。＝ほかに何か。
(not) anything	1-4	Ni+P	なにも＝何も +Neg.
anything	3-1	Ni+P	なんでも＝何でも
anytime	3-1	Ni+P	いつでも
(not to) anywhere	1-7	Ni+P	どこへも +Neg.
(to) apologize	4-7	V1	あやまる＝謝る [あやまります]
(to) apply (the medicine)	4-4	V2	つける [つけます]
(to) apply make-up	3-2	V3	(お) けしょう (を) する＝(お) 化粧 (を) する [-します]

(to) appreciate	2-15	V3	かんしゃ (を) する＝感謝 (を) する [-します]
appropriate	4-6	Na	てきとう＝適当
approximately	2-6	Adv	だいたい
April	1-3	N	しがつ＝四月
architect	4-6	N	けんちくか＝建築家
architecture	4-6	N	けんちく＝建築
area	2-13	N	へん＝辺
around that time	2-10	PN+N	そのころ＝その頃
(to) arrest	4-3	V3	たいほ (を) する＝逮捕 (を) する [-します]
arrival at (place)	4-8	Nd	(place) 〜ちゃく＝〜着
arrival time	4-8	N	とうちゃくじかん＝到着時間
(to) arrive (at a place)	2-4	V1	(place に) つく＝着く [つきます]
(to) arrive	4-8	V3	とうちゃく (を) する＝到着 (を) する [-します]
(to be) arrogant	4-7	V1	いばる＝威張る [いばります]
art	1-11	N	びじゅつ＝美術
art museum	2-13	N	びじゅつかん＝美術館
as it is	4-9	Nd	〜まま
as many/long as 〜	2-6	P	(counter) も
(not) as 〜 as	2-9	P	〜ほど (+ Neg.)
as 〜; for 〜	3-2	P+V	〜として
(to) ask (someone)	2-3	V1	(person に) きく＝聞く [ききます]
(to) ask [polite]	2-13	V1	うかがう＝伺う [うかがいます]
(to) ask a question	2-2	V3	しつもん (を) する＝質問 (を) する [-します]
(to) associate with 〜	3-6	V1	(〜と) つきあう [つきあいます]
at (location) [with existence verb]	1-10	P	に [with existence verb]
at (place) [with action verb]	1-4	P	で [with action verb]
at (specific time)	1-7	P	(specific time) に
(not) at all	1-5	Adv	ぜんぜん＝全然+Neg.
at last [after much effort]	2-11	Adv	とうとう
at least	4-6	Adv	すくなくとも＝少なくとも
at that time	2-15	N	そのとき＝その時
athletic field	2-10	N	うんどうじょう＝運動場
atomic bomb	4-4	N	げんばく＝原爆
(to) attack	4-3	V3	こうげき (を) する＝攻撃 (を) する [-します]
August	1-3	N	はちがつ＝八月
aunt	1-15	N	おばさん
(one's own) aunt	3-1	N	おば＝叔母
autumn	1-12	N	あき＝秋
avenue	2-13	N	とおり＝通り
award	4-9	N	しょう＝賞

<B>

baby	2-2	N	あかちゃん＝赤ちゃん
(to) babysit	4-2	V3	こもり (を) する＝子守り (を) する [-します]

back; behind	2-2	N	うしろ＝後ろ
back (side)	4-4	N	うら＝裏
(is) bad	1-6	A	わるい＝悪い
bag	1-2	N	バッグ
bag (paper)	2-9	N	ふくろ＝袋
baggage	4-8	N	にもつ＝荷物
balloon	1-15	N	ふうせん＝風船
ballpoint pen	1-2	N	ボールペン
bamboo shoot	3-8	N	たけのこ＝竹の子
bank	2-2	N	ぎんこう＝銀行
baseball	1-5	N	やきゅう
basement	2-9	N	ちか＝地下
basketball	1-5	N	バスケット (ボール)
bathroom	1-10	N	(お) トイレ; (お) てあらい＝(御) 手洗い
battery	4-9	N	でんち＝電池
be [polite equiv. of です]	4-1	C	～でございます
be [humble equiv. of いる]	4-1	V1	おる [おります]
be (for animate) [polite equiv. of いる]	2-6	V1	いらっしゃる [いらっしゃいます]
beach	1-7	N	うみ＝海
beard	1-6	N	ひげ＝髭
(to) beat (a drum)	3-6	V1	(ドラムを) たたく [たたきます]
(to) beat (someone)	4-2	V1	なぐる＝殴る [なぐります]
(is) beautiful	1-10	A	うつくしい＝美しい
(That's) because	4-2	SI	なぜなら
because of (noun)	2-6	P	(noun) で
because	1-11	Pc	(reason) から
(to) become calm	3-7	V1	おちつく＝落ち着く [おちつきます]
(to) become ～	2-12	V1	(～ に) なる [なります]
bed	1-10	N	ベッド
(Japanese) bedding	3-7	N	ふとん＝布団
bedroom	3-7	N	しんしつ＝寝室
beef	2-14	N	ぎゅうにく＝牛肉
beer	2-4	N	ビール
before	1-3	N	まえ＝前
before (not time)	1-12	P+N+P	～のまえに＝ ～の前に
before (time)	1-7	Nd	～まえ＝ ～前
Before (sentence)	3-6	N+P	(dic. form) まえに＝-前に
(to) begin (something)	1-4	V2	(～ を) はじめる＝始める [はじめます]
(to) begin doing ～	3-4	V2	(V stem) はじめる＝始める [-はじめます]
beginner level	3-4	N	しょきゅう＝初級
(at the) beginning	2-14	Adv	はじめに＝始めに
(something) begins	2-10	V1	(～ が) はじまる＝始まる [はじまります]
behind	2-2	N	うしろ＝後ろ

English	Lesson	Type	Japanese
(to) believe	4-2	V2	しんじる＝信じる [しんじます]
below	2-2	N	した＝下
Besides [Used at the beginning of a sentence.]	1-11	SI	それに
besides; what's more	3-4	Rc	ーし、
(the) best	3-8	N	さいこう＝最高
between [comparison]	2-9	P	～で
between [location]	2-2	N	あいだ＝間
beyond	2-13	N	むこう＝向こう
bicycle	1-7	N	じてんしゃ＝自転車
big	1-6	A	おおきい＝大きい
bill	2-5	N	(お) かんじょう＝(お) 勘定
bird	1-10	N	とり＝鳥
birthday	1-11	N	(お) たんじょうび＝(御) 誕生日
(is) bitter	3-8	A	にがい＝苦い
black	1-5	N	くろ＝黒
(pitch) black	4-4	N	まっくろ＝真っ黒
black tea	4-1	N	こうちゃ＝紅茶
(is) black	1-6	A	くろい＝黒い
(to) bleed	4-4	V2	ちがでる＝血が出る [でます]
(a) blind person	4-9	N	めがふじゆうなひと＝目が不自由な人
blood	4-4	N	ち＝血
(to) bloom	4-6	V1	さく＝咲く [さきます]
(to) blow (a trumpet)	3-6	V1	（トランペットを）ふく＝吹く [ふきます]
(to) blow away	2-11	V1	ふきとばす＝吹き飛ばす [ふきとばします]
blue	1-5	N	あお＝青
(is) blue	1-6	A	あおい＝青い
boat; ship	1-7	N	ふね＝船
body	1-6	N	からだ＝体
(to) boil (in broth); simmer	3-8	V2	にる＝煮る [にます]
boiled (in broth) foods	3-8	N	にもの＝煮物
bones	4-4	N	ほね＝骨
book	1-2	N	ほん＝本
bookstore	1-13	N	ほんや＝本屋
(to) boom	4-4	V3	ドーンとおとがする＝音がする [-します]
boring	1-11	A	つまらない
(be) born (in ～)	2-2	V2	(place で) うまれる＝生まれる [うまれます]
born in (month)	1-3	Nd	- がつうまれ＝- 月生まれ
(to) borrow	2-3	V2	かりる＝借りる [かります]
both	2-9	N	りょうほう＝両方
bottle	4-9	N	びん＝瓶
(plastic) bottle	4-9	N	ペットボトル
(to) bow	4-6	V3	おじぎ（を）する [-します]
Bow.	1-1	Exp	れい。＝礼。

(tea, rice) bowl	4-6	N	ちゃわん＝茶腕
- bowlful	1-14	Nd	- ぱい/- はい/- ばい＝ - 杯
box	2-9	N	はこ＝箱
box lunch	1-14	N	べんとう＝弁当
(a) box lunch sold at stations	4-8	N	えきべん＝駅弁
boy	1-10	N	おとこのこ＝男の子
boy's school	3-2	N	だんしこう＝男子校
(to) brag	4-7	V1	いばる＝威張る [いばります]
bread	1-4	N	パン
(a) break	1-11	N	やすみじかん＝休み時間
(something) breaks	3-7	V2	(〜が) こわれる＝壊れる [こわれます]
(to) break (something)	3-7	V1	(〜を) こわす＝壊す [こわします]
breakfast	1-4	N	あさごはん＝朝御飯
breakfast [formal]	3-1	N	ちょうしょく＝朝食
(a) bride	4-2	N	はなよめ＝花嫁
bridge	2-13	N	はし＝橋
(is) bright	2-11	A	あかるい＝明るい
(to) bring (animate)	2-7	V3	つれてくる＝連れて来る [つれてきます]
(to) bring (thing)	2-7	V3	もってくる＝持って来る [もってきます]
brown	1-5	N	ちゃいろ＝茶色
(is) brown	1-6	A	ちゃいろい＝茶色い
brown rice	4-7	N	げんまい＝玄米
(to) brush (teeth)	3-3	V1	(はを) みがく ＝(歯を) 磨く [みがきます]
(cold) buckwheat noodle dish	2-5	N	ざるそば
(a big image of) Buddha	4-8	N	だいぶつ＝大仏
Buddhism	4-6	N	ぶっきょう＝仏教
(to) build	3-7	V1	たてる＝建てる [たてます]
(to) build (a house or a building)	4-6	V3	けんちく (を) する＝建築 (を) する [-します]
building	1-10	N	たてもの＝建物
(a high tall) building	3-9	N	ビル
bullet train	3-9	N	しんかんせん＝新幹線
bullying	3-2	N	いじめ
(to) bully	3-2	V2	いじめる [いじめます]
(to get) burned	4-4	V3	やけど (を) する＝火傷 (を) する [-します]
(something) burns [intransitive]	4-9	V2	(〜が) もえる＝燃える [もえます]
bus	1-7	N	バス
bus stop	2-13	N	バスてい＝バス停
(is) busy	1-7	A	いそがしい＝忙しい
but	1-5	Pc	(sentence 1) が, (sentence 2)
But [Used at the beginning of the sentence.]	1-4	SI	でも
(to) buy	1-13	V1	かう＝買う [かいます]
by	2-2	N	そば＝傍
by (a certain time)	2-10	P	(time) までに

by (tool)	1-4	P	(tool) で
by (transportation facility)	1-7	P	(transportation) で
by 〜 [formal equiv. of 〜に]	4-6	P+V	〜によって
by all means	2-7	Adv	ぜひ＝是非
by far	2-9	Adv	ずっと
By the way	2-3	SI	ところで

<C>

cafeteria	1-4	N	カフェテリア
(to) call for	4-1	V1	よぶ＝呼ぶ [よびます]
(N2) called (N1)	3-2	P+V	N1 という N2
calligraphy	4-6	N	しょどう＝書道
calligraphy piece	4-6	N	しょ＝書
camera	1-15	N	カメラ
camp	1-7	N	キャンプ
can	4-9	N	かん＝缶
can do 〜; be able to do 〜	2-6	V2	できる＝出来る [できます]
can do well	1-5	Na	とくい＝得意
candy	1-2	N	あめ＝飴; キャンディ
canned food	4-3	N	かんづめ＝缶詰め
(It) cannot be helped.	2-6	Exp	しかたがありません。＝仕方がありません。
cannot hear	1-2	V2	きこえません＝聞こえません
cannot see	1-2	V2	みえません＝見えません
cap; hat	2-3	N	ぼうし＝帽子
car	1-7	N	くるま＝車; じどうしゃ＝自動車
(playing) cards	1-5	N	トランプ
(a) care/nursing home for the elderly	4-9	N	ろうじんホーム＝老人ホーム
(to be) careful	2-3	V2	きをつける＝気をつける [きをつけます]
carpet	3-7	N	カーペット
carriage (with two wheels on the sides)	4-4	N	だいはちぐるま＝大八車
carrot	3-1	N	にんじん＝人参
(to) carry	2-2	V1	もつ＝持つ [もちます]
(to) carry something on one's back	4-4	V1	せおう＝背負う [せおいます]
cash register	2-5	N	レジ
castle	4-8	N	しろ＝城
cat	1-10	N	ねこ＝猫
(to) catch a cold	2-6	V1	かぜをひく＝風邪を引く [ひきます]
(to) cause [transitive]	4-4	V1	(〜を) おこす＝起こす [おこします]
(to) celebrate	4-2	V1	いわう＝祝う [いわいます]
cellular phone	3-3	N	けいたいでんわ＝携帯電話
- cent(s)	1-13	Nd	- セント
center	4-4	N	まんなか＝真ん中
- century	4-6	Nd	- せいき＝- 世紀
ceramics	4-6	N	とうげい＝陶芸

EJ

(a) certain ~	2-11	PN	ある ～
(most) certainly	4-8	Adv	きっと
Certainly, Sir/Madam. [Used to acknowledge a request.]	4-1	Exp.	かしこまりました。
chair	1-10	N	いす＝椅子
change (from a larger unit of money)	2-9	N	おつり＝お釣
(to) change (something)	3-1	V2	かえる＝変える [かえます]
(to) change [i.e., shoes, pants, etc.]	3-2	V2	はきかえる＝履き替える [はきかえます]
(to) change over	2-6	V1	かわる＝代わる [かわります]
(a) charge	4-9	N	ゆうりょう＝有料
(to) chat	4-3	V3	おしゃべり (を) する [-します]
(a) chatterbox	4-3	N	おしゃべり
chatting	4-3	N	おしゃべり
(is) cheap; inexpensive	1-13	A	やすい＝安い
cheating	3-2	N	カンニング
(a) check; bill	2-5	N	(お) かんじょう＝(御) 勘定
(to) check; investigate	3-4	V2	しらべる＝調べる [しらべます]
(to) cheer	2-10	V3	おうえん (を) する＝応援 (を) する [-します]
Cheers!	3-8	Exp	かんぱい！＝乾杯
chemistry	3-1	N	かがく＝化学
cherry blossom	4-6	N	さくら＝桜
cherry blossom viewing	4-6	N	(お) はなみ＝(御) 花見
chew away	2-11	Adv	ガリガリ
(to) chew (gum)	2-3	V1	(ガムを) かむ [かみます]
chicken (meat)	2-14	N	とりにく＝鳥肉
chicken and egg over a bowl of steamed rice	2-5	N	おやこどんぶり＝親子丼
child	1-10	N	こども＝子供
China	1-3	N	ちゅうごく＝中国
Chinese language	1-4	N	ちゅうごくご＝中国語
Chinese noodle soup	2-5	N	ラーメン
Chinese reading (of a *kanji*)	3-4	N	おん (よみ)＝音 (読み)
chocolate	2-5	N	チョコレート
(to) choose	4-6	V1	えらぶ＝選ぶ [えらびます]
chopsticks	1-14	N	(お) はし＝(御) 箸
Christianity	2-7	N	キリストきょう＝キリスト教
Christmas	2-7	N	クリスマス
Christmas card	2-7	N	クリスマスカード
Christmas tree	2-7	N	クリスマスツリー
Chuo (Central) Line [orange colored train line in Tokyo]	3-9	N	ちゅうおうせん＝中央線
church	2-7	N	きょうかい＝教会
cigarettes	2-3	N	たばこ
circle	3-8	N	まる＝丸
(to) circle	3-8	V3	まる (を) する＝丸 (を) する [-します]

(a) citizen of a hostile (an enemy) country　4-3　N　てきこくじん＝敵国人

(large) city; metropolis　4-4　N　とかい＝都会

city　2-9　N　し＝市

class　1-11　N　じゅぎょう＝授業; クラス

classifier (of *kanji*)　3-4　N　ぶしゅ＝部首

classroom　1-10　N　きょうしつ＝教室

(to) clean up　2-7　V3　そうじ (を) する＝掃除 (を) する [-します]

(to) clean up; put away　2-14　V2　かたづける＝片付ける [かたづけます]

(is) clean　1-6　Na　きれい

(to) clean　2-14　V3　きれいにする [きれいにします]

clear (weather)　2-7　N　はれ＝晴れ

clearly　4-1　Adv　はっきり

(to) climb　4-8　V1　のぼる＝登る [のぼります]

clock; watch　1-13　N　とけい＝時計

(to) close (something)　1-13　V2　(〜を) しめる＝閉める [しめます]

close; near　1-10　A　ちかい＝近い

(Please) close.　1-2　Exp　しめてください。＝閉めて下さい。

(something, someplace) closes [intransitive]

　　　　　　4-4　V1　(〜が) しまる＝閉まる [しまります]

clothing　2-3　N　ふく＝服

cloud　2-11　N　くも＝雲

cloudy (weather)　2-7　N　くもり＝曇り

cloudy and occasionally clear　4-8　N　くもりいちじはれ＝曇り一時晴れ

club activity　3-2　N　ぶかつ (どう)＝部活 (動)

co-educational　3-2　N　(だんじょ) きょうがく＝(男女) 共学

cockroach　1-10　N　ごきぶり

coffee shop　1-13　N　きっさてん＝喫茶店

coffee　1-4　N　コーヒー

cola (drink)　1-4　N　コーラ

(a) cold　1-12　N　かぜ＝風邪

(is) cold (temperature)　1-1　A　さむい＝寒い

(is) cold (to the touch)　1-14　A　つめたい＝冷たい

(to) collect (something) [transitive]　4-3　V2　(〜を) あつめる＝集める [あつめます]

college　1-12　N　だいがく＝大学

college student　1-12　N　だいがくせい＝大学生

color　1-5　N　いろ＝色

(to) come　1-7　V3　くる＝来る [きます]

(to) come [honorific equiv. of 来る]　4-1　V1　いらっしゃる [いらっしゃいます]

(to) come [humble equiv. of 来る]　4-1　V1　まいる＝参る [まいります]

(Please) come again. [More polite than また、来て下さい。]

　　　　　4-1　Exp. また、いらしてください＝また、いらして下さい。

(Please) come in. [More polite than 入って下さい]

　　　　　4-1　Exp. おはいりください。＝お入り下さい。

come to do ～/come not to do ～	4-4	Na+P+V1	(Dic./NAI) ようになる
(to) come to pick up (someone)	2-10	V3	(person を) むかえにくる＝迎えに来る [-きます]
(to) come to pick up (thing)	2-10	V3	(thing を) とりにくる＝取りに来る [-きます]
(is) comfortable; feel good	2-14	A	きもちがいい＝気持ちがいい
(is) comfortable; easy	3-3	Na	らく＝楽
comics	3-4	N	まんが＝漫画
(to) command	4-3	V3	めいれい (を) する＝命令 (を) する [-します]
commercial	3-6	N	コマーシャル
(to) commute	3-2	V	かよう＝通う [かよいます]
company	1-7	N	かいしゃ＝会社
company employee (occupation)	1-3	N	かいしゃいん＝会社員
company employee	4-1	N	しゃいん＝社員
company president	4-1	N	しゃちょう＝社長
(to) compare	2-9	V2	くらべる＝比べる [くらべます]
competition [music]	2-15	N	コンクール
(to) complain	4-3	V1	ふへいをいう＝不平を言う [いいます]
(a) complaint	4-3	N	ふへい＝不平
complicated	3-4	Na	ふくざつ＝複雑
computer	1-4	N	コンピューター
concert	1-15	N	コンサート
condition is bad	2-6	A	ぐあいがわるい＝具合が悪い
confidence	4-7	N	じしん＝自信
(be) confident	4-7	V1	じしんがある＝自信がある [あります]
(to) congratulate	4-2	V1	いわう＝祝う [いわいます]
Congratulations.	1-15	Exp	おめでとうございます。
(under) construction (building)	4-6	N	けんちくちゅう＝建築中
(to) consult (someone)	3-3	V3	(someone に) そうだん (を) する＝相談 (を) する [-します]
(to) continue/keep doing ～	3-4	V2	(V Stem) つづける＝続ける [つづけます]
(something) continues [intransitive]	4-6	V1	(～が) つづく＝続く [つづきます]
convenience store	2-13	N	コンビニ
(is) convenient	3-7	Na	べんり＝便利
(to) cook	2-7	V3	りょうり (を) する＝料理 (を) する [-します]
cool [temperature]	1-1	A	すずしい＝涼しい
(to) cooperate	4-7	V3	きょうりょく (を) する＝協力 (を) する [-します]
cooperative	4-7	Na	きょうりょくてき＝協力的
corner	2-4	N	かど＝角
(is) correct	2-2	A	ただしい＝正しい
country	2-9	N	くに＝国
countryside	4-4	N	いなか＝田舎
courage	4-8	N	ゆうき＝勇気
cousin	1-15	N	いとこ
cram school	3-2	N	じゅく＝塾

crane (bird)	4-4	N	つる＝鶴
credit card	2-9	N	クレジットカード
(to) cross (over) ～	2-13	V1	(～を) わたる＝渡る [わたります]
(to get) crowded	2-13	V1	こむ＝込む [こみます]
(is) crowded	2-13	V1	こんでいる＝込んでいる [こんでいます]
(to) cry	2-15	V1	なく＝泣く [なきます]
(to) cry [lit., to shed tears]	4-7	V1	なみだをながす＝涙を流す [ながします]
culture	3-2	N	ぶんか＝文化
cup	1-14	N	コップ
- cupful	1-14	Nd	- ぱい/- はい/- ばい＝ - 杯
curry rice	2-5	N	カレーライス; ライスカレー
(floor) cushion	3-7	N	ざぶとん＝座布団
customer; guest	3-7	N	きゃく＝客
customer; guest [polite]	4-1	N	おきゃくさま＝御客様
(to) cut	2-14	V1	きる＝切る [きります]
cute	1-6	A	かわいい＝可愛い
<D>			
dance; dancing [Western]	1-5	N	ダンス
dance; dancing [Japanese]	3-6	N	おどり＝踊り
(to) dance	3-6	V1	おどる＝踊る [おどります]
(is) dangerous	2-4	A	あぶない＝危ない
(pitch) dark	4-4	N	まっくら＝真っ暗
(is) dark	2-11	A	くらい＝暗い
(own) daughter	2-11	N	むすめ＝娘
(someone else's) daughter	2-11	N	むすめさん＝娘さん
(the) day after tomorrow	1-11	N	あさって＝明後日
(the) day before yesterday	1-11	N	おととい＝一昨日
day of the month	1-11	Nd	- にち＝ - 日
day	1-15	N	ひ＝日
day off	1-7	N	(お) やすみ＝(お) 休み
- day(s)	2-6	Nd	- にち (かん) ＝- 日 (間)
daytime	1-4	N	(お) ひる＝(お) 昼
decade	4-2	N	- ねんだい＝- 年代 [1970 年代 means the 1970's.]
December	1-3	N	じゅうにがつ＝十二月
(to be) decided [intransitive]	4-2	V1	(～が) きまる＝決まる [きまります]
(to) decide [transitive]	4-2	V2	(～を) きめる＝決める [きめます]
decide on (something)	2-5	V3	(something に) する [します]
(to) decide to do ～	4-2	N+P+V3	(Dic./NAI) ことにする [します]
(to) decide to do ～	4-2	N+P+V2	(Dic./NAI) ことにきめる＝決める [きめます]
(It will be) decided that ～	4-2	N+P+V1	(Dic./NAI) ことになる
(It will be) decided that ～	4-2	N+P+V1	(Dic./NAI) ことにきまる＝決まる [きまります]
(to) decorate	3-7	V1	かざる＝飾る [かざります]

EJ

deer	4-8	N	しか＝鹿
definitely	2-7	Adv	ぜひ＝是非
- degree(s)	2-6	Nd	- ど＝- 度
(is) delicious	1-13	A	おいしい＝美味しい
(to) depart	4-8	V3	しゅっぱつ (を) する＝出発 (を) する [-します]
departing from (place)	4-8	Nd	～はつ＝～発
department store	1-7	N	デパート
departure time	4-8	N	しゅっぱつじかん＝出発時間
depending on ～	4-8	P+V	～によって
design	2-9	N	デザイン
desk	1-10	N	つくえ＝机
dessert	2-14	N	デザート
dialect	4-8	N	ほうげん＝方言
(a) diary	4-8	N	にっき＝日記
dictionary	1-2	N	じしょ＝辞書
(to) die	1-12	V1	しぬ＝死ぬ [しにます]
(to) differ	2-2	V1	ちがう＝違う [ちがいます]
(is) different	2-9	V1	ちがう＝違う [ちがいます]
(is) different; odd; unusual	3-8	V1	かわった＝変わった
(is) difficult	1-11	A	むずかしい＝難しい
difficult; hard	1-11	Na	たいへん＝大変
(to) dine; have a meal	1-7	V3	しょくじをする＝食事をする [-します]
dining	1-7	N	しょくじ＝食事
dinner	1-4	N	ばんごはん＝晩御飯
dinner [formal]	3-1	N	ゆうしょく＝夕食
(to) dip (object in thing)	2-14	V2	(object を thing に) つける [つけます]
- direction	3-9	N	- ほうめん＝- 方面
(movie) director; (baseball) manager	3-6	N	かんとく＝監督
(is) dirty	1-6	A	きたない
(to) disagree	4-4	V3	はんたい (を) する＝反対 (を) する [-します]
(How) disappointing! [on a future event]	1-11	Exp	ざんねんですねえ。＝残念ですねえ。
(How) disappointing! [on a past event]	1-11	Exp	ざんねんでしたねえ。＝残念でしたねえ。
(to) discriminate	4-3	V3	さべつ (を) する＝差別 (を) する [-します]
(racial) discrimination	4-3	N	じんしゅさべつ＝人種差別
(to) discuss	4-3	V1	はなしあう＝話し合う [はなしあいます]
dish	1-14	N	(お) さら＝(お) 皿
dislike	1-5	Na	きらい＝嫌い
dislike a lot	1-5	Na	だいきらい＝大嫌い
(to) divide	4-9	V2	わける＝分ける [わけます]
(to) divorce	2-15	V3	りこん (を) する＝離婚 (を) する [-します]
(to) do	1-4	V3	する [します]
(to) do [honorific equiv. of する]	4-1	V1	なさる [なさいます]

(to) do [humble equiv. of する]	4-1	V1	いたす [いたします]
(to) do (something in advance)	3-8	V1	(〜て) おく [おきます]
(to) do [informal form of する]	3-2	V1	やる [やります]
do one's best	1-12	V1	がんばる＝頑張る [がんばります]
(to) do 〜 completely [regret]	2-11	V1	(TE) しまう [しまいます]
(superior) do 〜 for me	3-3	E	(〜て) くださいます＝下さいます
(medical) doctor	1-3	N	いしゃ＝医者
(medical) doctor [polite]	1-3	N	おいしゃさん＝御医者さん
dog	1-10	N	いぬ＝犬
- dollar(s)	1-13	Nd	-ドル
(to) donate	4-7	V3	きふ (を) する＝寄付 (を) する [-します]
(〜 is) done	2-14	V2	(〜が) できました＝出来ました
door	1-10	N	ドア; と＝戸
dormitory	2-2	N	りょう＝寮
(to) draft (for military service)	4-3	V3	しょうしゅう (を) する＝召集 (を) する [-します]
(to) draw (a picture)	2-15	V1	(えを) かく＝(絵を) 描く [かきます]
drawing	1-5	N	え＝絵
dream	3-3	N	ゆめ＝夢
(one piece) dress	2-3	N	ワンピース
(the style of) dress	4-6	N	ふくそう＝服装
(a) drink	1-5	N	のみもの＝飲み物
(to) drink	1-4	V2	のむ＝飲む [のみます]
(to) drink [honorific equiv. of 飲む]	4-1	V1	めしあがる＝召し上がる [めしあがります]
(to) drink [humble equiv. of 飲む]	4-1	V1	いただく [いただきます]
(to) drive	2-3	V3	うんてん (を) する＝運転 (を) する [-します]
driver	2-4	N	うんてんしゅ＝運転手; ドライバー
driver's license	2-3	N	うんてんめんきょ＝運転免許
(to) drop (something) [transitive]	4-4	V1	(〜を) おとす＝落とす [おとします]
(to) drop by (a place)	2-10	V1	(place に) よる＝寄る [よります]
(something) drops [intransitive]	4-4	V2	(〜が) おちる＝落ちる [おちます]
drugs	3-2	N	まやく＝麻薬
(someone/something gets) dry [intransitive]	4-8	V1	(〜が) かわく＝乾く [かわきます]
Dust amassed will make a mountain.	3-1	Prov	ちりもつもればやまとなる ＝塵も積れば山となる

<E>

e-mail	3-3	N	でんしメール＝電子メール
(counter) each	4-4	ND	(counter) ずつ
ear	1-6	N	みみ＝耳
early [used with a verb]	1-12	Adv	はやく＝早く
early evening	1-4	N	ゆうがた＝夕方
(is) early	1-7	A	はやい＝早い
(to) earn/make (money)	4-2	V2	もうける＝儲ける [もうけます]
earrings	2-3	N	イヤリング

(the) earth	4-9	N	ちきゅう＝地球
(not) easily 〜	3-4	Adv	なかなか＋ Neg.
east	2-1	N	ひがし＝東
east coast	4-3	V3	ひがしかいがん＝東海岸
east entrance/exit	3-9	N	ひがしぐち＝東口
Eastern style	3-7	Na	とうようてき＝東洋的
(is) easy	1-11	A	やさしい＝易しい
(is) easy to do 〜	3-4	A	(Verb Stem) ＋やすい
(to) eat	1-4	V2	たべる＝食べる [たべます]
(to) eat [honorific equiv. of 食べる]	4-1	V1	めしあがる＝召し上がる [めしあがります]
(to) eat [humble equiv. of 食べる]	4-1	V1	いただく [いただきます]
Echo [A *shinkansen* that stops at most of the *shinkansen* stations.]	4-8	N	こだま
economics	3-4	N	けいざい＝経済
education	3-2	N	きょういく＝教育
egg	2-14	N	たまご＝卵
eight	1-1	N	はち＝八
eight [general counter]	1-2	N	やっつ＝八つ
eighteen	1-1	N	じゅうはち＝十八
(the) eighth day of the month	1-11	N	ようか＝八日
eighth grader	1-3	N	ちゅうがくにねんせい＝中学二年生
eighty	1-1	N	はちじゅう＝八十
(not) either	2-9	N	どちらも＋ Neg.
elderly man	1-3	N	おじいさん
elderly woman	1-3	N	おばあさん
(an) eldest daughter	4-2	N	ちょうじょ＝長女
(an) eldest son	4-2	N	ちょうなん＝長男
electric goods	3-7	N	でんきせいひん＝電気製品
electric train	1-7	N	でんしゃ＝電車
eleven	1-1	N	じゅういち＝十一
eleventh grader	1-3	N	こうこうにねんせい＝高校二年生
(to) embrace each other	4-3	V1	だきあう＝抱き合う [だきあいます]
Emperor	3-9	N	てんのう＝天皇
(is) employed (at 〜)	2-2	V2	(place に) つとめる＝勤める [つとめます]
empty	4-9	N	から＝空
empty [informal]	4-9	N	からっぽ＝空っぽ
(is) empty	2-13	V1	すいている [すいています]
(to get) empty	2-13	V1	すく [すきます]
empty can	4-9	N	あきかん＝空き缶
end (of a street)	3-9	N	つきあたり＝突き当たり
(something) ends [intransitive]	2-10	V1	(〜が) おわる＝終わる [おわります]
(the) end	2-11	N	おしまい
(at the) end	2-14	Adv	おわりに＝終わりに
endurance	4-2	N	がまん＝我慢

(to) endure	4-2	V3	がまん (を) する＝我慢 (を) する [-します]
enemy	4-3	N	てき＝敵
engineer	1-3	N	エンジニア
English language	1-4	N	えいご＝英語
English-Japanese dictionary	3-4	N	えいわじてん＝英和辞典
(to) enjoy	3-6	V1	たのしむ＝楽しむ [たのしみます]
(is) enjoyable	1-11	A	たのしい＝楽しい
enjoyment	4-9	N	たのしみ＝楽しみ
enough	4-9	Na/Adv	じゅうぶん＝十分
(to) enter (a place)	2-4	V1	(place に) はいる＝入る [はいります]
entertainment	3-6	N	ごらく＝娯楽
entrance	2-13	N	いりぐち＝入口
entrance way; foyer	3-7	N	げんかん＝玄関
envious	3-6	A	うらやましい＝羨ましい
environment	4-9	N	かんきょう＝環境
eraser [rubber]	1-2	N	けしごむ＝消しゴム
(to) escape	4-4	V2	にげる＝逃げる [にげます]
especially	2-2	Adv	とくに＝特に
(N1 and N2,) etc.	1-15	Nd	(N1) や (N2) など
～, etc. [informal]	4-9	Nd	～なんか
(not) even (one person) ～	4-7	N+P	ひとりも＋ Neg. ＝一人も＋ Neg.
even ～	4-3	Nd	～さえ
evening; night	1-4	N	ばん＝晩
event(s)	3-2	N	ぎょうじ＝行事
every month	1-12	N	まいつき＝毎月
every semester	3-2	N	まいがっき＝毎学期
every week	1-11	N	まいしゅう＝毎週
every year	1-15	N	まいとし＝毎年; まいねん＝毎年
everyday	1-4	N	まいにち＝毎日
everyone	1-15	N	みんな＝皆
everyone [polite]	1-15	N	みなさん＝皆さん
everyone	4-6	N	だれも＋affirmative ending [⇔だれも＋negative nobody]
everything	1-14	N	ぜんぶ＝全部
exam	1-2	N	しけん＝試験
(is) excited	2-10	V3	ドキドキする [ドキドキします]
Excuse me for going/doing something first.	3-1	Exp	おさきに。＝お先に。
Excuse me. [lit., I will commit a rudeness by troubling you. Used after one enters the host's home.]	4-1	Exp.	おじゃまします
Excuse me. I must be going now.	3-1	Exp	しつれいします。＝失礼します。
Excuse me. (apology)	1-1	Exp	すみません。
Excuse me. (to get attention)	1-13	Exp	すみません。
(to) exercise	2-10	V3	うんどう (を) する＝運動 (を) する [-します]

(to) exist (animate)	1-10	V1	いる [います]
(to) exist [honorific equiv. of いる]	2-6	V1	いらっしゃる [いらっしゃいます]
(to) exist [humble equiv. of いる]	4-1	V1	おる [おります]
exit	2-13	N	でぐち＝出口

(I) expect that he/she will do/will not do. He/She is expected to do/not to do

	2-6	Nd	(Dic./NAI) はずです
(is) expensive	1-13	A	たかい＝高い
(to) experience	3-7	V3	けいけん (を) する＝経験 (を) する [-します]
(to) experience (personally)	4-3	V3	たいけん (を) する＝体験 (を) する [-します]
(to) explain	3-9	V3	せつめい (を) する＝説明 (を) する [-します]
(an) explanation	3-9	N	せつめい＝説明
eye	1-6	N	め＝目
eyeglasses	1-2	N	めがね＝眼鏡

<F>

face	1-6	N	かお＝顔
fall (season)	1-12	N	あき＝秋
(rain, snow) fall	2-7	V1	ふる＝降る [ふります]
(to) fall in love (with person)	4-7	V3	(person に) こいをする＝恋をする [-します]
(own) family	1-3	N	かぞく＝家族
(someone's) family	1-3	N	ごかぞく＝御家族
famous	1-10	Na	ゆうめい＝有名
far away	2-2	N	とおく＝遠く
(is) far	1-10	A	とおい＝遠い
fare	3-9	N	りょうきん＝料金
farm; (vegetable) field	4-3	N	はたけ＝畑
fast	2-4	Adv	はやく＝速く
(is) fat	1-6	V1	ふとっている＝太っている [ふとっています]
(someone's) father	1-3	N	おとうさん＝お父さん
(own) father	1-3	N	ちち＝父
Father's Day	1-15	N	ちちのひ＝父の日
feast	4-8	N	ごちそう＝御馳走
February	1-3	N	にがつ＝二月
(to) feel	4-6	V2	かんじる＝感じる [かんじます]
(to) feel like ～	4-6	Na+P+V3	～ようなきがする＝～ような気がする
feel sick	2-6	A	ぐあいがわるい＝具合が悪い
female [formal]	3-6	N	じょせい＝女性
female; woman	1-10	N	おんな＝女
fermented soybeans	3-8	N	なっとう＝納豆
fever	1-12	N	ねつ＝熱
(a) few	1-10	Adv	すこし＝少し
(is) few	1-11	A	すくない＝少ない
(vegetable) field; garden	4-3	N	はたけ＝畑
field	4-7	N	のはら＝野原

fifteen	1-1	N	じゅうご＝十五
(the) fifth day of the month	1-11	N	いつか＝五日
fifty	1-1	N	ごじゅう＝五十
(to) fight	2-4	V3	けんか (を) する＝喧嘩 (を) する [-します]
(to) fight a battle	4-2	V1	たたかう＝戦う [たたかいます]
filial piety	4-2	Na	おやこうこう＝親孝行
finally	2-11	Adv	とうとう
finally	4-3	Adv	やっと
(to) find ～	3-4	V2	(～ を) みつける＝見つける [みつけます]
fine; healthy	1-1	Na	げんき＝元気
fine; healthy [polite]	1-1	Na	(お) げんき＝(御) 元気
finger	1-6	N	ゆび＝指
(to) finish doing ～	3-4	V1	(V Stem) おわる＝終わる [おわります]
(to) finish (something) [transitive]	1-1	V2	(～を) おわります＝終わります
(something) finishes [intransitive]	2-10	V1	(～が) おわる＝終わる [おわります]
fire; light; flame	4-4	N	ひ＝火
(a) fire	4-4	N	かじ＝火事
(to do) fireworks	2-7	V3	はなび (をする)＝花火 (をする) [-します]
(the) first day of the month	1-11	N	ついたち＝一日
first of all	2-14	SI	まず
first semester	3-2	N	いちがっき＝一学期
(at) first	3-8	Adv	さいしょに＝最初に
(Excuse me for going/doing something) first.	3-1	Exp	おさきに。＝お先に。
(for the) first time	2-7	N	はじめて＝始めて／初めて
(the) first	3-8	N	さいしょ＝最初
fish	1-10	N	さかな＝魚
five	1-1	N	ご＝五
five [general counter]	1-2	N	いつつ＝五つ
(to) fix	3-7	V1	なおす＝直す [なおします]
flammable garbage	4-9	N	もえるゴミ＝燃えるゴミ
(to) flash	4-4	V1	(ピカッと) ひかる＝光る [ひかります]
flavor	2-14	N	あじ＝味
floor	2-4	N	ゆか＝床
(wheat) flour	4-3	N	こむぎこ＝小麦粉
flower	1-10	N	はな＝花
flower arrangement	3-7	N	いけばな＝生け花
flower shop	1-13	N	はなや＝花屋
(to) fly	4-4	V1	とぶ＝飛ぶ [とびます]
folk tale	2-11	N	むかしばなし＝昔話
(to) follow (the rules)	4-3	V1	まもる＝守る [まもります]
food	1-5	N	たべもの＝食べ物
foot	1-6	N	あし＝足
football	1-5	N	フットボール

for (activity)	1-7	P	(activity) に
for everything	1-14	N	ぜんぶで＝全部で
For example	3-4	SI	たとえば＝例えば
foreign language	1-11	N	がいこくご＝外国語
forever	4-9	Adv	いつまでも
(to) forget	1-14	V2	わすれる＝忘れる [わすれます]
fork	1-14	N	フォーク
fortunately	4-2	Adv	うんよく＝運良く
forty	1-1	N	よんじゅう＝四十
(to be) found [intransitive]	3-4	V1	(〜 が) みつかる＝見つかる [みつかります]
four	1-1	N	し＝四; よん＝四
four [general counter]	1-2	N	よっつ＝四つ
4 1/2-mat room	3-7	N	よじょうはん＝四畳半
fourteen	1-1	N	じゅうし＝十四; じゅうよん＝十四
(the) fourteenth day of the month	1-11	N	じゅうよっか＝十四日
(the) fourth day of the month	1-11	N	よっか＝四日
fragrance	2-7	N	におい＝臭い
France	1-3	N	フランス
(is) free (time)	2-15	Na	ひま＝暇
(is) free; liberal	2-3	Na	じゆう＝自由
free of charge [formal]	4-9	N	むりょう＝無料
free of charge [informal]	4-9	N	ただ
french fries	1-14	N	フライドポテト
French language	1-4	N	フランスご＝フランス語
freshman (9th grader)	1-3	N	ちゅうがくさんねんせい＝中学三年生
Friday	1-7	N	きんようび＝金曜日
friend	1-4	N	ともだち＝友達
from now on	1-14	SI	これから
from 〜	1-11	P	〜から
from 〜 to 〜	2-13	P	〜から 〜まで
front	1-2	N	まえ＝前
front (side)	4-4	N	おもて＝表
fruit	2-14	N	くだもの＝果物
Fukuoka	2-1	N	ふくおか＝福岡
(I am) full.	1-14	Exp	おなかがいっぱいです。＝お腹が一杯です。
(is) fun	1-11	A	たのしい＝楽しい
funeral	4-2	N	(お) そうしき＝(御) 葬式
(is) funny	1-11	A	おもしろい＝面白い
furniture	4-9	N	かぐ＝家具
future	2-14	N	しょうらい＝将来
<G>			
game	1-15	N	ゲーム
(sports) game	1-12	N	しあい＝試合

garage	1-10	N	ガレージ
garden	1-10	N	にわ＝庭
garden (vegetable)	4-3	N	はたけ＝畑
garden [formal]	4-6	N	ていえん＝庭園
gardening	4-3	N	えんげい＝園芸
gas station	3-9	N	ガソリンスタンド
gate	2-3	N	もん＝門
(animate subjects) gather [intransitive]	4-3	V1	(〜が) あつまる＝集まる [あつまります]
generally	2-5	Adv	だいたい
(counter for) generations	4-2	Nd	- せい＝- 世
generous	4-7	Na	かんだい＝寛大
German language	1-4	N	ドイツご＝ドイツ語
Germany	1-3	N	ドイツ
(to) get	2-6	V1	とる＝取る [とります]
(to) get off (vehicle)	2-4	V2	(vehicle から/を) おりる＝降りる [おります]
(to) get up	1-7	V2	おきる＝起きる [おきます]
(to) get/receive (from 〜)	1-15	V1	(〜から/に) もらう [もらいます]
Ginza [a city in Tokyo]	3-9	N	ぎんざ＝銀座
girl	1-10	N	おんなのこ＝女の子
girl's school	3-2	N	じょしこう＝女子校
(to) give (to a superior)	2-9	V2	(superior に) さしあげる＝差し上げる [さしあげます]
(to) give (to equal)	1-15	V2	あげる [あげます]
(to) give (to inferior)	1-15	V2	やる [やります]
(to) give (to speaker or to speaker's family)	1-15	V2	くれる [くれます]
(to) give up	4-7	V2	あきらめる＝諦める [あきらめます]
(to be) glad	4-3	V1	よろこぶ＝喜ぶ [よろこびます]
(is) glad	1-11	A	うれしい＝嬉しい
- glassful(s)	1-14	Nd	- はい; - ばい; - ぱい＝ - 杯
(to) gnaw [onomatopoetic]	2-11	Adv	ガリガリ
(to) go	1-7	V1	いく＝行く [いきます]
(to) go [honorific equiv. of 行く]	4-1	V1	いらっしゃる [いらっしゃいます]
(to) go [humble equiv. of 行く]	4-1	V1	まいる＝参る [まいります]
(to) go down	3-7	V2	おりる＝下りる [おります]
(to) go out (from a place)	2-4	V2	(place を/から) でかける＝出かける [でかけます]
(to) go over 〜; cross over 〜	2-13	V1	(〜を) わたる＝渡る [わたります]
(to) go to bed	1-7	V2	ねる＝寝る [ねます]
(to) go to pick up (person)	2-10	V1	(person を) むかえにいく＝迎えに行く [-いきます]
(to) go to pick up (thing)	2-10	V1	(thing を) とりにいく＝取りに行く [-いきます]
gold	2-15	N	きん＝金
gold (color)	1-5	N	きんいろ＝金色
golf	1-5	N	ゴルフ
(is) good	1-2	A	いい; よい＝良い

(is) good [polite equiv. of いい]	4-1	A	よろしい
(be) good at	1-5	Na	じょうず＝上手
Good evening.	1-7	Exp	こんばんは＝今晩は
(That is a) good idea.	2-10	Exp	それはいいかんがえです。＝それはいい考えです。
(is) good looking	3-3	A	かっこいい＝格好いい
good-luck charm	4-8	N	おまもり＝御守り
Good luck.	1-12	Exp	がんばって。＝頑張って。
Good morning. [formal]	1-1	Exp	おはようございます。
Good morning. [informal]	1-1	Exp	おはよう。
Good night.	3-1	Exp	おやすみ (なさい)。＝お休み (なさい)。
Good-bye. [formal]	1-1	Exp	さようなら。
Good-bye. [informal]	1-14	Exp	バイバイ
grade	1-11	N	せいせき＝成績
gradually; step by step	4-4	Adv	だんだん
(to) graduate (school)	3-1	V3	(school を) そつぎょうする＝卒業する [-します]
graduate school	4-2	N	だいがくいん＝大学院
graduation ceremony	3-2	N	そつぎょうしき＝卒業式
(own) grandchild(ren)	4-2	N	まご＝孫
(other's) grandchild(ren)	4-2	N	おまごさん＝お孫さん
grandfather	1-3	N	おじいさん
(one's own) grandfather	3-1	N	そふ＝祖父
grandmother	1-3	N	おばあさん
(one's own) grandmother	3-1	N	そぼ＝祖母
grass	3-2	N	くさ＝草
(is) great (person)	2-11	A	えらい＝偉い
greed	4-7	N	よく＝欲
greedy (person)	4-7	Na	よくばり＝欲張り
green	1-5	N	みどり＝緑
green [traffic light]	2-2	N	あお＝青
green car [JR first class car]	4-8	N	グリーンしゃ＝グリーン車
(to) greet	4-1	V3	あいさつ (を) する＝挨拶 (を) する [-します]
grey	1-5	N	グレイ
(to) grill; roast; bake; toast; fry	3-11	V1	やく＝焼く [やきます]
grilled fish	3-8	N	やきざかな＝焼き魚
grilled skewered chicken	2-5	N	やきとり＝焼き鳥
guest	4-1	N	きゃく＝客
guest [polite]	4-1	N	おきゃくさま＝御客様
(to) guide	4-8	V3	あんない (を) する＝案内 (を) する [-します]
guitar	1-5	N	ギター
gum	2-3	N	ガム
gun	3-2	N	じゅう＝銃
gym	2-10	N	たいいくかん＝体育館

<H>

English	Lesson	Type	Japanese
hair	1-6	N	かみ (のけ)=髪 (の毛)
- half	1-7	Nd	- はん=- 半
(in) half	2-14	Adv	はんぶんに=半分に
hamburger	1-14	N	ハンバーガー
hand	1-6	N	て=手
(to) hand over	4-1	V1	わたす=渡す [わたします]
(to) hang	3-7	V2	かける=掛ける [かけます]
(something) happens [intransitive]	4-4	V2	(〜が) おきる=起きる [おきます]
happiness	4-7	N	こうふく=幸福
happy (life)	3-6	Na	しあわせ=幸せ
happy (life)	4-7	Na	こうふく=幸福
Happy New Year!	2-7	Exp	あけましておめでとうございます。=明けましておめでとうございます。
(is) happy [emotional]	1-11	A	うれしい=嬉しい
Harajuku [a city in Tokyo]	3-9	N	はらじゅく=原宿
harbor	4-3	N	みなと=港
(is) hard; difficult	1-11	Na	たいへん=大変
(is) hard to do 〜	3-4	A	(Verb Stem) にくい
(is) hard; stiff	3-8	A	かたい=硬い
(is) hard; bitter; painful	3-3	A	つらい=辛い
harmony, respect, purity and tranquility	4-6	N	わけいせいじゃく=和敬清寂
hat	2-3	N	ぼうし=帽子
hate	1-5	Na	だいきらい=大嫌い
have (part of body)	3-6	V	(part of body を) している [しています]
Have a nice weekend.	4-0	Exp	よいしゅうまつを。=良い週末を。
(I) have not seen you for a long time.	3-3	Exp	おひさしぶりです。
have to (do)	2-5	Dv	-なければなりません
have to (do) [informal]	4-9	Dv	-なきゃ／-なくちゃ (いけない／ならない)
(do not) have to (do)	2-5	Dv	-なくてもいいです
(to) have 〜	1-11	V1	(〜が) ある [あります]
(to) have 〜; hold; carry	2-2	V1	(〜を) もつ=持つ [もちます]
he; him; boyfriend	3-6	N	かれ=彼
head	1-6	N	あたま=頭
health	3-8	N	けんこう=健康
healthy	3-8	Na	けんこうてき=健康的
healthy; fine	1-1	Na	げんき=元気
healthy; fine [polite]	1-1	Na	(お) げんき=(御) 元気
(to) hear	1-4	V1	きく=聞く [ききます]
(I) heard that 〜.	3-6	Nd+ C	〜そうだ。[〜そうです。]
(I) heard that 〜 [informal]	4-9	SE	〜んだって。
heart; mind	1-6	N	こころ=心
(to) heat	2-14	V3	あつくする=熱くする [あつくします]

EJ

heaven	4-3	N	てんごく＝天国
(is) heavy	3-7	A	おもい＝重い
height	1-6	N	せ (い)＝背
hell	4-3	N	じごく＝地獄
Hello. [telephone]	2-6	Exp	もしもし
Hello; Hi.	1-1	Exp	こんにちは。
(to) help	2-7	V3	てつだう＝手伝う [てつだいます]
(to) help; rescue	2-15	V2	たすける＝助ける [たすけます]
here	1-2	N	ここ
here [polite equiv. of ここ]	1-2	N	こちら
Here! (attendance)	1-3	Exp	はい。
Here, please (take it).	1-2	Exp	はい、どうぞ。
(to) hesitate; be reserved	3-11	V3	えんりょ (を) する＝遠慮 (を) する [-します]
(to) hide (something)	2-11	V1	(〜を) かくす＝隠す [かくします]
high school	1-3	N	こうこう＝高校
high school student	1-3	N	こうこうせい＝高校生
hindrance	1-6	Na	じゃま＝邪魔
Hiroshima	2-1	N	ひろしま＝広島
history	3-1	N	れきし＝歴史
(to) hit (someone)	4-2	V1	(〜を) なぐる＝殴る [なぐります]
hobby	1-5	N	しゅみ＝趣味
Hokkaido	2-1	N	ほっかいどう＝北海道
(to) hold	2-2	V1	もつ＝持つ [もちます]
hole	2-11	N	あな＝穴

(I'm) home. [Used by a family member who has come home.] 3-1 Exp ただいま。

(Is anyone) home? [Used before one enters someone's home.]

	4-1	Exp.	ごめんください。
homeroom	1-11	N	ホームルーム
(do a) homestay	2-2	V3	ホームステイ (をする) [-します]
hometown	4-4	N	いなか＝田舎
homework	1-2	N	しゅくだい＝宿題
honest	4-7	Na	しょうじき＝正直
honorifics	4-1	N	けいご＝敬語
Honshu	2-1	N	ほんしゅう＝本州

Hope [A *shinkansen* that stops at only the largest *shinkansen* stations.] 4-8 N のぞみ

(I) hope/wish that 〜.	4-9	Exp	〜 といい (です)。
hospital	1-3	N	びょういん＝病院
(is) hot [temperature]	1-1	A	あつい＝暑い
(is) hot and humid	1-1	A	むしあつい＝蒸し暑い
hot spring	4-8	N	おんせん＝温泉
hotdog	1-14	N	ホットドッグ
- hour(s)	2-6	Nd	- じかん＝- 時間
house [building]	2-2	N	いえ＝家

(someone's) house [polite]	2-6	N	おたく＝お宅
house; home	1-4	N	うち
household chore; housework	3-3	N	かじ＝家事
housewife	1-3	N	しゅふ＝主婦
How?	3-9	N	どうやって（＝どう）
how? [Polite]	1-13	Ni	いかが
How are you?	1-1	Exp	おげんきですか。＝お元気ですか。
How do you do?	1-1	Exp	はじめまして。
How do you say 〜 in Japanese?	1-2	Exp	〜はにほんごでなんといいますか。 ＝〜は日本語で何と言いますか。
How far is it? [distance]	2-13	Exp	どのぐらいありますか。
How is it? [informal]	1-11	Exp	どうですか。
How long does it take? [time]	2-13	Exp	どのぐらいかかりますか。
How long/far is it?	2-13	Exp	どのぐらいですか。
how many [birds]?	1-10	Ni	なんわ＝何羽
how many [bound objects]?	1-15	Ni	なんさつ＝何冊
how many [long cylindrical objects]?	1-10	Ni	なんぼん＝何本
how many [mechanized goods]?	1-10	Ni	なんだい＝何台
how many [small animals]?	1-10	Ni	なんびき＝何匹
how many cups?	1-14	Ni	なんばい＝何杯
how many people?	1-3	Ni	なんにん＝何人
how many? [general counter]	1-2	Ni	いくつ
how much? [price]	1-13	Ni	（お）いくら
how old? [age]	1-3	Ni	なんさい＝何歳; 何才; （お）いくつ
How pitiful.	1-12	Exp	かわいそうに。＝可愛そうに。
How ridiculous!	2-11	Exp	とんでもない。
how to do 〜	2-14	N	(Verb stem) かた＝方
how to make 〜	2-14	N	（〜の）つくりかた＝作り方
However [Formal expression of でも]	2-15	SI	しかし
Huh?	2-11	SI	えっ
humble	4-7	Na	けんきょ＝謙虚
humble language	4-1	N	けんじょうご＝謙譲語
hundred thousand	1-13	N	じゅうまん＝十万
hundred	1-1	N	ひゃく＝百
(I got) hungry.	1-14	Exp	おなかがすきました。＝お腹が空きました。
(I am) hungry.	1-14	Exp	おなかがペコペコです。＝お腹がペコペコです。
Hurray!	2-10	Exp	ばんざい！＝万歳！
Hurry!	1-1	Exp	はやく＝速く
(someone else's) husband	3-6	N	ごしゅじん＝ご主人
(own) husband	3-6	N	しゅじん＝主人

<I>

I	1-1	N	わたし＝私
I (used by males)	1-1	N	ぼく＝僕

I see!	2-11	Exp	なるほど
(It is) I, (not you.) [emphasis]	3-1	Exp	こちらこそ。
I. D.	2-3	N	しょうめいしょ＝証明書
ice cream	2-4	N	アイスクリーム
(That is a good) idea.	2-10	Exp	それはいいかんがえです。＝それはいい考えです。
If	3-7	Adv	もし
If something happens twice, it will happen three times.	3-2	Prov	にどあることはさんどある＝二度あることは三度ある
Ikebukuro [a city in Tokyo]	3-9	N	いけぶくろ＝池袋
illness	1-12	N	びょうき＝病気
immigrant	4-2	N	いみん＝移民
immoral	4-7	Na	ふどうとく＝不道徳
Imperial Palace	4-8	N	こうきょ＝皇居
important	1-12	Na	だいじ＝大事
(That's) impossible!	2-11	Exp	とんでもない（です）。
impression	4-3	N	いんしょう＝印象
impressive	4-3	Na	いんしょうてき＝印象的
in (location)	1-10	P	(location) に
in (place) [with action verb]	1-4	P	(place) で [with action verb]
in [tool particle]	1-4	P	(tool) で
in order to do/not to do	4-2	N	(Dic./NAI form) ため（に）
in spite of 〜; although 〜 [reverse result]	3-3	Rc	〜のに
(is) in the way	1-6	Na	じゃま＝邪魔
inappropriate	4-6	Na	ふてきとう＝不適当
incense stick	4-2	N	せんこう＝線香
(is) inconvenient	3-7	Na	ふべん＝不便
Indeed!	2-11	Exp	なるほど
Indeed!; Just as I thought.	4-8	SI	やはり
Indeed!; Just as I thought. [informal]	4-8	SI	やっぱり
(person of) inferior status [lit., a person below your eye level]	4-1	N	めしたのひと＝目下の人
inflammable garbage	4-9	N	もえないゴミ＝燃えないゴミ
influence	4-6	N	えいきょう＝影響
(to) influence	4-6	V2	えいきょうをあたえる＝影響を与える [あたえます]
(to be) influenced	4-6	V2	えいきょうをうける＝影響を受ける [うけます]
(to) inform	4-3	V2	しらせる＝知らせる [しらせます]
information booth	4-8	N	あんないしょ＝案内所
ingredients	3-8	N	ざいりょう＝材料
(to get) injured	4-4	V3	けが（を）する＝怪我（を）する [-します]
(Japanese) inn	4-8	N	りょかん＝旅館
innocent	4-4	Na	むじつ＝無実
inside	2-2	N	なか＝中
inside; home	3-7	N	うち＝内

(personal) interest	3-4	N	きょうみ＝興味
(is) interesting	1-11	A	おもしろい＝面白い
intermediate level	3-4	N	ちゅうきゅう＝中級
intermediate school student	1-3	N	ちゅうがくせい＝中学生
intermediate school	1-3	N	ちゅうがく＝中学
internment camp	4-3	N	しゅうようじょ＝収容所
(to) interpret	4-3	V3	つうやく (を) する＝通訳 (を) する [-します]
intersection	2-13	N	こうさてん＝交差点
(to) introduce	2-2	V3	しょうかい (を) する＝紹介 (を) する [-します]
irresponsible	4-2	Na	むせきにん＝無責任
(It) is not so. [formal]	1-1	Exp	そうではありません。
(It) is not so. [informal]	1-1	Exp	そうじゃありません。
island	2-9	N	しま＝島
Isn't it 〜?	2-7	C	-でしょう [rising intonation]
(〜,) isn't it? [emphasis and confirmation]	4-7	C	(plain form) じゃない。
isn't it? [sentence ending particle]	1-6	SP	ね
It is like 〜.	4-3	P+NA+C	〜のようだ。
(Yes,) it is.	1-1	Exp	そうです。
It's me. [used on the telephone]	2-6	Exp	かわりました。
itinerary	4-8	N	にっていひょう＝日程表

<J>

jacket	1-13	N	ジャケット
January	1-3	N	いちがつ＝一月
Japan	1-3	N	にほん＝日本
Japan Railway	3-9	N	ＪＲ〔ジェイアール〕
Japan Railway ticket window	3-10	N	みどりのまどぐち＝みどりの窓口
Japan-U.S.	4-3	N	にちべい＝日米
Japanese citizen	1-3	N	にほんじん＝日本人
(person of) Japanese descent	4-2	N	にっけい (じん)＝日系 (人)
Japanese language	1-4	N	にほんご＝日本語
Japanese meal	3-11	N	わしょく＝和食
Japanese military	4-3	N	にほんぐん＝日本軍
Japanese reading (of *kanji*)	3-4	N	くん (よみ)＝訓 (読み)
Japanese-English dictionary	3-4	N	わえいじてん＝和英辞典
Japanese-style room	3-7	N	わしつ＝和室
(to) jilt	4-7	V1	ふる [ふります]
job	1-3	N	(お) しごと＝(御) 仕事
jogging	1-5	N	ジョギング
joke	2-10	N	じょうだん＝冗談
journal	4-8	N	にっき＝日記
juice	1-4	N	ジュース
July	1-3	N	しちがつ＝七月
June	1-3	N	ろくがつ＝六月

| junior (in high school) | 1-3 | N | こうこうにねんせい＝高校二年生 |

<K>

kabuki theater	3-9	N	かぶきざ＝歌舞伎座
Kanda [a city in Tokyo]	3-9	N	かんだ＝神田
kanji dictionary	3-4	N	かんじじてん＝漢字辞典
Kansai Airport	4-8	N	かんさいくうこう＝関西空港

Kansai area [region of western Honshu including Osaka and Kyoto]

| | 4-8 | N | かんさい＝関西 |

Kanto area [region of eastern Honshu including Tokyo]　4-8　N　かんとう＝関東

kendo [Japanese fencing]	3-2	N	けんどう＝剣道
key	2-4	N	かぎ＝鍵
(Are you) kidding?	2-10	Exp	うそでしょう。
(to) kill	4-4	V1	ころす＝殺す [ころします]

Kill two birds with one stone.　3-11　Prov　いっせきにちょう＝一石二鳥

(summer cotton) kimono	4-8	N	ゆかた＝浴衣
(is) kind	1-6	A	やさしい＝優しい
(is) kind; considerate	3-3	Na	しんせつ＝親切
kindergarten	3-1	N	ようちえん＝幼稚園
kitchen	2-14	N	だいどころ＝台所
knife	1-14	N	ナイフ
(do not) know	1-1	V1	しりません＝知りません
(to) know	2-2	V1	しっている＝知っている [しっています]

(Do you) know?　[honorific equiv. of 知っていますか]

	4-1	V	ごぞんじですか＝御存知ですか
Kobe	2-1	N	こうべ＝神戸
Korea	1-3	N	かんこく＝韓国
Korean language	1-4	N	かんこくご＝韓国語
Kyoto	2-1	N	きょうと＝京都
Kyushu	2-1	N	きゅうしゅう＝九州

<L>

language	2-15	N	ことば＝言葉
large size	1-14	N	エルサイズ
last month	1-12	N	せんげつ＝先月
last night	1-12	N	ゆうべ
last semester	3-2	N	せんがっき＝先学期
last week	1-11	N	せんしゅう＝先週
last year	1-15	N	きょねん＝去年
(the) last; final	3-8	N	さいご＝最後
(at) last; finally	3-8	Adv	さいごに＝最後に
late (+ verb)	1-12	Adv	おそく＝遅く
late afternoon	1-4	N	ゆうがた＝夕方
(is) late	1-7	A	おそい＝遅い
(to) laugh	2-15	V1	わらう＝笑う [わらいます]

(to do) laundry	2-7	V3	せんたく (を) する＝洗濯 (を) する [-します]
lawn	3-2	N	しばふ＝芝生
lawyer	1-3	N	べんごし＝弁護士
(to) lay out the bedding	4-8	V1	ふとんをしく＝布団を敷く [しきます]
lazy person	4-7	N	なまけもの＝怠け者
leaf	4-6	N	は (っぱ) ＝葉 (っぱ)
(to) learn	2-2	V1	ならう＝習う [ならいます]
(to) leave (a boyfirend/girlfriend)	4-7	V1	ふる [ふります]
(to) leave (a place)	2-4	V2	(place を) でる＝出る [でます]
(to) leave; put (a thing)	2-5	V1	おく＝置く [おきます]
(autumn) leaves	4-6	N	こうよう＝紅葉
left	2-2	N	ひだり＝左
leftovers	4-8	N	のこり＝残り
leg	1-6	N	あし＝脚
(Please) lend me.	1-14	V1	かしてください。＝貸して下さい。
less than ～	4-4	Nd	～いか＝～以下
Let me see . . .	2-1	SI	ええと . . . ; あのう . . . ; そうですねえ . . .
Let's begin.	1-1	Exp	はじめましょう。＝始めましょう。
Let's do ～. [suggestion]	1-4	Dv	-ましょう。
Let's eat. [informal form of 食べましょう]	3-1	V2	たべよう。＝食べよう。
Let's finish.	1-1	Exp	おわりましょう。＝終わりましょう。
letter	1-4	N	てがみ＝手紙
leukemia	4-4	N	はっけつびょう＝白血病
liar	4-7	N	うそつき
liberal; free	2-3	Na	じゆう＝自由
library	1-4	N	としょかん＝図書館
(a) lie	2-10	N	うそ＝嘘
life; living	3-3	N	せいかつ＝生活
(a) lifetime	4-2	N	じんせい＝人生
Light [A *shinkansen* that stops at major *shinkansen* stations.]	4-8	N	ひかり
(is) light (in weight)	3-7	A	かるい＝軽い
like (something)	1-5	Na	(～が) すき＝好き
like ～	4-3	P+Na+P	～のように
(Do you) like it? [polite]	2-9	Exp	おすきですか。＝お好きですか。
(N2) like (N1)	3-6	P+Nd+C	N1 のような N2
like very much	1-5	Na	だいすき＝大好き
line is busy	2-6	Exp	はなしちゅう＝話し中
(to) line up	4-8	V1	ならぶ＝並ぶ [ならびます]
lipstick	4-6	N	くちべに＝口紅
liquor (in general)	2-14	N	(お) さけ＝(お) 酒
(to) listen	1-4	V1	きく＝聞く [ききます]
(Please) listen.	1-2	Exp	きいてください。＝聞いて下さい。
literature	3-1	N	ぶんがく＝文学

(to) litter	2-3	V2	(ごみを) すてる [すてます]
(a) little [formal]	1-4	Adv	すこし=少し
(a) little [more colloquial than すこし]	1-4	Adv	ちょっと
(is a) little; few	1-11	A	すくない=少ない
(to) live	4-2	V2	いきる=生きる [いきます]
(to) live (in 〜)	2-2	V1	(place に) すむ=住む [すみます]
lively	3-6	Na	にぎやか=賑やか
living room; family room	3-7	N	いま=居間
location	2-10	N	ばしょ=場所
locker	1-10	N	ロッカー
(is) lonely	3-6	A	さびしい=寂しい
long ago	2-11	N	むかしむかし=昔々
(is) long	1-6	A	ながい=長い
(I have not seen you for a) long time.	3-3	Exp	(お) ひさしぶり (です)。=(お) 久しぶり (です)。
(to) look	1-4	V2	みる=見る [みます]
(to) look [honorific equiv. of 見る]	4-1	V1	ごらんになる=御覧になる [ごらんになります]
(to) look [humble equiv. of 見る]	4-1	V3	はいけんする=拝見する [はいけんします]
(to) look for; search for	3-4	V1	さがす=探す [さがします]
(to) look up a word (in a dictionary)	3-4	V1	(じしょを) ひく=(辞書を) 引く [ひきます]
(Please) look.	1-2	Exp	みてください。=見て下さい。
(Please) look. [More polite than 見て下さい。]	4-1	Exp.	ごらんください。=御覧下さい
(I am) looking forward to 〜.	1-15	Exp	(〜を) たのしみにしています。=(〜を) 楽しみにしています。
(It) looks 〜	2-5	SI	(V stem) そうです
(to) lose	1-12	V2	まける=負ける [まけます]
(to get) lost	3-9	V1	まいごになる=迷子になる [なります]
(a) lot	1-10	Adv	たくさん=沢山
love	2-15	N	あい=愛
(to be in) love	2-15	V1	あいしている=愛している [あいしています]
love; like very much	1-5	Na	だいすき=大好き
luckily	4-2	Adv	うんよく=運良く
(is) lucky	4-2	A	うんがいい=運がいい
lunch	1-4	N	ひるごはん=昼御飯
lunch [formal]	3-1	N	ちゅうしょく=昼食
luxurious	4-7	Na	ぜいたく=贅沢

<M>

(is) made of/from 〜	4-6	P+V2+V2	(〜で／から) できている=出来ている [できています]
magazine	1-4	N	ざっし=雑誌
mail box	3-9	N	ポスト

(to) mail; send	2-7	V1	おくる＝送る [おくります]
mainland	4-3	N	ほんど＝本土
(to) major (in ～)	3-1	V3	(～を) せんこうする＝専攻する [-します]
(to) make	1-15	V1	つくる＝作る [つくります]
(to) make a mistake	2-6	V2	まちがえる＝間違える [まちがえます]
(to) make a phone call	2-6	V2	でんわをかける＝電話をかける [かけます]
(to) make a reservation	2-5	V3	よやく (を) する＝予約 (を) する [-します]
(to) make an effort to do/not to do ～	4-3	Na+P+V3	(Dic./NAI) ようにする
(to) make efforts	4-7	V3	どりょく (を) する＝努力 (を) する [-します]
(to) make someone drink [causative form]	4-4	V2	のませる＝飲ませる [のませます]
male	1-10	N	おとこ＝男
male [formal]	3-6	N	だんせい＝男性
man	1-10	N	おとこのひと＝男の人
many times	2-6	Adv	なんども＝何度も
(are) many	1-11	A	おおい＝多い
many; a lot (+ verb)	1-10	Adv	たくさん＝沢山
map	2-13	N	ちず＝地図
maple leaves	4-6	N	もみじ＝紅葉
March	1-3	N	さんがつ＝三月
(to) marry ～	2-2	V3	(person と) けっこん (を) する [-します]
math	1-11	N	すうがく＝数学
May I help you?	2-9	N	なにをさしあげましょうか。＝何を差し上げましょうか。
May	1-3	N	ごがつ＝五月
may ～; might ～	3-7	E	～かもしれない
(city) mayor	4-4	N	しちょう＝市長
meal	1-7	N	しょくじ＝食事
(have a) meal	1-7	V3	しょくじ (を) する＝食事 (を) する [-します]
(What does it) mean?	3-4	Exp	どういういみですか。＝どういう意味ですか。
meaning	3-4	N	いみ＝意味
(It) means ～.	3-4	Exp	(～という) いみです。＝(～という) 意味です。
meat grilled on fire	2-5	N	やきにく＝焼肉
medicine	1-12	N	くすり＝薬
medium (size)	1-14	N	エムサイズ
(to) meet (someone)	1-12	V1	(person に) あう＝会う [あいます]
Meiji Period (1868 - 1912)	4-2	N	めいじじだい＝明治時代
memories	4-8	N	おもいで＝思い出
(to) memorize	2-6	V2	おぼえる＝覚える [おぼえます]
menu	2-5	N	メニュー
(is) messy	1-6	A	きたない
messy; confusing; incorrect	3-4	Na	めちゃくちゃ
metropolis	4-4	N	とかい＝都会
microwave oven	3-7	N	でんしレンジ＝電子レンジ
middle	4-4	N	まんなか＝真ん中

might ～; may ～	3-7	E	～かもしれない
military	4-3	N	ぐん＝軍
military personnel	4-3	N	ぐんじん＝軍人
military police [MP]	4-3	N	けんぺい＝憲兵
(mother's) milk	4-4	N	(お)ちち＝(お)乳
(cow's) milk	1-4	N	ぎゅうにゅう＝牛乳; ミルク
milk carton	4-9	N	ぎゅうにゅうパック＝牛乳パック
(one) million	1-13	N	ひゃくまん＝百万
(I do not) mind if . . .	2-3	V1	かまいません
mine	1-2	N	わたしの＝私の
- minute(s)	1-7	Nd	- ふん/- ぷん＝- 分
Monday	1-7	N	げつようび＝月曜日
money	1-2	N	(お)かね＝(お)金

money received mainly by children from adults at New Year's

	2-7	N	おとしだま＝お年玉
- month(s)	2-6	Nd	- かげつ＝- か月
moral	4-7	N	どうとく＝道徳
(is) moral	4-7	Na	どうとくてき＝道徳的
more	2-9	Adv	もっと
(one) more (cup)	1-14	Adv	もう (いっぱい)＝もう (一杯)
more than ～	4-4	Nd	～いじょう＝～以上
(the) more ～, the more ～	4-6	E+P	～ば、～ほど
more than ～	2-9	P	～より
Moreover	1-11	SI	それに
morning	1-4	N	あさ＝朝
(the) most	2-9	Adv	いちばん＝一番
(the) most	4-6	Adv	もっとも＝最も
(the) most	3-8	Adv	さいこうに＝最高に
(own) mother	1-3	N	はは＝母
(someone's) mother	1-3	N	おかあさん＝お母さん
Mother's Day	1-15	N	ははのひ＝母の日
mountain	1-7	N	やま＝山
mouse	1-10	N	ねずみ＝鼠
moustache	1-6	N	ひげ＝髭
mouth	1-6	N	くち＝口
(be) moved	4-7	V3	かんどう (を) する＝感動 (を) する [-します]
(thing) moves	2-11	V1	(thing が) うごく＝動く [うごきます]
(to) move (one's residence)	4-2	V1	ひっこす＝引っ越す [ひっこします]
(to) move (one's residence)	4-2	V3	ひっこし (を) する＝引っ越し (を) する [-します]
movie	1-5	N	えいが＝映画
movie theater	2-3	N	えいがかん＝映画館
Mr./Mrs./Ms.	1-1	Nd	～さん

Mr./Mrs./Ms./Dr. (teacher, doctor, statesman)   1-1   N   ～せんせい＝～先生

much; plentiful	1-11 A	おおい＝多い
muscles	4-7 N	きんにく＝筋肉
museum	3-9 N	はくぶつかん＝博物館
music	1-5 N	おんがく＝音楽
musical piece; song	3-6 N	きょく＝曲
must be ～	4-8 E	～にちがいない
must not do ～	2-3 V2	(TE form+は) いけません

<N>

Nagoya	2-1 N	なごや＝名古屋
Naha	2-1 N	なは＝那覇
naked	4-8 N	はだか＝裸
name	1-3 N	なまえ＝名前
(someone's) name	1-3 N	おなまえ＝御名前
napkin	1-14 N	ナプキン
Nara	2-1 N	なら＝奈良
narrator	2-11 N	ナレーター
(is) narrow; small [a place]	1-10 A	せまい＝狭い
nation	2-9 N	くに＝国
nature	3-8 N	しぜん＝自然
(is) near	1-10 A	ちかい＝近い
nearby	2-2 N	ちかく＝近く；そば＝傍
neat	1-6 Na	きれい
necessary	4-6 Na	ひつよう＝必要
neck	1-6 N	くび＝首
necklace	2-3 N	ネックレス
need ～	1-14 V1	(～が) いる＝要る [いります]
neighbor	4-3 N	きんじょのひと＝近所の人
neither	2-9 N	どちらも＋ Neg.
(to become) nervous	4-8 V3	きんちょう (を) する＝緊張 (を) する [-します]
(is) nervous	2-10 V3	ドキドキする [ドキドキします]
never + Neg.	2-4 Adv	けっして＋ Neg.
New Year	2-7 N	(お) しょうがつ＝(お) 正月
New Year's card	2-7 N	ねんがじょう＝年賀状
(is) new	1-10 A	あたらしい＝新しい
newspaper	1-4 N	しんぶん＝新聞
next	1-11 N	つぎ＝次
next (+ verb)	2-14 Adv	つぎに＝次に
next [location]; neighboring	2-2 N	となり＝隣
next month	1-12 N	らいげつ＝来月
next semester	3-2 N	らいがっき＝来学期
next week	1-11 N	らいしゅう＝来週
next year	1-15 N	らいねん＝来年
Nice to meet you.	1-1 Exp	どうぞよろしく。

(is) nice; kind	1-6	A	やさしい＝優しい
nice; pretty	1-6	Na	きれい
(How) nice! [on a future event]	1-11	Exp	いいですねえ。
(How) nice! [on a past event]	1-11	Exp	よかったですねえ。＝良かったねえ。
night	1-4	N	よる＝夜
- night(s)	4-8	Nd	- はく；- ぱく ＝- 泊
(one) night, two days	4-8	N	いっぱくふつか＝一泊二日
nine	1-1	N	く＝九; きゅう＝九
nine [general counter]	1-2	N	ここのつ＝九つ
nineteen	1-1	N	じゅうく＝十九; じゅうきゅう＝十九
ninety	1-1	N	きゅうじゅう＝九十
(the) ninth day of the month	1-11	N	ここのか＝九日
ninth grader	1-3	N	ちゅうがくさんねんせい＝中学三年生
No [formal]	1-1	SI	いいえ
No [informal]	2-4	SI	ううん
No [Stronger negation than いいえ.]	2-11	SI	いや (っ)
no good	1-2	Na	だめ
no need to (do)	2-5	Dv	-なくてもいいです
No parking. [negative command form]			
	4-3	V3	ちゅうしゃ (を) するな。＝駐車 (を) するな。
no smoking	4-8	N	きんえん＝禁煙
No, thank you.	1-14	Exp	いいえ、けっこうです。
(is) noisy	1-6	A	うるさい
non-reserved seat	4-8	N	じゆうせき＝自由席
non-smoking car	4-8	N	きんえんしゃ＝禁煙車
(thick white) noodles in broth	2-5	N	うどん
north	2-1	N	きた＝北
north entrance/exit	3-9	N	きたぐち＝北口
nose	1-6	N	はな＝鼻
(is) nostalgic	3-6	A	なつかしい＝懐かしい
(is) not at home	2-6	N	るす＝留守
not only 〜, but also 〜	4-6	E	〜だけでなく〜も
Not yet.	1-14	Exp	まだです。
notebook	1-2	N	ノート
November	1-3	N	じゅういちがつ＝十一月
now	1-3	N	いま＝今
nude	4-8	N	はだか＝裸
nuisance	1-6	Na	じゃま＝邪魔
number - [order]	2-10	Nd	- ばん ＝- 番

<O>

- o'clock	1-7	Nd	- じ＝ - 時
occasionally	2-15	Adv	たまに
ocean	1-7	N	うみ＝海

Ochanomizu [a city in Tokyo]	3-9	N	おちゃノみず＝御茶ノ水
October	1-3	N	じゅうがつ＝十月
of course	2-6	SI	もちろん
office	1-10	N	じむしょ＝事務所
often	1-4	Adv	よく
Oh!	2-13	SI	ああ
oil	2-14	N	あぶら＝油
Okinawa	2-1	N	おきなわ＝沖縄
(is) old (age)	1-6	V1	としをとっている＝年を取っている [-います]
old (not for person's age)	1-10	A	ふるい＝古い
old person(s)	4-9	N	(お) としより＝(お) 年寄り
(my) older brother	1-3	N	あに＝兄
(someone's) older brother	1-3	N	おにいさん＝お兄さん
(my) older sister	1-3	N	あね＝姉
(someone's) older sister	1-3	N	おねえさん＝お姉さん
on the way	4-4	N	とちゅう＝途中
on; top	2-2	N	うえ＝上
once in a while	2-15	Adv	たまに
one	1-1	N	いち＝一
one (person)	1-3	N	ひとり＝一人
one [general counter]	1-2	N	ひとつ＝一つ
one more time	1-1	Adv	もういちど＝もう一度
one night, two days	4-8	N	いっぱくふつか＝一泊二日
oneself	2-15	N	じぶん＝自分
only child	2-15	N	ひとりっこ＝一人っ子
only ～	2-3	Nd	～だけ
only ～ [a lot]	3-8	Nd	～ばかり
only ～ [emphasis]	3-1	Nd	～しか + Neg.
(to) open	1-13	V2	あける＝開ける [あけます]
(Please) open.	1-2	Exp	あけてください。＝開けて下さい。
(something, someplace) opens	4-4	V1	(～が) あく＝開く／あきます [あきます]
opinion	3-3	N	いけん＝意見
Or	1-6	SI	それとも
orange (color)	1-5	N	オレンジいろ＝オレンジ色
(to) order	2-5	V3	ちゅうもん (を) する＝注文 (を) する [-します]
(to) order; command	4-3	V3	めいれい (を) する＝命令 (を) する [-します]
(What is your/May I take your) order?	2-5	Exp	ごちゅうもんは。＝御注文は。
ordinary; average; regular	3-3	N	ふつう＝普通
Osaka	2-1	N	おおさか＝大阪
other	2-9	N	ほか
other side	2-13	N	むこう＝向こう
other side (of)	3-9	N	むかいがわ＝向かい側
outside	1-10	N	そと＝外

EJ

over there	1-2	N	あそこ
over there [polite equiv. of あそこ]	2-5	N	あちら
overseas travel	3-2	N	かいがいりょこう＝海外旅行

<P>

p.m.	1-7	N	ごご＝午後
P.E.	1-11	N	たいいく＝体育
painful	4-2	A	くるしい＝苦しい
(is) painful; sore	1-12	A	いたい＝痛い
(to) paint (a picture)	2-15	V1	(えを) かく＝(絵を) 描く [かきます]
painting	1-5	N	え＝絵
pan	2-14	N	なべ＝鍋
panda	3-9	N	パンダ
pants [Used by younger people.]	1-13	N	パンツ
pants	2-3	N	ズボン
paper	1-2	N	かみ＝紙
paper (report)	1-4	N	レポート
(own) parents	1-2	N	りょうしん＝両親
(someone else's) parents	1-2	N	ごりょうしん＝御両親
park	2-2	N	こうえん＝公園
(to) park	4-3	V3	ちゅうしゃ (を) する＝駐車 (を) する [-します]
parking lot	2-13	N	ちゅうしゃじょう＝駐車場
(to) participate (in ～)	4-9	V3	(～に) さんか (を) する＝参加 (を) する [-します]
(to) participate (in a sports game)	2-10	V2	(しあいに) でる＝(試合に) 出る [でます]
party	1-7	N	パーティー
(to) pass an exam	4-9	V3	(school に) ごうかく (を) する＝合格 (を) する [-します]
(to) pass away; die [polite form of しぬ]	3-5	V1	なくなる＝亡くなる [なくなります]
(to) pass (something)	3-8	V1	(～を) わたす＝渡す [わたします]
(Please) pass me ～.	3-8	Exp	(～を) とってください。＝取って下さい。
passport	2-3	N	パスポート
(to) paste; glue; attach	3-3	V1	はる＝貼る [はります]
(to be) patient	4-2	V3	がまん (を) する＝我慢 (を) する [-します]
patient	4-2	A	がまんづよい＝我慢強い
patrol car	2-4	N	パトカー
(to) pay	2-5	V1	はらう＝払う [はらいます]
peace; peaceful	3-2	N/Na	へいわ＝平和
Pearl Harbor	4-3	N	しんじゅわん＝真珠湾
pencil	1-2	N	えんぴつ＝鉛筆
pencil sharpener	1-10	N	えんぴつけずり＝鉛筆削り
pepper	2-14	N	こしょう＝胡椒
per ～	2-6	P	～に
- percent	2-5	Nd	-パーセント
perfectionist	4-7	N	かんぜんしゅぎしゃ＝完全主義者

(to) perm (one's hair)	3-2	V2	パーマをかける [かけます]
person	1-10	N	ひと＝人
person [polite form of ひと]	1-10	Nd	- かた＝- 方
personality	3-3	N	せいかく＝性格
photo	1-2	N	しゃしん＝写真
physics	3-1	N	ぶつり＝物理
piano	1-5	N	ピアノ
(to) pick up	4-9	V1	ひろう＝拾う [ひろいます]
pickled turnip	3-8	N	たくわん＝沢庵
pickled vegetables	3-8	N	つけもの＝漬け物
picnic	1-7	N	ピクニック
pierced (earrings)	2-3	N	ピアス
pig	1-10	N	ぶた＝豚
pine tree	4-7	N	まつ＝松
pink	1-5	N	ピンク
pizza	1-14	N	ピザ
place	2-2	N	ところ＝所
place of origin	4-1	N	(ご) しゅっしん＝(御) 出身
place; location	2-10	N	ばしょ＝場所
place of embarkment	3-9	N	のりば＝乗り場
(a) plan	4-8	N	けいかく＝計画
(to) plan	4-8	V3	けいかく (を) する＝計画 (を) する [-します]
plan to do/do not plan to do	2-6	Nd	(Dic./NAI) つもりです
plantation	4-2	N	プランテーション
plastic	4-9	N	プラスチック
plate	1-14	N	(お) さら＝(お) 皿
platform	3-9	N	ホーム
(to) play (a string instrument)	2-6	V1	ひく＝弾く [ひきます]
(to) play (for fun)	1-15	V1	あそぶ＝遊ぶ [あそびます]
(to) play (sports)	1-15	V3	する [します]
(to) play (a game)	1-15	V3	(ゲームを) する [します]
(stage) play	2-12	N	げき＝劇
(to give/put on a stage) play	2-12	V3	げきをする＝劇をする [げきをします]
(sports) player	2-10	N	せんしゅ＝選手
(is) pleasant	2-14	A	きもちがいい＝気持ちがいい
(Here) please (take it).	1-2	Exp	はい、どうぞ。
Please come again.	2-9	Exp	また、どうぞ。
Please come again. [More polite than また、来て下さい。]	4-1	Exp	また、いらしてください。 ＝また、いらして下さい。
Please come in. [More polite than 入って下さい。]	4-1	Exp	おはいりください。＝お入り下さい。
Please give me 〜.	1-2	Exp	〜をください＝〜を下さい

EJ

Please look. [More polite than 見て下さい.] 4-1 Exp ごらんください。＝御覧下さい。
Please step up. [More polite than 上がって下さい.]

	4-1	Exp	おあがりください。＝お上がり下さい。
Please. [request]	1-1	Exp	おねがいします＝御願いします
poem	4-7	N	し＝詩
poet	4-7	N	しじん＝詩人
point	3-2	N	ところ
- point(s) [score]	2-10	Nd	- てん＝ - 点
police officer	2-4	N	けいかん＝警官
polite	4-1	NA	ていねい＝丁寧
polite language	4-1	N	ていねいご＝丁寧語
pollution	4-9	N	こうがい＝公害
pond	1-10	N	いけ＝池
pool	1-10	N	プール
poor	2-11	Na	びんぼう＝貧乏
(be) poor [formal word of びんぼう]	4-3	A	まずしい＝貧しい
(be) poor at	1-5	Na	へた＝下手
(be) popular	3-6	V1	にんきがある＝人気がある [にんきがあります]
population	4-4	N	じんこう＝人口
pork	2-14	N	ぶたにく＝豚肉
pork cutlet	2-5	N	とんかつ＝豚カツ
port	4-3	N	みなと＝港
(as 〜 as) possible	4-7	Adv	できるだけ〜＝出来るだけ〜
post office	2-13	N	ゆうびんきょく＝郵便局
(picture) postcard	3-3	N	(え) はがき＝(絵) 葉書
pot	2-14	N	なべ＝鍋
potato chips	2-4	N	ポテトチップ
(to) pour over; sprinkle	3-8	V2	かける [かけます]
poverty	4-3	N	まずしさ＝貧しさ
powder	4-4	N	こな＝粉
powdered green tea	4-6	N	まっちゃ＝抹茶
power	2-11	N	ちから＝力
(to) practice	1-12	V3	れんしゅう (を) する＝練習 (を) する [-します]
(to) praise	4-2	V2	ほめる＝褒める [ほめます]
prayer	3-8	N	(お) いのり＝(お) 祈り
(to) pray	3-8	V1	いのる＝祈る [いのります]
(to get) pregnant	4-2	V3	にんしん (を) する＝妊娠 (を) する [-します]
(to) prepare	4-3	V3	じゅんび (を) する＝準備 (を) する [-します]
(a) present	1-15	N	プレゼント
(to) present; announce	3-3	V3	はっぴょう (を) する＝発表 (を) する [-します]
president (of country)	4-3	N	だいとうりょう＝大統領
(is) pretty	1-6	Na	きれい
price	2-9	N	(お) ねだん＝(お) 値段

private (school)	3-2	N	しりつ＝私立
prize	4-9	N	しょう＝賞
probably	2-7	Adv	たぶん＝多分
probably ～	2-7	C	-でしょう [falling intonation]
probably is [informal form of でしょう]	3-1	C	-だろう
problem	2-6	N	もんだい＝問題
professional baseball	3-6	N	プロやきゅう＝プロ野球
(TV) program	3-6	N	(テレビ) ばんぐみ＝(テレビ) 番組
(a) promise	3-9	N	やくそく＝約束
(to make a) promise	3-9	V3	やくそく (を) する＝約束 (を) する [-します]
(to) pronounce	3-4	V3	はつおん (を) する＝発音 (を) する [-します]
pronunciation	3-4	N	はつおん＝発音
proper	4-6	Na	てきとう＝適当
(to) protect	4-3	V1	まもる＝守る [まもります]
proverb	3-1	N	ことわざ＝諺
public (school, library, etc.)	3-2	N	こうりつ＝公立
public phone	2-13	N	こうしゅうでんわ＝公衆電話
(to) pull	4-4	V1	ひく＝引く [ひきます]
purple	1-5	N	むらさき＝紫
(to) push	4-4	V1	おす＝押す [おします]
(to) put	2-5	V1	おく＝置く [おきます]
(to) put away	2-14	V2	かたづける＝片付ける [かたづけます]
(to) put in ～	2-9	V2	(～ に) いれる＝入れる [いれます]

<Q>

question	2-2	N	しつもん＝質問
(I have a) question. [polite]	2-13	Exp	ちょっとうかがいますが . . .
quickly	2-4	Adv	はやく＝速く
quiet	1-6	Na	しずか＝静か
(is) quiet (refers to people only)	3-3	A	おとなしい
(to) quiet down	1-13	V3	しずかにする＝静かにする [しずかにします]
(Please be) quiet.	1-2	Exp	しずかにしてください。＝静かにして下さい。
(to) quit; discontinue	3-2	V2	やめる＝辞める [やめます]
quite; fairly	3-3	Adv	ずいぶん＝随分
quiz	1-2	N	しょうテスト＝小テスト

<R>

(ethnic) race	4-3	N	じんしゅ＝人種
radio	1-4	N	ラジオ
(JR) railpass (for foreigners)	4-8	N	レールパス
rain	1-1	N	あめ＝雨
(to) raise (a person/pet)	4-2	V2	そだてる＝育てる [そだてます]
(to) raise (a pet)	3-3	V1	(ペットを) かう＝飼う [かいます]
rapidly	4-4	Adv	どんどん
(is) rare; unusual	3-11	A	めずらしい＝珍しい

raw egg	2-14	N	なまたまご＝生卵
(to) read	1-4	V1	よむ＝読む [よみます]
(Please) read.	1-2	Exp	よんでください。＝読んで下さい。
reading	1-5	N	どくしょ＝読書
(〜 is) ready	2-14	V2	(〜 が) できました＝出来ました
really	2-3	Adv	ほんとうに＝本当に
Really! [conversational]	4-9	Exp	へ〜え。
(to) recall	3-4	V2	おもいだす＝思い出す [おもいだします]
(to) receive	1-15	V1	もらう [もらいます]
(to) receive [action]	3-3	V1	うけとる＝受け取る [うけとります]
(to) receive [humble equiv. of もらう]	4-1	V1	いただく [いただきます]
(I will) receive your serving. [tea ceremony]	4-6	Exp	おてまえちょうだいいたします。＝お手前ちょうだいいたします。
recently	3-4	Adv	さいきん＝最近
(to) recommend	4-9	V3	すいせん (を) する＝推薦 (を) する [-します]
recommendation	4-9	N	すいせんじょう＝推薦状
recycling	4-9	N	リサイクル
red	1-5	N	あか＝赤
(bright) red	4-4	N	まっか＝真っ赤
(is) red	1-6	A	あかい＝赤い
refrigerator	3-7	N	れいぞうこ＝冷蔵庫
regulation	2-3	N	きそく＝規則
(no) relation	4-3	Exp	かんけい (がない)＝関係 (がない)
relationship	4-3	N	かんけい＝関係
relatives	1-15	N	しんせき＝親戚
(to become) relieved	4-8	V3	あんしん (を) する＝安心 (を) する [-します]
religion	4-6	N	しゅうきょう＝宗教
(something) remains [intransitive]	4-9	V1	(〜が) のこる＝残る [のこります]
(to) remarry	4-2	V3	さいこん (を) する＝再婚 (を) する [-します]
(to) remove clothing [i.e., shoes, dress, hat]	3-2	V1	ぬぐ＝脱ぐ [ぬぎます]
(to) rent (from)	2-3	V2	かりる＝借りる [かります]
(to) repeat	3-9	V1	くりかえす＝繰り返す [くりかえします]
(to) report	4-3	V2	しらせる＝知らせる [しらせます]
report; paper	1-4	N	レポート
(to) require	2-9	V1	かかる [かかります]
(to) rescue	2-15	V2	たすける＝助ける [たすけます]
reserved seat	4-8	N	していせき＝指定席
residence	2-6	N	おたく＝お宅
(to) respect	3-3	V3	そんけい (を) する＝尊敬 (を) する [-します]
respect language	4-1	N	そんけいご＝尊敬語
responsibility	4-2	N	せきにん＝責任
(to be) responsible	4-2	V1	せきにんかんがある＝責任感がある [あります]
(to) rest	1-12	V1	やすむ＝休む [やすみます]

restaurant	1-7	N	レストラン
restroom	1-10	N	(お) トイレ; (お) てあらい＝(御) 手洗い
(to) retire (from a job)	4-2	V3	たいしょく (を) する＝退職 (を) する [-します]
return (home); (on one's) way home	4-1	N	かえり＝帰り
(to) return (something)	2-5	V1	かえす＝返す [かえします]
(to) return (to a place)	1-7	V1	かえる＝帰る [かえります]
(to) return to pick up (person)	2-10	V1	(person を) むかえにかえる＝迎えに帰る [むかえにかえります]
(to) return to pick up (thing)	2-10	V1	(thing を) とりにかえる＝取りに帰る [とりにかえります]
rice wine	2-14	N	(お) さけ＝(お) 酒
(cooked) rice	1-4	N	ごはん＝ご飯
riceball	1-14	N	(お) むすび; おにぎり
rich person	2-11	N	(お) かねもち＝(お) 金持ち
(to) ride 〜	2-4	V1	(vehicle に) のる＝乗る [のります]
right side	2-2	N	みぎ＝右
ring	2-3	N	ゆびわ＝指輪
river	1-7	N	かわ＝川
road	2-4	N	みち＝道
robber	4-2	N	どろぼう＝泥棒
rock garden	4-6	N	せきてい＝石庭
roof	4-4	N	やね＝屋根
room	1-10	N	へや＝部屋
room where guests are received	3-7	N	きゃくま＝客間
(is) round	3-8	A	まるい＝丸い
rubbish	1-2	N	ごみ
rule	2-3	N	きそく＝規則
rumor	3-6	N	うわさ
(to) run	1-12	V1	はしる＝走る [はしります]

\<S\>

(is) sad	1-11	A	かなしい＝悲しい
(is) safe	2-4	Na	あんぜん＝安全
(for the) sake of 〜	4-2	N	(〜の) ため (に)
salad	1-14	N	サラダ
salary; pay	3-6	N	きゅうりょう＝給料
(for) sale	2-9	N	セール中
salt	2-14	N	しお＝塩
(is) salty	2-14	A	からい＝辛い; しおからい＝塩辛い
same	2-9	N	おなじ＝同じ
sandwich	1-14	N	サンドイッチ
Sapporo	2-1	N	さっぽろ＝札幌
Saturday	1-7	N	どようび＝土曜日
(to) say	1-13	V1	いう＝言う [いいます]

(to) say [honorific equiv. of 言う] 4-1　V1　おっしゃる [おっしゃいます]
(to) say [humble equiv. of 言う]　4-1　V1　（〜と）もうす＝申す [もうします]
say that 〜　　　　　　　　4-8　E　　〜ようにいう＝〜ように言う
Say, "Cheese."　　　　　　1-15 Exp　はい、チーズ。
Say, "Peace."　　　　　　　1-15 Exp　はい、ピース。
(is) scary　　　　　　　　2-4　A　　こわい＝恐い
(to) scatter (handbills)　　4-4　V1　（ビラを）まく [まきます]
scenery　　　　　　　　　4-8　N　　けしき＝景色
scholarship　　　　　　　4-9　N　　しょうがくきん＝奨学金
school　　　　　　　　　1-3　N　　がっこう＝学校
school bus　　　　　　　　2-4　N　　スクールバス
science　　　　　　　　　1-11 N　　かがく＝科学
science [school subject]　　3-1　N　　りか＝理科
(to) scold　　　　　　　　2-15 V1　しかる＝叱る [しかります]
score　　　　　　　　　　2-10 N　　スコア
sea　　　　　　　　　　　1-7　N　　うみ＝海
season　　　　　　　　　3-8　N　　きせつ＝季節
seasonings　　　　　　　　3-8　N　　ちょうみりょう＝調味料
(a) second daughter　　　　4-2　N　　じじょ＝次女
(the) second day of the month　1-11 N　ふつか＝二日
second generation　　　　　4-2　N　　にせい＝二世
second serving　　　　　　3-11 N　　おかわり＝お代わり
(a) second son　　　　　　4-2　N　　じなん＝次男
(Will you have) seconds?　　3-8　Exp　おかわりは？＝お代わりは？
(to) see　　　　　　　　　1-4　V2　　みる＝見る [みます]
(to) see [honorific equiv. of 見る] 1-4　V1　ごらんになる＝御覧になる [ごらんになります]
(to) see [humble equiv. of 見る]　4-1　V3　はいけんする＝拝見する [はいけんします]
(Well then,) see you later.　1-14 Exp　（じゃ、）またあとで。＝（じゃ、）また後で。
seems 〜; It is like 〜　　　4-3　Na　〜よう（だ）。
seems 〜 [informal equiv. of 〜よう（だ）] 4-9　Na　〜みたい（だ）。
(It) seems that 〜　　　　　3-8　Da　〜らしい
(to) select　　　　　　　　4-6　V1　えらぶ＝選ぶ [えらびます]
selfish; self-centered　　　4-7　Na　わがまま
(to) self-introduce　　　　　2-2　V3　じこしょうかい（を）する＝自己紹介（を）する [-します]
(to) sell　　　　　　　　　2-9　V1　うる＝売る [うります]
semester　　　　　　　　　3-2　N　　がっき＝学期
(to) send　　　　　　　　　2-7　V1　おくる＝送る [おくります]
Sendai　　　　　　　　　2-1　N　　せんだい＝仙台
(high school) senior　　　　1-3　N　　こうこうさんねんせい＝高校三年生
senior citizen(s)　　　　　4-8　N　　（お）としより＝（お）年寄り
sentence　　　　　　　　　3-4　N　　ぶん＝文
separate　　　　　　　　　4-9　N　　べつ（べつ）
(to) separate [intransitive]　3-6　V2　わかれる＝別れる [わかれます]

separately	4-9	Adv	べつ (べつ) に
September	1-3	N	くがつ＝九月
(is) serious	3-3	NA	まじめ＝真面目
seven	1-1	N	しち＝七; なな＝七
seven [general counter]	1-2	N	ななつ＝七つ
seventeen	1-1	N	じゅうしち; じゅうなな＝十七
(the) seventh day of the month	1-11	N	なのか＝七日
seventh grader	1-3	N	ちゅうがくいちねんせい＝中学一年生
seventy	1-1	N	ななじゅう; しちじゅう＝七十
several people	4-3	N	なんにんも＝何人も
shade	4-7	N	かげ＝陰
shadow	4-4	N	かげ＝影
shake hands	4-1	V3	あくしゅ (を) する＝握手 (を) する [-します]
shape	3-4	N	かたち＝形
she; her; girlfriend	3-6	N	かのじょ＝彼女
Shibuya [a city in Tokyo]	3-9	N	しぶや＝渋谷
Shikoku	2-1	N	しこく＝四国
Shinagawa [a city in Tokyo]	3-9	N	しながわ＝品川
Shinjuku [a city in Tokyo]	3-9	N	しんじゅく＝新宿
Shintoism	4-6	N	しんとう＝神道
ship	1-7	N	ふね＝船
shirt	1-13	N	シャツ
shoes	1-13	N	くつ＝靴
shoji (rice paper) door	3-7	N	しょうじ＝障子
(to) shop	1-7	V3	かいもの (を) する＝買い物 (を) する [-します]
shopping	1-7	N	かいもの＝買い物
(is) short (height)	1-6	A	ひくい＝低い
(is) short [not for height]	1-6	A	みじかい＝短い
shorts	2-3	N	ショーツ; ショートパンツ
should (do)	2-5	Dv	-なければなりません
should /should not do ～	4-4	N+C	(Dic.) べきだ／べきではない
(to) show	1-13	V2	みせる＝見せる [みせます]
(Please) show.	1-2	Exp	みせてください。＝見せて下さい。
shredded *konnyaku*	2-14	N	いとこんにゃく＝糸こんにゃく
shrine (Shinto)	2-7	N	じんじゃ＝神社
(my) sibling(s)	1-3	N	きょうだい＝兄弟
sickness	1-12	N	びょうき＝病気
(to) sightsee	4-8	V3	けんぶつ (を) する＝見物 (を) する [-します]
sightseeing tour	4-8	N	かんこうりょこう＝観光旅行
silver	2-15	N	ぎん＝銀
silver color	1-5	N	ぎんいろ＝銀色
simple	3-4	NA	かんたん＝簡単
since (reason)	1-11	Pc	(reason) から

since 〜; because 〜 [expected result];　〜, so　3-3　Rc　〜ので

sincere	4-7	Na	せいじつ＝誠実
(to) sing	1-15	V1	うたう＝歌う [うたいます]
singer	3-6	N	かしゅ＝歌手
singing	1-5	N	うた＝歌
(to) sit	1-13	V1	すわる＝座る [すわります]
(to) sit properly	3-7	V3	せいざ (を) する＝正座 (を) する [-します]
Sit. [ceremony]	1-4	Exp	ちゃくせき。＝着席。
(Please) sit.	2-2	Exp	すわってください。＝座って下さい。
six	1-1	N	ろく＝六
six [general counter]	1-2	N	むっつ＝六つ
sixteen	1-1	N	じゅうろく＝十六
(the) sixth day of the month	1-11	N	むいか＝六日
sixty	1-1	N	ろくじゅう＝六十
size	1-14	N	サイズ
skillful	1-5	Na	じょうず＝上手
skirt	2-3	N	スカート
sky	4-4	N	そら＝空
(to) sleep	1-7	V2	ねる＝寝る [ねます]
(to) sleep [honorific equiv. of 寝る]	4-1	V1	おやすみになる＝お休みになる [おやすみになります]
(is) sleepy	1-12	A	ねむい＝眠い
(to) slice	2-14	V1	きる＝切る [きります]
slowly	1-1	Adv	ゆっくり

small [formal use of 小さい and used only before a noun]　4-3　Na　ちいさな＝小さな

(This is a) small gift. [Used when giving someone a gift.]

	4-1	Exp.	これはすこしですが＝これは少しですが . . .
small size	1-14	N	エスサイズ
(is) small	1-6	A	ちいさい=小さい
(is) small; narrow	1-10	A	せまい=狭い
smell	2-7	N	におい＝臭い
(is) smelly	3-11	A	くさい＝臭い
(to) smile	2-15	V1	わらう＝笑う [わらいます]
smilingly [onomatopoetic]	2-15	Adv	ニコニコ
(to) smoke (cigarettes)	2-3	V1	(たばこを) すう [すいます]
snack bar	1-4	N	スナックバー
snacks	4-7	N	おやつ
snow	2-7	N	ゆき＝雪
(reson,) so (result).	1-11	Pc	(reason) から、(result)。
so, so	1-5	Adv	まあまあ
(Is that) so?	1-3	Exp	そうですか。
(to) soak; dip	3-8	V2	つける＝漬ける [つけます]

Sobu Line [yellow colored train line in Tokyo]　3-9　N　そうぶせん＝総武線

soccer	1-5	N	サッカー
social studies; society	1-11	N	しゃかい＝社会
social welfare	4-9	N	しゃかいふくし＝社会福祉
socks	2-3	N	くつした＝靴下; ソックス
(is) soft; tender	3-8	A	やわらかい＝柔らかい
(to) solve	4-9	V3	かいけつ (を) する＝解決 (を) する [-します]
(〜 or) something	4-1	C+P	〜でも
something	2-15	N	なにか＝何か
something 〜	4-6	N	なにか〜もの＝何か〜物
sometimes	1-4	Adv	ときどき＝時々
(own) son	2-11	N	むすこ＝息子
(someone else's) son	2-11	N	むすこさん＝息子さん
song	1-5	N	うた＝歌
sophomore; 10th grader	1-3	N	こうこういちねんせい＝高校一年生
(is) sore	1-12	A	いたい＝痛い
Sorry to be late.	2-14	Exp	おそくなりました。＝遅くなりました。
(I am) sorry to have inconvenienced you.			
	3-1	Exp	しつれいしました。＝失礼しました。
Sorry, but . . .	2-6	Exp	ざんねんですが. . .＝残念ですが. . .
(I am) sorry.	4-0	Exp	ごめんなさい。
(I am) sorry. [polite]	1-1	Exp	すみません。
(I am) sorry. [formal]	4-1	Exp	もうしわけございません。＝申し訳ございません。
(I am) sorry. [sympathy - formal]	2-6	Exp	(お) きのどくに。＝(御) 気の毒に。
(to) sort	4-9	V2	わける＝分ける [わけます]
sound	3-3	N	おと＝音
soup flavored with *miso*	2-5	N	(お) みそしる＝(御) 味噌汁
(is) sour	2-14	A	すっぱい＝酸っぱい
south	2-1	N	みなみ＝南
south entrance/exit	3-9	N	みなみぐち＝南口
souvenir gift	2-9	N	(お) みやげ＝(御) 土産
space	4-3	N	ひろさ＝広さ
(is) spacious	1-10	A	ひろい＝広い
Spain	1-3	N	スペイン
Spanish language	1-4	N	スペインご＝スペイン語
(to) speak	1-4	V1	はなす＝話す [はなします]
special	3-3	Na	とくべつ＝特別
(to) speed	2-4	V1	スピードをだす＝スピードを出す [だします]
(is) spicy	2-14	A	からい＝辛い
spoon	1-14	N	スプーン
- spoonful	1-14	Nd	- はい／- ぱい／- ばい＝- 杯
sports shoes	2-10	N	うんどうぐつ＝運動靴
sports	1-5	N	スポーツ
sports	2-10	N	うんどう＝運動

spring	1-12	N	はる＝春
square	3-8	N	しかく＝四角
(is) square (shaped)	3-8	A	しかくい＝四角い
stairs	3-7	N	かいだん＝階段
stamp	3-3	N	きって＝切手
(to) stand	1-13	V1	たつ＝立つ [たちます]
Stand. [ceremony]	1-1	Exp	きりつ。＝起立。
(Please) stand.	1-2	Exp	たってください。＝立って下さい。
(to) start 〜	4-3	V1	(Verb stem) だす＝出す [だします]
(to) start (something) [transitive]	2-10	V2	(〜を) はじめる＝始める [はじめます]
(something) starts [intransitive]	2-10	V1	(〜 が) はじまる＝始まる [はじまります]
state	2-9	N	しゅう＝州
station employee	3-9	N	えきいん＝駅員
(to) stay overnight	4-8	V1	とまる＝泊まる [とまります]
(to) steal	4-2	V1	ぬすむ＝盗む [むすみます]
step by step	4-4	Adv	だんだん
(to) step up	3-7	V1	あがる＝上がる [あがります]
(Please) step up. [More polite than 上がって下さい]			
	4-1	Exp.	おあがりください。＝御上がり下さい。
(to) stick	4-4	V1	ささる [ささります]
still	2-2	Adv	まだ + Aff.
stomach	1-6	N	おなか＝お腹
(something) stops [intransitive]	4-3	V1	(〜が) やむ＝止む [やみます]
(to) stop (at a place)	2-4	V1	(place で/に) とまる＝止まる [とまります]
(to) stop by	2-10	V1	(place に) よる＝寄る [よります]
Stop. [command form]	4-3	V1	とまれ。＝止まれ。
store	1-13	N	(お) みせ＝(お) 店
store clerk	4-1	N	てんいん＝店員
straight	2-13	Adv	まっすぐ
strange; unusual	2-6	Na	へん＝変
straw	1-14	N	ストロー
straw mat	3-7	N	たたみ＝畳
strawberry	2-14	N	いちご＝苺
street; avenue	2-13	N	とおり＝通り
street; road	2-4	N	みち＝道
strength	2-11	N	ちから＝力
(I am very) stressed.	2-6	Exp	ストレスがいっぱいです。
(is) strict	1-6	A	きびしい＝厳しい
stroke order	3-4	N	かきじゅん＝書き順
- stroke(s)	3-4	N	- かく＝- 画
(be) strong in	1-5	Na	とくい＝得意
(is) strong	1-12	A	つよい＝強い
strong; healthy	4-7	Na	じょうぶ＝丈夫

student [college]	1-3	N	がくせい＝学生
student [pre-college]	1-3	N	せいと＝生徒
(to) study	1-4	V3	べんきょう (を) する＝勉強 (を) する [-します]
(to) study abroad	3-2	V3	りゅうがく (を) する＝留学 (を) する [-します]
Study. [polite command]	4-3	V3	べんきょう (を) しなさい。＝勉強 (を) しなさい。
subject	1-12	N	かもく＝科目
(to) submit	2-4	V1	だす＝出す [だします]
(to) subtract	4-4	V1	ひく＝引く [ひきます]
subway	1-7	N	ちかてつ＝地下鉄
success	3-6	N	せいこう＝成功
(to) succeed	3-6	V3	せいこう (を) する＝成功 (を) する [-します]
suddenly	2-4	Adv	きゅうに＝急に
suddenly; unexpectedly	4-3	Adv	とつぜん＝突然
(to) suffer	4-2	V3	くろう (を) する＝苦労 (を) する [-します]
sugar	2-14	N	さとう＝砂糖
sugar cane	4-2	N	さとうきび
sukiyaki	2-14	N	すきやき＝鋤焼き
summer	1-12	N	なつ＝夏
summer cotton *kimono*	4-8	N	ゆかた＝浴衣
sun [polite]	2-11	N	おひさま＝お日様
Sunday	1-7	N	にちようび＝日曜日
sunglasses	2-3	N	サングラス
(a) superior [lit., a person above your eye level]	4-1	N	めうえのひと＝目上の人
supermarket	1-13	N	スーパー
supper	1-4	N	ばんごはん＝晩御飯
supper [formal]	3-1	N	ゆうしょく＝夕食
supporter	4-3	N	みかた＝味方
surely	4-8	Adv	きっと
(to be) surprised	4-2	V1	おどろく＝驚く [おどろきます]
sushi shop/bar	1-13	N	すしや＝寿司屋
sweater	2-3	N	セーター
(is) sweet	2-14	A	あまい＝甘い
(Japanese) sweets	4-6	N	わがし＝和菓子
(to) swim	1-15	V1	およぐ＝泳ぐ [およぎます]
swimming	1-5	N	すいえい＝水泳
sword	4-6	N	かたな＝刀

<T>

T-shirt	2-3	N	Ｔシャツ
TV	1-4	N	テレビ
table	2-5	N	テーブル
(to) take	1-15	V1	とる＝取る [とります]
(to) take (animate)	2-7	V1	つれていく＝連れて行く [つれていきます]
(to) take (medicine)	1-12	V1	のむ＝飲む [のみます]

(to) take (thing)	2-7	V1	もっていく＝持って行く [もっていきます]
(to) take (time)	2-9	V1	かかる [かかります]
(to) take (a bath)	3-3	V1	(ふろに) はいる＝(風呂に) 入る [はいります]
(to) take (a shower)	3-3	V2	(シャワーを) あびる [あびます]
(to) take a walk	2-15	V3	さんぽ (を) する＝散歩 (を) する [-します]
(to) take (an exam)	3-3	V2	(しけんを) うける＝(試験を) 受ける [うけます]
(to) take care of 〜	3-3	V3	(〜の) せわ (を) する＝世話 (を) する [-します]
(to) take care of (a sick person)	4-7	V3	かんびょう (を) する＝看病 (を) する
(to) take good care of 〜; value	4-6	V3	(〜を) たいせつ／だいじにする ＝(〜を) 大切／大事にする [-します]
(to) take out	2-4	V1	だす＝出す [だします]
(to) take out (the garbage)	2-7	V1	ごみをだす＝ごみを出す [だします]
(to) take/bring (animate) back home	2-7	V1	つれてかえる＝連れて帰る [つれてかえります]
(to) take/bring (inanimate) back home	2-7	V1	もってかえる＝持って帰る [もってかえります]
talent; ability	4-7	N	さいのう＝才能
(to) talk; speak	1-4	V1	はなす＝話す [はなします]
(is) tall	1-6	A	たかい＝高い
tape	1-4	N	テープ
(He/She is) tardy; late.	1-1	Exp	ちこくです。＝遅刻です。
(to) taste	4-6	V1	あじわう＝味わう [あじわいます]
taste; flavor	2-14	N	あじ＝味
tatami	3-7	N	たたみ＝畳
(counter for *tatami*)	3-7	C	-じょう＝-畳
tax	2-9	N	ぜいきん＝税金
taxi	1-7	N	タクシー
tea	1-4	N	(お) ちゃ＝(お) 茶
tea ceremony	4-6	N	ちゃどう; さどう＝茶道
tea ceremony room	4-6	N	(お) ちゃしつ＝(御) 茶室
tea poured over a bowl of rice	3-8	N	(お) ちゃづけ＝(御) 茶漬け
(to) teach	2-4	V2	おしえる＝教える [おしえます]
teacher	1-1	N	せんせい＝先生
teaching	4-6	N	おしえ＝教え
team	1-12	N	チーム
telephone	1-4	N	でんわ＝電話
telephone number	1-15	N	でんわばんごう＝電話番号
(weather) temperature	2-7	N	おんど＝温度
temple (Buddhist)	2-7	N	(お) てら＝(御) 寺
ten	1-1	N	じゅう＝十
ten [general counter]	1-2	N	とお＝十
ten thousand	1-13	N	いちまん＝一万
tennis	1-5	N	テニス

(the) tenth day of the month	1-11	N	とおか＝十日
tenth grader	1-3	N	こうこういちねんせい＝高校一年生
(be on good) terms with ～	4-7	A	(～と) なかがいい＝仲がいい
(be on bad) terms with ～	4-7	A	(～と) なかがわるい＝仲が悪い
(is) terrible	1-11	A	ひどい＝酷い
(is) terrific	1-13	A	すごい＝凄い
textbook	1-2	N	きょうかしょ＝教科書; テキスト
Thank you.	1-1	Exp	どうも, ありがとう。

Thank you for allowing me to trouble you. [Used when leaving after a visit. lit., I have committed a rudeness.] 4-1 Exp. おじゃましました。

Thank you very much (for your service.) [Generally used by superior as an expression of gratitude for a service or favor done by a person of lesser status.]
4-9 Exp ごくろうさま。＝御苦労様。

Thank you very much (for your hard work). [Generally used to express gratitude to an equal or superior who has done something that has required considerable effort.]
4-9 Exp おつかれさま。＝お疲れ様。

Thank you for your kind help. 3-3 Exp おせわになりました。＝お世話になりました。

thank you letter	3-3	N	(お) れいじょう＝(お) 礼状
Thank you very much.	1-1	Exp	ありがとうございます。

Thank you very much. [used after one has received something]
1-2 Exp ありがとうございました。＝有難うございました。

(to) thank	2-15	V3	かんしゃ (を) する＝感謝 (を) する [-します]
Thanks to you.	3-3	Exp	おかげさまで。＝お陰様で。
thanks; gratitude; appreciation	3-3	N	(お) れい＝(お) 礼
that one	1-1	N	それ
that one [polite equiv. of それ]	2-9	N	そちら
that one over there	1-1	N	あれ
that one over there [polite equiv. of あれ]	2-9	N	あちら
that ～	1-2	PN	その～
that ～ over there	1-2	PN	あの～
That's all.	2-5	Exp	それだけです。
That's impossible!; That's ridiculous! [strong negation]	2-11	Exp	とんでもない (です)。
there	1-2	N	そこ
there [polite equiv. of そこ]	2-5	N	そちら
there is (animate object)	1-10	V2	(～が) いる [います]
there is (inanimate object)	1-10	V1	(～が) ある [あります]
Therefore [Formal]	2-11	SI	ですから
Therefore [Informal]	2-11	SI	だから
Thereupon	2-13	SI	すると
these [plural of これ]	4-6	N	これら
(is) thick (in width; size)	3-8	A	ふとい＝太い
thick white noodles in broth	2-5	N	うどん
thick (+ verb)	2-14	Adv	あつく＝厚く

(is) thick	2-14	A	あつい＝厚い
thief	4-2	N	どろぼう＝泥棒
thin (+ verb)	2-14	Adv	うすく＝薄く
(is) thin	2-14	A	うすい＝薄い
(is) thin (person)	1-6	V2	やせている＝痩せている [やせています]
(is) thin and long	3-8	A	ほそながい＝細長い
(is) thin; slender	3-8	A	ほそい＝細い
thing [intangible]	1-5	N	こと＝事
thing [tangible]	1-5	N	もの＝物
(to) think	2-11	V1	おもう＝思う [おもいます]
third daughter	4-2	N	さんじょ＝三女
(the) third day of the month	1-11	N	みっか＝三日
third son	4-2	N	さんなん＝三男
(I got) thirsty.	1-14	Exp	のどがかわきました。＝喉が渇きました。
(I am) thirsty.	1-14	Exp	のどがカラカラです。＝喉がカラカラです。
thirteen	1-1	N	じゅうさん＝十三
thirty	1-1	N	さんじゅう＝三十
This is a small gift. [Used when handing someone a gift.]			
	4-1	Exp	これはすこしですが . . .＝これは少しですが . . .
this month	1-12	N	こんげつ＝今月
this morning	1-12	N	けさ＝今朝
this one	1-1	N	これ
this one [polite equiv. of これ]	1-3	N	こちら
this semester	3-2	N	こんがっき＝今学期
this side (of)	3-9	N	てまえ＝手前
This way, please.	2-5	Exp	どうぞ、こちらへ。
this week	1-11	N	こんしゅう＝今週
this year	1-15	N	ことし＝今年
this ～	1-2	PN	この ～
thousand	1-13	N	せん＝千
three	1-1	N	さん＝三
three [general counter]	1-2	N	みっつ＝三つ
throat	1-6	N	のど＝喉
through ～	2-4	P	～を
throughout	2-15	Adv	ずっと
(to) throw away (garbage)	2-3	V2	(ごみを) すてる＝捨てる [すてます]
Thursday	1-7	N	もくようび＝木曜日
ticket	1-15	N	きっぷ＝切符
ticket gate	3-9	N	かいさつぐち＝改札口
ticket vending machine	3-9	N	けんばいき＝券売機
(JR) ticket window	4-8	N	みどりのまどぐち＝みどりの窓口
time	2-10	N	じかん＝時間
time table	4-8	N	じこくひょう＝時刻表

- time(s)	2-6	Nd	- ど＝- 度
- time(s) [informal]	3-4	Nd	- かい＝- 回
tip	2-5	N	チップ
(I am) tired.	1-12	Exp	つかれています。＝疲れています。
(I got) tired.	1-12	Exp	つかれました。＝疲れました。
tissue	1-2	N	ティッシュ
to (place)	1-7	P	(place) へ; (place) に
(from ～) to ～	1-11	P	(～から) ～まで
to ～	2-13	P	～まで
tobacco	2-3	N	たばこ; タバコ
today	1-4	N	きょう＝今日
toe	1-6	N	ゆび＝指
together	1-4	Adv	いっしょに＝一緒に
Tokyo	2-1	N	とうきょう＝東京
Tokyo Station	3-9	N	とうきょうえき＝東京駅
tomorrow	1-4	N	あした＝明日
tonight	1-7	N	こんばん＝今晩
too ～	2-14	V2	(stem+) すぎる＝過ぎる [すぎます]
tooth	1-6	N	は＝歯
top	2-2	N	うえ＝上
(be) touched (by ～)	4-7	V3	(～に) かんどう (を) する＝感動 (を) する [-します]
tough; hard	3-8	A	かたい＝硬い
(to) tour	4-8	V3	かんこう (を) する＝観光 (を) する [-します]
tour	4-8	N	かんこう＝観光
tour bus	4-8	N	かんこうバス＝観光バス
tourist	4-8	N	かんこうきゃく＝観光客
town	2-13	N	まち＝町
track number ～	3-9	N	- ばんせん＝- 番線
tradition	3-7	N	でんとう＝伝統
traditional	3-7	Na	でんとうてき＝伝統的
traffic accident	2-4	N	こうつうじこ＝交通事故
traffic lights	2-4	N	しんごう＝信号
train station	2-13	N	えき＝駅
(to) translate	3-4	V1	やくす＝訳す [やくします]
translation	3-4	N	やく＝訳
trash can	1-10	N	ごみばこ＝ごみ箱
(to) travel	1-7	V3	りょこう (を) する＝旅行 (を) する [-します]
traveler's check	2-9	N	トラベラーズチェック
traveling	1-7	N	りょこう＝旅行
tray	4-9	N	トレー
(to) treat (someone) to a meal	2-5	V3	ごちそう (を) する＝御馳走 (を) する [-します]
tree	1-10	N	き＝木
triangle	3-8	N	さんかく＝三角

trip	1-7	N	りょこう＝旅行
trouble; worry [personal]	4-7	N	なやみ＝悩み
(be) troubled	3-3	V1	こまる＝困る [こまります]
true	1-3	N	ほんとう＝本当
(Is it) true/real?	2-3	Exp	ほんとうですか。＝本当ですか。
truly	2-3	Adv	ほんとうに＝本当に
(to) trust	4-2	V2	しんじる＝信じる [しんじます]
try doing ～	2-5	Dv	(-て) みる [みます]
Tuesday	1-7	N	かようび＝火曜日
tuition	3-2	N	じゅぎょうりょう＝授業料
(to) turn (something) around	4-6	V1	まわす＝回す [まわします]
(to) turn at/along (place)	2-4	V1	(place で/を) まがる＝曲がる [まがります]
(to) turn in; hand in	1-13	V1	だす＝出す [だします]
(Please) turn in.	1-2	Exp	だしてください。＝出して下さい。
(something) turns off [intransitive]	4-4	V2	(～が) きえる＝消える [きえます]
(something) turns on [intransitive]	4-4	V1	(～が) つく [つきます]
twelfth grader	1-3	N	こうこうさんねんせい＝高校三年生
twelve	1-1	N	じゅうに＝十二
(the) twentieth day of the month	1-11	N	はつか＝二十日
twenty	1-1	N	にじゅう＝二十
(the) twenty fourth day of the month	1-11	N	にじゅうよっか＝二十四日
twenty years old	1-3	N	はたち＝二十歳
twins	2-15	N	ふたご＝双児
two	1-1	N	に＝二
two (persons)	1-3	N	ふたり＝二人
two [general counter]	1-2	N	ふたつ＝二つ
two story house	3-7	N	にかいだて＝二階建て
(to) type	1-4	V3	タイプ (を) する [-します]

<U>

U.S.	1-3	N	アメリカ
U.S. [formal]	4-3	N	べいこく＝米国
U.S. citizen	1-3	N	アメリカじん＝アメリカ人
udon topped with beef	2-5	N	にくうどん＝肉うどん
Ueno [a city in Tokyo]	3-9	N	うえの＝上野
(is) unappetizing; tasteless	1-13	A	まずい
uncle	1-15	N	おじさん
(own) uncle	3-1	N	おじ＝叔父
(is) uncomfortable	2-14	A	きもちがわるい＝気持ちが悪い
under	2-2	N	した＝下
(to) understand	1-1	V1	わかる＝分かる [わかります]
unfortunately	4-2	Adv	うんわるく＝運悪く
unhappy	4-7	Na	ふこう＝不幸
(sports) uniform	2-10	N	ユニフォーム

uniform	2-3	N	せいふく＝制服
(is) uninteresting	1-11	A	つまらない
university	1-12	N	だいがく＝大学
unluckily	4-2	Adv	うんわるく＝運悪く
unlucky	4-2	A	うんがわるい＝運が悪い
(is) unpleasant	2-14	A	きもちがわるい＝気持ちが悪い
unskillful	1-5	Na	へた＝下手
unusual	2-6	Na	へん＝変
(to) use	3-1	V1	つかう＝使う [つかいます]
(to be) useful	4-9	V1	やくにたつ＝役に立つ [やくにたちます]
usually	1-4	Adv	たいてい＝大抵
(with one's) utmost effort	2-11	Adv	いっしょうけんめい＝一生懸命

\<V\>

vacation	1-7	N	(お) やすみ＝(お) 休み
(sense of) value	4-7	N	かちかん＝価値観
(to) value ～	4-6	V3	(～を) たいせつ／だいじにする ＝(～を) 大切／大事にする [-します]
various	2-9	Na	いろいろ
vegetable	2-14	N	やさい＝野菜
vehicle	1-7	N	くるま＝車; じどうしゃ＝自動車
veranda	3-7	N	ベランダ
very	1-5	Adv	とても
very soon	1-15	Adv	もうすぐ
(not) very	1-5	Adv	あまり ＋ Neg.
vicinity	2-2	N	ちかく＝近く
video	1-4	N	ビデオ
video game	1-5	N	テレビゲーム
view	4-8	N	けしき＝景色
village chief	4-3	N	そんちょう＝村長
vinegar	2-14	N	す＝酢
vinegared vegetables	3-8	N	すのもの＝酢の物
vinyl	4-9	N	ビニール
(to) visit ～	4-1	V3	(～を) ほうもんする＝訪問する [-します]
voice	1-6	N	こえ＝声
volleyball	1-5	N	バレー(ボール)
volunteer	4-7	N	ボランティア

\<W\>

| (to) wait | 1-13 | V1 | まつ＝待つ [まちます] |
| (Please) wait a minute. | 1-1 | Exp | ちょっとまってください。＝ちょっと待って下さい。 |

(Please) wait a minute. [More polite than ちょっと待って下さい.]

| | 4-1 | Exp | しょうしょうおまちください。 ＝少々お待ち下さい。 |
| waiter | 2-5 | N | ウェイター |

waitress	2-5	N	ウェイトレス
(to) wake up	1-7	V2	おきる＝起きる [おきます]
(to) walk	1-7	V1	あるく＝歩く [あるきます]
walkman	1-4	N	ウォークマン
wall	2-11	N	かべ＝壁
wallet	1-2	N	さいふ＝財布
want (something)	1-11	A	(something が) ほしい＝欲しい
want (to do)	1-12	Da	(verb stem) -たい
(someone else) wants 〜	4-4	V1	(〜を) ほしがる [ほしがります]
war	4-2	N	せんそう＝戦争
(is) warm	1-14	A	あたたかい＝暖かい
(Japanese) warrior	3-6	N	さむらい＝侍
(to) wash	2-7	V1	あらう＝洗う [あらいます]
wasteful	4-9	Exp	もったいない
(a) watch	1-13	N	とけい＝時計
(to) watch	1-4	V2	みる＝見る [みます]
water	1-4	N	(お) みず＝(お) 水
(on one's) way home	4-1	N	かえり＝帰り
we	1-12	N	わたしたち＝私達
we [Used by males.]	1-12	N	ぼくたち＝僕達
We did it!	2-10	Exp	やったあ！
(be) weak in 〜	1-5	Na	(〜が) にがて＝苦手
(is) weak	1-12	A	よわい＝弱い
(to) wear [above the waist or on the entire body]	2-3	V2	きる＝着る [きます]
(to) wear [accessories]	2-3	V3	する [します]
(to) wear [below the waist]	2-3	V1	はく＝履く [はきます]
(to) wear [glasses]	2-3	V2	(めがねを) かける [かけます]
(to) wear [on or draped over the head]	2-3	V2	かぶる [かぶります]
(to) wear a seat belt	2-4	V3	シートベルトをする [します]
weather	1-1	N	(お) てんき＝(御) 天気
weather forecast	3-6	N	てんきよほう＝天気予報
Wednesday	1-7	N	すいようび＝水曜日
- week(s)	2-6	Nd	- しゅうかん＝- 週間
weekend	1-11	N	しゅうまつ＝週末
weird	2-6	Na	へん＝変
Welcome. [Used when greeting others into one's home or other personal space.]	4-1	Exp.	いらっしゃい。
Welcome. [polite]	2-5	Exp	いらっしゃいませ。
(You are) welcome.	1-1	Exp	どういたしまして。
well	1-4	Adv	よく
Well done.	1-2	Exp	よくできました。＝良く出来ました。
Well . . . [Used when one does not know or is unsure of the answer.]	2-9	SI	さあ...

Well . . . [Used when one is unsure of the answer.]   2-1 SI ええと... あのう...
(a) well-known product (of a given area) 4-8 N めいぶつ＝名物
Well then [formal]   1-14 Exp では
Well then [informal]   1-14 Exp じゃ
Welcome home.   3-1 Exp おかえりなさい。＝お帰りなさい。
west   2-1 N   にし＝西
west coast   4-3 N   にしかいがん＝西海岸
west entrance/exit   3-9 N   にしぐち＝西口
Western style   3-7 Na   せいようてき＝西洋的
Western style meal   3-8 N   ようしょく＝洋食
Western-style cooking   3-8 N   せいようりょうり＝西洋料理
Western-style room   3-7 N   ようしつ＝洋室
(someone/something gets) wet [intransitive] 4-8 V2 （～が）ぬれる＝濡れる [ぬれます]
what?   1-1 Ni   なに＝何; なん＝何
what color?   1-5 N   なにいろ＝何色
(the) what day of the month? 1-11 Ni なんにち＝何日
what day of the week?   1-7 Ni   なんようび＝何曜日
What does it mean?   3-4 Exp どういういみですか。＝どういう意味ですか。
what grade?   1-3 N   なんねんせい＝何年生
What happened?   1-12 Exp どうしましたか。
what kind of ～?   1-5 PN   どんな～
what language?   1-4 Ni   なにご＝何語
what month?   1-3 Ni   なんがつ＝何月
what nationality?   1-3 Ni   なにじん＝何人
What should I do?   3-3 Exp どうしたら、いいですか。
what time?   1-7 Ni   なんじ＝何時
wheelchair   4-9 N   くるまいす＝車いす
when?   1-7 Ni   いつ
where?   1-3 Ni   どこ
where? [polite equiv. of どこ] 2-5 Ni どちら
which (one of two)? [informal] 2-9 Ni どっち
which (one of two)? [polite] 2-9 Ni どちら
which one (of three or more)? 1-13 Ni どれ
which ～?   1-13 Nd   どの～
which ～? [polite]   2-9 Nd   どちらの～
(for a) while   4-8 Adv しばらく
While ～   3-6 N+P ～あいだに＝～間に
While ～ [Describing a person's simultaneous or concurrent actions.]
                          3-6 Rc   (verb stem) ながら
(pure) white   4-4 N   まっしろ＝真っ白
white   1-5 N   しろ＝白
(is) white   1-6 A   しろい＝白い
who?   1-3 Ni   だれ＝誰

why?	1-11 Ni	なぜ; どうして
(is) wide	1-10 A	ひろい＝広い
width	4-3 N	ひろさ＝広さ
(own) wife	3-6 N	かない＝家内
(someone else's) wife	3-6 N	おくさん＝奥さん
(to) win	1-12 V1	かつ＝勝つ [かちます]
(to) win a championship	2-10 V3	ゆうしょう (を) する＝優勝 (を) する [-します]
wind	2-7 N	かぜ＝風
window	1-10 N	まど＝窓
winter	1-12 N	ふゆ＝冬
with (person)	1-4 P	(person) と (いっしょに)
with (tool)	1-4 P	(tool) で
Without doing 〜	4-7 E	〜ないで; 〜ずに
Without reservation/hesitation, please (have some).		
	3-8 Exp	(ご) えんりょなく、どうぞ。 ＝(御) 遠慮なく、どうぞ。
woman	1-10 N	おんなのひと＝女の人
woman (middle-aged)	1-15 N	おばさん
(We) won! (We) won!	2-10 Exp	かった！かった！＝勝った！勝った！
won't do	2-3 V2	いけません
(it) won't do [formal]	2-5 V1	なりません
Won't you do 〜? [invitation]	1-7 Dv	-ませんか
(I) wonder if 〜 [used by female]	3-2 SP	〜かしら。
(I) wonder if 〜 [used by male and female]	3-2 SP	〜かな。
(is) wonderful	1-13 A	すばらしい＝素晴らしい
words	2-15 N	ことば＝言葉
(to) work (at 〜)	2-2 V1	(place で) はたらく＝働く [はたらきます]
(to) work part-time (at 〜)	2-2 V3	(place で) アルバイト (を) する [-します]
worksheet	1-2 N	ワークシート
world	2-9 N	せかい＝世界
World War II	4-3 N	だいにじせかいたいせん＝第二次世界大戦
(to be) worried [personal]	4-7 V1	なやむ＝悩む [なやみます]
(to) worry	2-4 V3	しんぱい (を) する＝心配 (を) する [-します]
Would/Won't you do 〜?	4-1 E	(-て) くださいませんか。
	4-1 E	(-て) いただけませんか。
Wow!	1-13 SI	わあ
(to) write	1-4 V1	かく＝書く [かきます]
(Please) write.	1-2 Exp	かいてください。＝書いて下さい。
(is) wrong	2-2 V1	ちがう＝違う [ちがいます]

\<Y>

Yamanote Line [green colored train line in Tokyo]	3-9 N	やまのてせん＝山手線
(a) yard	1-10 N	にわ＝庭
- year	1-15 Nd	- ねん＝- 年

- year(s) (duration)	2-6	Nd	- ねんかん＝- 年間
yellow	1-5	N	きいろ＝黄色
(is) yellow	1-6	A	きいろい＝黄色い
yen	1-13	Nd	- えん＝- 円
Yes [formal]	1-1	SI	はい
Yes [informal]	2-4	SI	うん
Yes [less formal than はい]	1-1	SI	ええ
yesterday	1-4	N	きのう＝昨日
you [used to an inferior by male]	4-3	N	おまえ
You are welcome.	1-1	Exp	どういたしまして。
you know [sentence ending particle]	1-6	SP	よ
you	1-2	N	あなた
young lady [informal]; daughter	2-11	N	むすめ＝娘
young lady [polite]; (someone's) daughter	2-11	N	むすめさん＝娘さん
(is) young	1-6	A	わかい＝若い
(own) younger brother	1-3	N	おとうと＝弟
(someone's) younger brother	1-3	N	おとうとさん＝弟さん
(my) younger sister	1-3	N	いもうと＝妹
(someone's) younger sister	1-3	N	いもうとさん＝妹さん
youngest child (in a family)	4-2	N	すえっこ＝末っ子
yours	1-2	N	あなたの＝あなたの
Yummm . . .	2-5	SI	う～ん

<Z>

Zen (Buddhism)	4-6	N	ぜん＝禅
(seated) Zen meditation	4-6	N	ざぜん＝座禅
zoo	2-13	N	どうぶつえん＝動物園

日本語1−1か

1-1　わたし<u>は</u>　やまもと<u>です</u>。
　　　I am Yamamoto.

1-4　これは　<u>なんですか</u>。
　　　What is this?

1-6　<u>これ／それ／あれ</u> は　〜です。
　　　This/That/That one over there is 〜.

1-6　これは　<u>お</u>です<u>か</u>。
　　　Is this *O*?

1-7　あついです<u>ねえ</u>。
　　　It is hot!

日本語1−2か

2-1　わかり<u>ます</u>。
　　　I understand.

2-1　わかり<u>ません</u>。
　　　I do not understand.

2-4　これは　わたし<u>の</u>です。
　　　This is mine.

2-4　<u>この／その／あの</u>おかねは　わたしのです。
　　　This/That/That money over there is mine.

2-5　ワークシートWAAKUSHIITO<u>を</u>　にまい　<u>ください</u>。
　　　Please give me two worksheets.

2-5　ティッシュTISSHUは　<u>ここ／そこ／あそこ</u>です。
　　　The tissue is here/there/over there.

日本語1−3か

3-1　あに<u>の</u>　なまえは　マイクMAIKUです。
　　　My older brother's name is Mike.

3-2　ベンBENさん<u>と</u>　リサRISAさんは　おやすみです。
　　　Ben and Lisa are absent.

3-2　あなた<u>は</u>？
　　　How about you?

3-2　ちちは　４３さいです。<u>そして</u>、ははは　３８さいです。
　　　My father is 43. And my mother is 38 years old.

3-3　わたしは　こうこうせい<u>では</u>　ありません。
I am not a high school student.

3-3　わたし<u>も</u>　１４さいです。
I am 14 years old, too.

3-3　ちち<u>も</u>　はは<u>も</u>　４０さいです。
Both my father and mother are 40 years old.

3-5　ちちは　まえ　かいしゃいん<u>でした</u>。
My father was a company employee before.

3-5　わたしは　まえ　この　がっこうの　せいと<u>では　ありませんでした</u>。
I was not a student of this school before.

日本語１－４か

4-1　ははは　にほんご<u>を</u>　はなします。
My mother speaks Japanese.

4-1　わたしは　うち<u>で</u>　にほんごを　はなします。
I speak Japanese at home.

4-1　おばあさんは　にほんごを　<u>よく</u>　はなします。
My grandmother speaks Japanese well.

4-1　これは　わたしのです。<u>でも</u>、それは　あなたのです。
This is mine. But that is yours.

4-2　わたしは　にほんごを　はなします。でも、ちゅうごくご<u>は</u>　はなしません。
I speak Japanese. But I do not speak Chinese.

4-3　あなたは　あさごはんを　たべ<u>ました</u>か。
Did you eat breakfast?
いいえ、たべ<u>ませんでした</u>。
No, I did not eat (breakfast).

4-3　<u>なにも</u>　たべませんでした。
I did not eat anything.

4-3　わたしは　<u>きのう</u>　なにも　たべませんでした。
I did not eat anything yesterday.

4-3　きのう　ばんごはん<u>に</u>　おすしを　たべました。
I ate sushi for dinner yesterday.

4-4　ともだち<u>と</u>　いっしょに　たべます。
I eat together with my friend.

4-4　としょかんで　<u>べんきょう(を)</u>　しました。
I studied at the library.

4-4 なにを　べんきょうしましたか。
What did you study?

4-5 しけんを　えんぴつで　かきます。
I will write the exam in pencil.

5-2 すきです。
(I) like (it).

5-2 すきでは／じゃありません。
(I) do not like (it).

5-2 すきでした。
(I) liked (it).

5-2 すきでは／じゃありませんでした。
(I) did not like (it).

5-2 わたしは　どくしょが　すきです。
I like reading (books).

5-2 あなたは　どんな　たべものが　すきですか。
What kind of food do you like?

5-3 ちちは　ゴルフGORUFUが　じょうずですが、ははは　へたです。
My father is good at golf, but my mother is poor at it.

5-4 おばあさんは　にほんごが　とても　じょうずです。
My grandmother is very good at speaking Japanese.

5-4 ぼくは　バスケットBASUKETTOが　ちょっと　にがてです。
I am a little weak at basketball.

5-4 ははは　にほんごが　あまり　じょうずでは　ありません。
My mother is not very good at speaking Japanese.

5-4 ぼくは　テニスTENISUが　ぜんぜん　じょうずでは　ありません。
I am not good at tennis at all.

6-1 わたしは　すこし　せが　ひくいです。　　　　I am a little short.
6-2 たかいです。　　　　(I) am tall.
6-2 たかくないです。／たかくありません。　　　　(I) am not tall.
6-2 たかかったです。　　　　(I) was tall.
6-2 たかくなかったです。／たかくありませんでした。　(I) was not tall.
6-2 いいです。／よいです。　　　　(It) is good.
6-2 よくないです。／よくありません。　　　　(It) is not good.
6-2 よかったです。　　　　(It) was good.

6-2 よくなかったです。／よくありませんでした。 (It) was not good.

6-3 ぼくの　ぼうしは　あかです。 My cap is a red color.

6-3 ぼくの　ぼうしは　あかいです。 My cap is red.

6-3 ぼくの　ぼうしは　あかと　しろです。 My cap is red and white.

6-5 「あなたは　あたまが　いいですね。」 "You are smart, aren't you?"
「いいえ、よくないですよ。」 "No, I am not smart, you know."

日本語1－7か

7-1 おひるごはんを　たべましょう。
Let's eat lunch!

7-1 ジュースJUUSUを　のみませんか。
Won't you drink some juice?

7-1 わたしは　どようびに　えいがを　みました。
I watched a movie on Saturday.

7-3 ぼくは　きょう　7じはんに　がっこうへ　きました。
I came to school at 7:30 today.

7-3 どようびの　7じはんに　えいがに　いきました。
I went to a movie at 7:30 on Saturday.

7-3 6じに　おきました。それから、あさごはんを　たべました。
I got up at 6:00. And then I ate breakfast.

7-4 ははは　くるまで　かいしゃに　いきます。
My mother goes to her company by car.

7-5 にほんへ　りょこう（を）しましょう。
Let's travel to Japan.

7-5 ちちは　にちようびに　いつも　ゴルフGORUFUを　します。
My father always plays golf on Sundays.

7-5 どこへも　いきませんでした。
I did not go anywhere.

日本語1－10か

10-1 えんぴつけずりは　あそこに　あります。
The pencil sharpener is over there.

10-1 ジョンさんは　そとに　います。
John is outdoors.

10-1 ごみばこは　あそこです。
The rubbish can is over there.

10-1 ジョンさんは　そとです。
John is outdoors.

115

文法

10-2 あそこに　プールが　あります。
There is a pool over there.

10-2 あそこに　かわいい　おんなの　こが　いますよ。
There is a cute girl over there.

10-2 いま　おひるごはんを　たべましょうか。
Shall we eat lunch now?

10-3 あそこに　おおきい　きが　いっぽん　あります。
There is a big tree over there.

日本語1－11か

11-2 あした　しけんが　あります。
I have an exam tomorrow.

11-2 わたしは　10じから　11じまで　えいごの　じゅぎょうが　あります。
I have (my) English class from 10:00 to 11:00.

11-4 きのうの　しけんは　むずかしかったです。
Yesterday's exam was difficult.

11-4 その　せんせいは　ぜんぜん　きびしくなかったです。
That teacher was not strict at all.

11-4 にほんごは　おもしろい（です）から、すきです。
Japanese is interesting, so I like it.

11-4 「なぜ　せいせきが　わるかったですか。」「べんきょうしませんでしたから。」
"Why was your grade bad?"　　　　　　"It is because I did not study."

11-5 いま　おみずが　ほしいです。
I want water now.
　　コーヒーは　ほしくないです。
I don't want coffee.

11-5 すうがくは　しゅくだいが　とても　おおいです。
There is a lot of math homework.

11-5 おとこの　がくせいは　すくないですね。
There are few male students, aren't there?

日本語1－12か

12-2 いま　テレビを（or が）　みたいです。
I want to watch TV now.

12-2 おちゃは（or を）　のみたくありません。
I do not want to drink tea.

12-2 ゆうべ　フットボールを　みたかったです。
I wanted to watch football last night.

文法　　　　　　　　　116

12-2 ゆうべ　フットボール<u>は</u>（or <u>を</u>）　みたくなかったです。
I did not want to watch football last night.

12-3 <u>つよい</u>　チームでした。
(They) were a strong team.

12-4 あした　だいじ<u>な</u>　しあいが　あります。
I have an important game tomorrow.

12-5 ダンスは　カフェテリア<u>で</u>　あります。
The dance will be at the cafeteria.

日本語1－13か

13-2 ゆっくり　<u>はなして</u>　ください。
Please speak slowly.

13-3 ジュース<u>か</u>　おみずを　のみます。
I will drink juice or water.

13-3 トイレへ　<u>いっても</u>　いいですか。
May I go to the restroom?

13-4 おおきい<u>の</u>を　ください。
Please give me a big one.

日本語1－14か

14-1 「<u>もう</u>　おひるごはんを　たべましたか。」「いいえ、<u>まだです</u>。」
"Did you already eat lunch?"　　　　　　"No, not yet."

14-2 ははは　テニスが　すき<u>で</u>、ちちは　ゴルフが　すきです。
My mother likes tennis and my dad likes golf.

14-2 この　シャツは　2まい<u>で</u>　30ドルです。
This shirt is $30 for two.

14-3 この　しゅくだいを　えんぴつ<u>で</u>　かきました。
I wrote this homework with a pencil.

14-4 にほんごは　おもしろ<u>くて</u>、たのしいです。
Japanese is interesting and fun.

14-5 あさごはんを　<u>たべて</u>、しんぶんを　よみます。
I eat breakfast and read the newspaper.

日本語1－15か

15-2 ともだちは　わたし<u>に</u>　ふうせんを　くれました。
My friend gave me balloons.

15-2 わたしは　ともだち<u>に</u>　おかねを　もらいました。
I received some money from my friend.

117

文法

15-3 これを　あなたに　あげます。

I will give this to you.

15-3 ははは　いぬに　たべものを　やります。

My mother gives food to the dog.

15-3 しんぶんや　ざっしなど　よみました。

I read newspapers, magazines, etc.

15-3 ははに　あげました。いもうとにも　やりました。

I gave it to my mother. I gave it to my younger sister, too.

15-3 ちちは　にほんへ　いきました。ちゅうごくへも　いきました。

My father went to Japan. He went to China, too.

日本語２－１課

2-1 ベンさんは　今<ruby>今<rt>いま</rt></ruby>　走<ruby>走<rt>はし</rt></ruby>って　います。

Ben is running now.

2-1 姉<ruby>姉<rt>あね</rt></ruby>は　結婚<ruby>結婚<rt>けっこん</rt></ruby>して　います。

My older sister is married.

2-2 猫<ruby>猫<rt>ねこ</rt></ruby>が　車<ruby>車<rt>くるま</rt></ruby>の　上<ruby>上<rt>うえ</rt></ruby>に　います。

The cat is on the car.

2-2 犬<ruby>犬<rt>いぬ</rt></ruby>が　ドアの　ところに　います。

The dog is where the door is.

2-3 赤<ruby>赤<rt>あか</rt></ruby>ちゃんは　まだ　一才<ruby>一才<rt>さい</rt></ruby>です。

The baby is still a year old.

2-3 兄<ruby>兄<rt>あに</rt></ruby>は　もう　サンフランシスコに　住<ruby>住<rt>す</rt></ruby>んで　いません。

My older brother is not living in SF any more.

2-3 Verb Dictionary form

2-4 母<ruby>母<rt>はは</rt></ruby>は　歌<ruby>歌<rt>うた</rt></ruby>を　歌<ruby>歌<rt>うた</rt></ruby>うの／ことが　好<ruby>好<rt>す</rt></ruby>きです。

My mother likes to sing.

2-4 日本語<ruby>日本語<rt>にほんご</rt></ruby>を　勉強<ruby>勉強<rt>べんきょう</rt></ruby>するの／ことは　楽<ruby>楽<rt>たの</rt></ruby>しいです。

Studying Japanese is fun.

日本語２－３課

3-1 父<ruby>父<rt>ちち</rt></ruby>は　青<ruby>青<rt>あお</rt></ruby>い　シャツを　着<ruby>着<rt>き</rt></ruby>ています。

My father is wearing a blue shirt.

3-1 あの　生徒<ruby>生徒<rt>せいと</rt></ruby>は　黒<ruby>黒<rt>くろ</rt></ruby>いズボンを　はいて　います。

That student is wearing black pants.

3-1 姉<ruby>姉<rt>あね</rt></ruby>は　白<ruby>白<rt>しろ</rt></ruby>いネックレス　して　います。

My older sister is wearing a white necklace.

3-1 弟は いつも ぼうしを かぶって います。

My younger brother always wears a hat.

3-1 母は めがねを かけて います。

My mother is wearing glasses.

3-2 この学校では Tシャツを 着ても いいです。

You may wear T-shirts at this school.

3-2 プレゼントは 高くても かまいません。

I don't mind if the present is expensive.

3-2 パーティーは 一時でも いいです。

I don't mind if the party is at 1 o'clock.

3-2 教室で 食べては いけません。

You may not eat in the classroom.

3-2 ショートパンツは 短くては いけません。

Shorts should not be (too) short.

3-2 この 本では だめです。

This book will not do.

3-3 図書館へ 本を 借りに 来ました。

I came to the library to borrow a book.

3-3 旅行に 行きます。

I will go on a trip.

3-4 「昨日は 海に 行きませんでしたか。」 「はい、行きませんでした。」

"Yesterday, didn't you go to the beach?"　"No, I didn't go."

3-4 ピアスを 一つだけ しても いいです。

You may wear only one pierced earring.

3-4 結婚したいんです。

I really want to get married.

日本語２－４課

4-1 Verb NAI form

4-1 Informal conversation

4-1 「行く？」 「うん、行く。」

"Are you going? " "Yes, I will go."

4-1 「今 お昼 食べる？」

"Are you going to eat lunch now?"

「ううん、今 食べない。」

"No, I am not eating now."

4-2 宿題を　忘れないで　下さい。

Please don't forget (your) homework.

4-2 今日　おそく　起きました。

I got up late today.

4-2 漢字を　もっと　きれいに　書いて　下さい。

Please write the *kanji* more neatly.

日本語２－５課

5-1 ぼくは　ピザと　コーラに　します。

I will have pizza and a coke.

5-1 わあ、おいしそうですねえ。

Wow, that looks delicious, doesn't it!

5-1 あの　学生は　とても　頭が　よさそうですね。

That student over there looks very smart, doesn't he?

5-1 あの　人は　テニスが　上手そうですねえ。

That person looks skillful at tennis!

5-1 今日　雨が　ふりそうですねえ。

It looks like it will rain today.

5-1 私の　朝ご飯は　毎日　パンに　コーヒーです。

Every day my breakfast is bread and coffee.

5-2 今　授業に　行かなければ　なりません。

I have to go to class now.

5-2 お昼ご飯を　食べなくても　いいです。

I don't have to eat lunch.

5-3 おすしを　食べて　みましょう。

Let's try eating *sushi*.

5-3 この　くつを　はいて　みて　ください。

Please try wearing these shoes.

日本語２－６課

6-1 母は　少し　日本語が　出来ます。

My mom can speak a little Japanese.

6-1 手が　いたくて、書くことが　出来ません。

My hands hurt, and I cannot write.

6-2 「私　ゆみですが、こうじさん　いますか。」

"I am Yumi. Is Koji there?"

6-2 「山田ですが . . . 」

"I am Yamada." [Expecting a response from the listener.]

文法　　　　　　　　　120

6-3　来年　日本へ　<u>行くつもりです</u>。

Next year, I plan to go to Japan.

6-3　今晩　十二時まで　<u>寝ないつもりです</u>。

Tonight, I don't plan to go to bed until 12 o'clock.

6-3　明日　試験が　<u>あるはずです</u>。

Tomorrow, there is supposed to be an exam.

6-3　明日　試験は　<u>ないはずです</u>。

Tomorrow, there is not supposed to be an exam.

6-3　父は　仕<u>事で</u>　東京へ　行きました。

My father went to Tokyo for work.

6-4　学校を　三日<u>も</u>　休みました。

I was absent from school for as many as three days.

6-4　一日<u>に</u>　何時間ぐらい　勉強しますか。

How many hours a day do you study?

日本語２－７課

7-1　Verb TA form

7-1　この　本を　<u>読んだことが　あります</u>。

I have read this book.

7-1　まだ　日本へ　<u>行ったことが　ありません</u>。

I have not gone to Japan yet.

7-2　Verb NAKATTA form

7-2　明日は　たぶん　くもり<u>でしょう</u>。

It will probably be cloudy tomorrow.

7-2　昨日は　雪が　ふらなかった<u>でしょう</u>。

It probably did not snow yesterday.

7-2　お天気は　わるかった<u>でしょう</u>。

The weather was probably bad.

7-2　この　音楽を　知って　いる<u>でしょう</u>？

You know this music, don't you?

7-4　友達を　パーティーに　<u>連れて　行っても</u>　いいですか。

May I bring my friends to your party?

7-4　ぜひ　友達を　<u>連れて　来て</u>　下さい。

By all means, please bring your friends.

7-4　ケーキを　クラスに　<u>持って　来ても</u>　いいですか。

May I bring cake to class?

7-4 おばあさんの　うちに　プレゼントを　持^もって　行きました。

I took a present to my grandmother's house.

日本語２－９課

9-1 犬と　猫^{ねこ}と　どちらの方^{ほう}が　好きですか。

Which do you like better, dogs or cats?

9-1 私は　猫^{ねこ}より　犬の方^{ほう}が　好きです。

I like dogs more than cats.

9-2 アメリカは　中国ほど　広^{ひろ}くありません。

America is not as spacious as China.

9-2 お好きですか。

Do you like it?

9-3 魚^{さかな}と　豚肉^{ぶたにく}と　チキンで　何が　一番^{ばん}　いいですか。

Which is best, fish, pork, or chicken?

9-3 この　クラスで　だれが　一番^{ばん}　背^せが　高^{たか}いですか。

In this class, who is the tallest?

9-3 この　中で　これが　一番^{ばん}　好きです。

Among these, I like this best.

日本語２－１０課

10-1 しあいが　はじまります。

The game will start. [Intransitive Verb]

10-1 しあいを　はじめます。

(Someone) will start the game. [Transitive Verb]

10-1 試合^{しあい}の　始^{はじ}まる時間^{かん}は　何時ですか。

What time does the game start?　[lit., What time is the game starting time?]

10-1 今日　試合が　ありますが、行きませんか。

There is a game today. Won't you go?

10-2 だれが　あなたを　学校へ　迎^{むか}えに　来ますか。

Who comes to pick you up at school?

10-2 宿題^{しゅくだい}を　取^とりに　行っても　いいですか。

May I go to get my homework?

10-3 Verb Potential Form

10-3 父は　中国語が　話せますが、私は　話せません。

My father can speak Chinese, but I cannot.

10-3 母は　さしみが　食べられません。

My mother cannot eat *sashimi*.

10-3 うるさくて、勉強 出来ません。

   It is noisy, so I cannot study.

10-4 私は チームに かって ほしいです。

   I want the team to win.

日本語2−11課

11-2 この 本を 全部 読んでしまいました。

   I read this entire book.

11-2 疲れていましたから、ゆうべは 早く 寝てしまいました。

   I was tired, so I ended up going to bed early last night.

11-2 昨日は 病気でした。ですから、宿題が 出来ませんでした。

   I was sick yesterday. Therefore, I could not do my homework.

11-2 母は 仕事で 東京へ 行きました。だから、私が 料理しなければ なりません。

   My mother went to Tokyo for work. Therefore, I have to cook.

11-3 デレックさんは 「こんにちは。」と 言いました。 Derek said, "Hello."

11-4 明日 日本語の 試験が あると 思います。

   I think there is a Japanese exam tomorrow.

11-4 母は 今 四十五才だと 思います。

   I think my mother is 45 years old now.

11-4 父は 前 ピアノが 上手だったと 聞きました。

   I heard that my father was good at the piano before.

日本語2−12課

12-1 医者に なりたいです。

   I want to be a doctor.

日本語2−13課

13-2 右に まがると、動物園が あります。

   If you turn right, the zoo is (right) there.

13-3 家から 学校まで どのぐらい かかりますか。

   How long does it take from home to school?

13-3 家から 学校まで どのぐらい ありますか。

   How far is it from home to school?

13-3 バスで 行くのと タクシーで 行くのと どちらの方が 速いですか。

   Which is faster, going by bus or going by taxi?

13-3 バスで 行く方が 歩くより 速いです。

   It is faster to go by bus than to walk.

13-3 バスで 学校へ 行くのは 車で 行くほど 速くありません。

   Going to school by bus is not as fast as going by car.

14-1 すき焼きの　作り方を　教えて　下さい。

Please teach me how to make *sukiyaki*.

14-2 かみの　けを　短く　して　下さい。

Please make (cut) my hair short.

14-2 ここを　きれいに　して　下さい。

Please clean up this place.

14-2 牛肉を　薄く　切って　下さい。

Please slice the beef thin.

14-2 糸こんにゃくを　半分に　切って　下さい。

Please cut the shredded *konnyaku* in half.

14-3 背が　高く　なりましたねえ。

You've grown tall, haven't you!

14-3 私は　将来　医者に　なりたいです。

I want to become a doctor in the future.

14-4 父は　お酒を　飲みすぎます。

My father drinks too much *sake*.

14-4 この　犬は　頭が　良すぎます。

This dog is too smart.

14-4 あの　人は　テニスが　下手すぎます。

That person is too unskillful at tennis.

14-4 勉強しすぎないで　下さい。

Please do not study too hard.

15-2 休みには　映画に　行ったり　コンサートに　行ったり　します。

I do such things as go to the movies and concerts on my days off.

15-2 私の　成績は　良かったり　悪かったり　します。

My grades are sometimes good and sometimes bad.

15-2 生徒は　上手だったり　下手だったり　します。

Some students are skillful and some students are unskillful.

15-2 日本語の　先生は　日本人だったり　アメリカ人だったり　します。

Teachers of Japanese are sometimes Japanese and sometimes American.

15-3 日本へ　行ったら、いろいろな　物を　見たいです。

When (if) I go to Japan, I want to see various things.

15-3 休みが　もっと　長かったら、嬉しいです。

If the vacation is longer, I will be happy.

15-3 日本語が　上手だったら、仕事が　あります。

If I am good at Japanese, I will have a job.

15-4 私は　母に　晩御飯を　作って　あげました。

I made dinner for my mother.

15-4 妹に　本を　読んで　やりました。

I read a book to my younger sister.

15-4 父は　私を　学校に　連れて行って　くれます。

My father takes me to school.

15-4 僕は　友達に　お金を　貸して　もらいました。

I had my friend lend me some money (as a favor.)

日本語3－1課

1. 妹のケリーはまだ小学生です。

   My younger sister Kelly is still an elementary school student.

2. 母は高校で先生をしています。

   My mother is a teacher at a high school.

3. 家族では父しか日本語を話しません。

   No one but my father speaks Japanese in my family.

4. Verb OO form

   今、行こうか。　　　　　　　　　　Shall we go now?

   うん、行こう。　　　　　　　　　　Yes, let's go.

5. Informal/Plain Speech Style

6. Male & Female Speech Style

   これ、食べるか（い）？　　　　　Will you eat this?　[male]

   今日はかつぞ。　　　　　　　　　I'll win today!　[male]

   新聞を持って来てくれ。　　　　　Bring me a newspaper.　[male]

   今日、おすしにするわ。　　　　　I will have *sushi* today!　[female]

   手紙を書くの。　　　　　　　　　I'm going to write a letter.　[female]

   今、帰るわよ。　　　　　　　　　I'll go home now!　[female]

日本語3－2課

1. 「トトロ」という映画を見たことがありますか。

   Have you ever seen the movie called "Totoro"?

2. 日本とか中国（とか）に行ってみたいです。

   I want to try to go to Japan and China (among other places).

3. 私は、家へ帰ると、服を着かえます。

   When I return home, I change my clothes.

4. 試合が（or の）始まる時間は、四時です。

The game's starting time is 4:00.

5. クッキーが（or の）好きな人は　だれですか。

Who is the person who likes cookies?

6. 日本レストランへ行った時に、おすしを食べました。

When I went to a Japanese restaurant, I ate *sushi*.

7. 中学一年生の時に、私は日本語をぜんぜん話せませんでした。

I could not speak Japanese at all when I was in the seventh grade.

8. ひまな時に、家へ遊びに来て下さい。

Please come to my house to play when you are free.

日本語３－３課

1. 私は、まだ１６才なので、お酒を飲んではいけません。

Since I am still 16 years old, I am not allowed to drink alcohol.

2. 明日、試験があるので、今晩、勉強しなければなりません。

Since I will have an exam tomorrow, I have to study tonight.

3. ジーンズは楽なので、私はいつもジーンズをはいています。

Since jeans are comfortable, I always wear them.

4. 妹は、小学生なのに、料理がとても上手です。

Although my younger sister is an elementary school student, she is very skillful at cooking.

5. 私がケーキを作ったのに、だれも食べてくれませんでした。

Even though I baked a cake, no one ate it.

6. 友達が麻薬を使っているんですよ。　My friend is using drugs.

7. あの人が好きなんです。　I like him/her.

8. 寒くなってきました。　It has become cold.

9. 暖かくなっていくでしょう。　It will become warm.

10. 早く寝た方がいいでしょう。

It's probably better to go to bed early.

11. たばこはすわない方がいいと思います。

I think it's better not to smoke.

日本語３－４課

1. 私は三年前に日本語を取り始めました。

I started to take Japanese three years ago.

2. 昨日やっとこの本を読み終わりました。

I finally finished reading this book yesterday.

文法　　　　126

3. 漢字を書きつづけていたので、手が痛くなりました。
   Since I kept writing *kanji*, my hand became sore.
4. このシャツはとても着やすいです。
   This shirt is very easy to wear.
5. このペンは書きにくいですねえ。
   This pen is hard to write with, isn't it?
6. 昼食を食べてから、映画を見に行こう。
   Let's go to watch a movie after eating lunch.
7. 森田君は頭もいいし、スポーツも上手です。
   Mr. Morita is smart; what's more, he is also good at sports.
8. このジャケットは楽だし、とっても安かったのよ。
   This jacket is comfortable; what's more, it was very cheap.
9. ベンさんは宿題もしなかったし、教科書を持って来るのも忘れました。
   Ben did not do homework; what's more, he also forgot to bring his textbook.

日本語３－６課
1. 弟がテレビを見ている間に、私は宿題をしてしまいました。
   I finished doing my homework while my younger brother was watching TV.
2. 冬休みの間に、日本へ旅行するつもりです。
   I am planning to take a trip to Japan during winter vacation.
3. 長い間、私は日本料理を食べていません。
   I have not eaten Japanese food for a long time.
4. 静かな間、よく勉強出来ました。
   I could study well while it was quiet.
5. 姉は、いつも音楽を聞きながら、勉強しています。
   My older sister always studies while she listens to music.
6. あの俳優は三度目の結婚をしたそうです。
   I heard that that actor got married for the third time.
7. 新聞によると、この冬はとても寒いそうだよ。
   According to the newspaper, (I understand that) it will be very cold this winter.
8. 日本人は食べた後で、「ごちそうさま。」と言います。
   Japanese say "*GOCHISOSAMA*" after eating.
9. このクラスの後で、お昼を一緒に食べましょう。
   Let's eat lunch together after this class.
10. この後で、何をしますか。
    What are you going to do after this?

文法

11. 日本人は食べる前に、「いただきます。」と言います。

Japanese say "*ITADAKIMASU*" before they eat.

12. 冬休みの前に、ビデオを貸して下さい。

Please lend me some videos before winter vacation.

日本語３－７課

1. BA form / NAKEREBA form   if 〜/if not 〜

日本語が話せれば、旅行は楽しいです。

If you can speak Japanese, the trip will be fun.

あなたが行かなければ、私も行きません。

If you won't go, I won't go either.

もし安ければ、買います。

If it is cheap, I will buy it.

映画が好きなら、おもしろい映画をたくさん知っているはずです。

If he likes movies, he should know lots of interesting movies.

学生なら、安いですよ。

If you are a student, it is cheap.

2. 友子さんからの電話はいつもとても長いんです。

Telephone calls from Tomoko are always very long.

3. パーティーの食べ物はもう買ってあります。

The food for the party has already been bought.

4. 明日、雨が降るかもしれません。

It might rain tomorrow.

5. 昨日おそく家へ帰り、すぐ寝ました。

I returned home late yesterday and went to bed immediately.

日本語３－８課

1. 弟は毎日テレビゲームばかりしています。

My younger brother is playing only computer games every day.

2. ベンさんは来年日本へ行くらしいです。

It seems that Ben is going to Japan next year.

3. 明日、パーティーをするので、今日食べ物を買っておきました。

Since we are going to have a party tomorrow, I bought food today ahead of time.

4. 大学に行っても、日本語を勉強しようと思っています。

I am thinking of studying Japanese even when I go to college.

文法   128

1. 田中さんがパーティーに来る<u>かどうか</u>、知りません。

   I do not know if Mr. Tanaka will come to the party or not.

2. 田中さんがパーティーに来る<u>か来ないか</u>、知りません。

   I do not know if Mr. Tanaka will come or will not come to the party.

3. 東京駅までいくら<u>か</u>、知っていますか。

   Do you know how much it is to Tokyo Station?

4. <u>いつ</u>日本語の試験がある<u>か</u>、おぼえていますか。

   Do you remember when we are having our Japanese exam?

5. 右に<u>まがると</u>、大きいデパートがあります。

   If you turn right, there will be a large department store.

6. 早く<u>終わったら</u>、買い物に行きましょう。

   If we finish early, let's go shopping.

7. 雨が<u>降らなければ</u>、ピクニックをします。

   If and only if it does not rain, we will have a picnic.

日本語４－１課

1. 「先生、もうお昼を<u>食べられました</u>か。」

   "Teacher, did you eat lunch already?"

2. 「社長、新聞を<u>読まれます</u>か。」

   "President, are you going to read the newspaper?"

3. 「お客様はゴルフを<u>されます</u>か。」

   "Do you (customer) play golf?"

4. 「先生、この紙に<u>サインしてくださいませんか</u>。」

   "Teacher, would you please sign this paper?"

5. 「先生、大学の推薦状(recommendation)を<u>書いていただけませんか</u>。」

   "Teacher, would you write a college recommendation for me?"

6. 学生：「先生、お昼をもう<u>めしあがりました</u>か。」

   Student: "Teacher, have you already eaten lunch?"

   先生：「ええ、もう食べましたよ。」

   Teacher: "Yes, I've already eaten."

7. ウェイトレス：「何に<u>なさいます</u>か。」

   Waitress: "What will you have?"

   客：「おすしにします。」

   Customer: "I will have *sushi*."

8. 旅行会社 ：「どちらに<u>いらっしゃいます</u>か。」

   Travel agent: "Where are you going?"

文法

客：「京都に行きたいんです。」

Customer: "I want to go to Kyoto."

9. 店員：「こちらのシャツをを<u>ごらんになりますか</u>。」

Store clerk: "Would you like to see this shirt?"

客：「ええ、見せて下さい。」

Customer: "Yes, please show it to me."

10. 社員：「社長、田中様を<u>ご存知ですか</u>。」

Company employee: "President, do you know Mr. Tanaka?"

社長：「いいや、知らないよ。」

Company president: "No, I don't know him."

11. 学生：「先生、今日は何時ごろ<u>お帰りになりますか</u>。」

Student: "Teacher, about what time will you go home today?"

先生：「五時ごろ帰ります。」

Teacher: "I will go home at around 5:00."

12. 社員：「社長、今日のミーティングは十時<u>でございます</u>。」

Company employee: "President, the today's meeting is at 10:00."

社長：「ああ、分かった。」

Company president: "Yes, I understand."

13. 店員：「Mサイズで<u>よろしい</u>ですか。」

Store clerk: "Is the medium size o.k.?"

客　：「ええ、いいです。」

Customer: "Yes, it's o.k."

14. 「どうぞ、<u>お入り下さい</u>。」

"Please come in."

15. 社長：「ビールを飲むかい？」

Company president: "Will you drink some beer?"

社員：「はい、<u>いただきます</u>。」

Company employee: "Yes, I will (drink some)."

16. 社長：「何にするかい？」

Company president: "What are you going to have?"

社員：「天ぷらに<u>いたします</u>。」

Company employee: "I will decide on *tenpura*."

17. 先生：「どこから来ましたか。」

Teacher: "Where did you come from?"

学生：「アメリカから<u>まいりました</u>。」

Student: "I came from the U.S."

18. 先生：「今、どこに住んでいますか。」

Teacher: "Where do you live now?"

学生：「学校の近くに住んでおります。」

Student: "I live near school"

19. 先生：「お名前は。」

Teacher: "What is your name?"

学生：「田中と申^{もう}します。どうぞよろしく。」

Student: "I am Tanaka. Glad to meet you."

20. 先生：「この写真を見ますか。」

Teacher: "Will you look at these photos?"

学生：「はい、はいけんします。」

Student: "Yes, I will look (at them)."

21. スチュワーデス：「お水をお持ちいたしました。」

Stewardess: "I brought some water for you."

客：「どうもすみません。」

Customer: "Thank you very much."

日本語４－２課

1. 教科書がぬすまれた。

My textbook was stolen.

2. お弁当は犬に食べられた。

My box lunch was eaten by my dog.

3. 兄はどろぼうに自動車をぬすまれた。

My older brother had his car stolen by a thief.

4. 母は父に死なれて、生活は大変だったそうだ。

I heard that after my father died my mother was left and life was difficult (for her).

5. 両親は子供の教育のために、家を引^ひっ越^こしたそうだ。

I heard that the parents moved to a different location for the sake of their children's education.

6. いい大学へ行くためには、いい成績^{せいせき}がいる。

I need good grades in order to go to a good college.

7. 学校にちこくしないために、夜は早く寝る。

In order not to be late to school, I go to bed early at night.

8. 兄はニューヨークの大学に行くことにした。

My older brother decided to go to a college in New York.

131

文法

9. 私の家族はコロラドに引っ越しをすることに決めた。

My family decided to move to Colorado.

10. 学校でTシャツを着てはいけないことになった。

It has been decided that we can no longer wear t-shirts in school.

11. 次の試合は私達の学校ですることに決まったらしい。

It seems that it was decided to have the next game at our school.

12. 私は医者になりたい。なぜなら、病気の人達を助けたいからだ。

I want to become a doctor. It's because I want to help sick people.

13. 日本語を三年間勉強しても、まだあまり上手に話せません。

Even though I have studied Japanese for three years, I still cannot speak it well.

14. 漢字の勉強はむずかしくても、おもしろいと思います。

Even if the study of *kanji* is difficult, I think it is interesting.

15. パーティーが日曜日の夜でも、田中さんは来るでしょう。

Even if the party is on Sunday night, Mr. Tanaka will probably come.

16. 山本君は、あまり勉強しなくても、成績がいいです。

Even though Mr. Yamamoto does not study much, his grades are good.

17. この本はおもしろくなくても、読まなければなりません。

Even though this book is not interesting, I have to read it.

18. ダンスが好きではなくても、ダンスパーティーに行きましょう。

Even though you don't like dancing, let's go to the dance party.

19. いい天気じゃなくても、キャンプへ行きますよ。

Even if the weather is not good, we will go camping.

日本語4－3課

1. 父はいつももっと勉強しろと言う。

My father always tells me to study harder.

2. 私が運転する時、両親はいつもスピードを出すなと言う。

When I drive a car, my parents always tell me not to speed.

3. 日本の道によく止まれと書いてある。

"Stop" is often written on the roads (road signs) in Japan.

4. 私が外へ出かける時、母はいつも気をつけなさいと言う。

When I go out, my mother always tells me to be careful.

5. 花子さんのような人が好きだ。

I like people like Hanako.

6. 日本人のように日本語を話したい。

I want to speak Japanese like a Japanese.

7. マイクさんはお父さんのようだ。

Mike is like his father.

8. 教室で日本語を話すようにしよう。

Let's make an effort to speak Japanese in the classroom.

9. 先生となるべく英語で話さないようにする。

I try to make an effort not to speak English to my teacher as much as possible.

10. 両親とよく話し合って、西海岸の大学へ行くことにした。

I discussed it well with my parents and decided to go to a college on the West Coast.

11. アメリカ本土の広さには驚いた。

I was very surprised at the spaciousness of the mainland U.S.

12. この学校の良さは、教育レベルがとても高いことだ。

The good point of this school is that its educational level is very high.

13. 雨が急に降り出した。

It started to rain suddenly.

14. 貧しくて、パンさえ買えない人がいる。

There are people who are poor and cannot even buy bread.

15. 母はスーパーへさえ一人で行かない。

My mother doesn't go alone even to a supermarket.

16. 友達の家にはテレビが四台もあって、台所にさえある。

My friend's house has as many as four TVs and there is even one in the kitchen.

17. 田村君は私におはようとさえ言わない。

Mr. Tamura does not even say "good morning" to me.

18. とてもいい映画だったので、何度も見に行った。

Because it was a very good movie, I went to see it many times.

19. キャンプに入れられた人が何人もいた。

There were many people who were put in the internment camp.

20. クッキーがおいしかったから、いくつも食べた。

Since the cookies were delicious, I ate many of them.

21. 今朝、日本語の試験があったので、ゆうべは何時間も勉強した。

Since I had a Japanese exam this morning, I studied for it for many hours last night.

日本語4－4課

1. クラスは9時に始まるはずなのに、先生はいつも遅く始める。

The class is supposed to begin at 9:00, but the teacher always starts late.

133   文法

2. ドアが壊れているけど、だれが壊したか知っていますか。

The door is broken. Do you know who broke it?

3. 原爆が落とされた時、屋根が落ちた。

When the atomic bomb was dropped, the roof fell in.

4. 事故が起きたのを見ていたら、私も事故を起こしてしまった。

While I was watching the accident happen, I caused an accident, too.

5. 図書館は午前七時から午後四時まで開いている。

The library is open from 7:00 a.m. to 4:00 p.m.

6. レストランは昨日、閉まっていた。

The restaurant was closed yesterday.

7. このコンピューターは夜もずっとついていた。

This computer was on throughout the night.

8. 私の時計は今、こわれている。

My watch is broken now.

9. 先生は生徒にたくさん漢字を書かせる。

Our teacher makes students write *kanji* a lot.

10. 両親は私を(or に)日本旅行に行かせてくれた。

My parents let me go to a trip to Japan.

11. 疲れているので、私をここで寝させて下さい。

Because I am tired, please let me sleep here.

12. 子守りをすれば、子供に 食べさせなければならない。

When you babysit, you have to feed the children.

13. 母は私に毎日二時間ピアノを練習させる。

My mother makes me practice the piano for two hours every day.

14. 「すみません。お待たせしました。」

"I'm sorry for making you wait (for me)."

15. 皆はのどがかわいていたので、水をほしがった。

Since everyone was thirsty, they seemed to want water.

16. 弟は冷蔵庫の中のケーキを食べたがっている。

My younger brother appears to want to eat the cake in the refrigerator.

17. 姉は、東海岸の大学へ行きたがっていたのに、行けなかった。

Although my older sister seemed to want to go to a college on the East Coast, she could not go.

18. マイクは日本語を話したがらない。

Mike does not seem to want to speak Japanese.

19. 日本語が話せる<u>ようになりました</u>。

I became able to speak Japanese.

20. 兄は、大学へ行って、肉を食べない<u>ようになりました</u>。

After my older brother went to college, he no longer eats meat.

21. あなたは大学へ行く<u>べきだ</u>と思う。

I think you should go to college.

22. 悪い友達とつきあう<u>べきではない</u>と思う。

I think you should not associate with bad friends.

23. あなたは日本語のＳＡＴの試験を受ける<u>べきだった</u>。

You should have taken the Japanese SAT exam.

|日本語４－６課|

1. 日本の文化を<u>習えば習うほど</u>、日本の事をもっと知りたくなる。

The more I learn Japanese culture, the more I want to know about Japanese things.

2. <u>寒ければ寒いほど</u>、暖かい飲み物がほしくなる。

The colder it is, the more I want warm drinks.

3. 図書館が<u>静かなら静かなほど</u>、よく勉強出来る。

The more quiet the library is, the more I can study.

4. 日本語<u>って</u>、とってもむずかしいね。

Japanese is very difficult, isn't it? [informal]

5. この本はイギリス人<u>によって</u>書かれた。

This book was written by an English person.

6. <u>どこか</u>美しい海が見える<u>所</u>へ行きたいですね。

I want to go somewhere where I can see the beautiful ocean.

7. <u>何か</u>少しからい<u>物</u>を食べたいですね。

I want to eat something a little spicy.

8. <u>だれか</u>かっこいい<u>人</u>とダンスに行きたいなあ。

I want to go dancing with someone good-looking.

9. <u>どこか</u>静かな<u>所</u>に行きたい。

I want to go somewhere where it is quiet.

10. <u>いつか</u>お金がある<u>時</u>に、日本に行こうと思っている。

I am thinking of going to Japan sometime when I have some money.

11. 僕は<u>だれも</u>皆好きだよ。

I like everyone.

12. 今日レストランはどこもこんでいた。

All the restaurants were crowded today.

135

文法

13. 私<u>だけでなく</u>、姉<u>も</u>チョコレートケーキが好きなんですよ。

Not only I, but my older sister also likes chocolate cake.

14. 漢字は数が多い<u>だけでなく</u>、読み方<u>も</u>いろいろある。

Not only are there many Chinese characters, but there are also various ways to read them.

15. 祖母は日本の食べ物が好きな<u>だけでなく</u>、日本の音楽<u>も</u>大好きだ。

My grandmother likes not only Japanese food, but also Japanese music.

16. 大統領はリーダーシップがある<u>だけでなく</u>、性格<u>も</u>良くなければならない。

The country's president should have not only leadership ability, but also has to have a good personality.

17. しょうじやふすま<u>は</u>木と紙<u>で</u>出来ている。

Shoji doors and *fusuma* doors are made from wood and paper.

18. 抹茶はお茶の葉っぱ<u>から</u>作られている。

Powdered green tea is made from tea leaves.

19. 何かを習い始めたら、<u>少なくとも</u>三年は勉強し続けた方がいい。

Once you start learning something, you had better continue studying it for at least three years.

20. 女の先生：「レポートは<u>遅くとも</u>金曜日の三時半までに出しなさい。」

Female teacher: "Turn in the report by 3:30 on Friday at latest."

21. 日本へ行けば、もっと日本文化が分かる<u>ような気がする</u>。

I have a feeling that if we go to Japan, we will better understand the Japanese culture.

22. 日本へ夏に行くととても暑い<u>ような気がする</u>。

I have a feeling that if we go to Japan in summer, it will be very hot.

23. 花子さんは太郎君が好きな<u>ような気がする</u>。

I have a feeling that Hanako likes Taro.

24. ケンさんのお父さんは白人の<u>ような気がする</u>。

I have a feeling that Ken's father is Caucasian.

日本語４－７課

1. 今朝、朝食を<u>食べないで</u>、学校へ来た。

I came to school without eating breakfast this morning.

2. <u>運動せずに</u>食べてばかりいると、太ってしまうよ。

If you just eat without exercising, you will gain weight, you know!

3. 今朝、朝食を<u>食べずに</u>、学校へ来た。

I came to school without eating breakfast this morning.

4. 今日、数学の試験があったので、ゆうべ<u>寝ずに</u>勉強した。

Because there was a math exam today, I studied without sleeping last night.

5. 次郎君は頭が<u>良さそう</u>だ。 ＊ Previously introduced.

Jiro looks like he is smart.

6. このシャツは<u>安くなさそう</u>だ。 ＊

This shirt doesn't look cheap.

7. 祖母も祖父もとても<u>元気そう</u>だ。 ＊

Both of my grandparents look very healthy.

8. このドアは<u>壊れそう</u>だ。 ＊

This door looks like it is about to break.

9. <u>死にそうな人</u>がいれば、助けてあげるべきだ。

If there is a person who looks as if he is dying, we should help him.

10. まりさんはお母さんに死なれて、毎日、<u>悲しそうな顔</u>をしている。

Since Mari's mother died, Mari looks sad every day.

11. 太郎君は<u>じょうぶそうな歯</u>をしている。

Taro looks like he has strong teeth.

12. 父が昔、日本に住んでいた<u>と</u>知らなかった。

I didn't know that my father was living in Japan before.

13. 日本人とのインタビューから、移民の一番の問題は言葉だ<u>と</u>知った。

I learned from an interview with a Japanese that the biggest problem of immigrants is language.

14. 父が屋根からドーン<u>と</u>落ちた。

My father fell from the roof with a crash.

15. 兄は北海道へ行かなかった。沖縄<u>へも</u>行かなかった。 ＊ Previously introduced.

My older brother did not go to Hokkaido. He didn't go to Okinawa, either.

16. 兄<u>も</u>姉も北海道へ行かなかった。 ＊

Neither my older brother nor my older sister went to Hokkaido.

17. 兄は東京へ行った。<u>また</u>、東京で働いた。 ＊

My older brother went to Tokyo. And also, he worked in Tokyo.

18. 両親は漢字を一つ<u>も</u>知らない。

My parents don't know even a single *kanji*.

19. ゆうべおそく帰ったので、お風呂に<u>も</u>入らなかった。

Since I came home late last night, I did not even take a bath.

20. 今日、数学の試験があったので、ゆうべ五時間<u>も</u>勉強した。 ＊

Since there was a math exam today, I studied for as long as five hours last night.

137

21.　あなたは日本語がよく分かる<u>じゃない</u>。
　　You understand Japanese well, don't you?

日本語4－8課

　1.　スコットは今日の約束（やくそく）を忘れた<u>にちがいない</u>。
　　Scott must have forgotten today's appointment.

　2.　日本旅行は楽しい<u>にちがいない</u>。
　　The Japan trip will most certainly be fun.

　3.　村田君は英語が上手<u>にちがいない</u>。
　　Mr. Murata must be good at English.

　4.　先生の御主人はアメリカ人<u>にちがいない</u>。
　　My teacher's husband must be American.

　5.　鹿（しか）は何でも食べる<u>みたい</u>で、私が持っていた紙も食べてしまった。
　　The deer seem to eat anything and even ate up the paper I had.

　6.　日本の伝統的（でんとう）な物は高い<u>みたいだ</u>。
　　It seems that traditional Japanese things are expensive.

　7.　この手紙はとても大事<u>みたい</u>だ。
　　This letter looks very important.

　8.　旅館の温泉（おんせん）は広くて、プール<u>みたい</u>だった。
　　The hot spring at the Japanese inn was spacious and looked like a pool.

　9.　人<u>によって</u>意見が違う。
　　Depending on the person, opinions are differ.

10.　日本は季節（きせつ）<u>によって</u>、違う花が咲（さ）く。
　　In Japan, different flowers bloom depending on the season.

11.　祖父は、私にいつも正直（じき）な人になる<u>ように</u>言っていた。
　　My grandfather was always telling to me to become an honest person.

12.　朝、家を出かける時、祖母はいつも気をつける<u>ように</u>（と）言う。
　　When I leave home in the morning, my grandmother always tells me to be careful.

13.　両親は、いつもあぶない所へ行かない<u>ように</u>（と）言う。
　　My parents always tell me not to go to dangerous places.

14.　<u>だれに</u>話して<u>も</u>、だれも私の意見に賛成（さんせい）してくれなかった。
　　No matter who I talked to, nobody agreed with my opinion.

15.　百円ショップでは、<u>何を</u>買って<u>も</u>、百円だ。
　　No matter what you buy at the hundred yen shop, it is a hundred yen.

16.　日本では、<u>どこへ</u>行って<u>も</u>、トイレにペーパータオルはなかった。
　　No matter where I went to in Japan, there were no paper towels in the bathrooms.

文法　　　　　　　　138

17. いつ聞い<u>て</u><u>も</u>、私はこの音楽に感動する。

No matter when I listen to it, this music moves me.

18. どう考え<u>て</u><u>も</u>、あなたの考えは、間違っていると思う。

No matter how I think about it, I think your idea is wrong.

日本語4－9課

1. 「夏休み、どこへ行こうか。」「ハワイ<u>なんか</u>どう？」

"Where shall we go during the summer vacation?"　"How about somewhere like Hawaii?"

2. 「この手紙を英語に訳して。」「私<u>なんか</u>出来ないよ。」

"Please translate this letter to English." "A person like me cannot do it."

3. 「明日の朝、早く<u>起きなきゃいけない</u>から、すぐ寝るよ。」

"Because I have to get up early tomorrow morning, I will go home soon."

4. 「明日、日本語の試験があるから、今晩<u>勉強しなくちゃ</u>。」

"Because there is a Japanese exam tomorrow, I have to study tonight."

5. 「聞いた？　マイクがハーバード大学に合格した<u>んだって</u>。」

"Did you hear?　I heard that Mike was accepted by Harvard University."

6. 「チェスが上手な<u>んだって</u>？　今度いっしょにやろうよ。」

"I heard you are good at playing chess. Let's play together next time."

7. 「社長、今日、田中様はいらっしゃらない<u>そうです</u>。」＊ Previously introduced.

"President, I heard that Mr. Tanaka won't come today."

8. 「プリンストン大学に合格出来る<u>といいね</u>。」

"I hope you can get into Princeton University."

9. 「大学の先生達がやさしい<u>といいね</u>。」

"I hope your college teachers are nice."

10. 「図書館が静かだ<u>といいね</u>。」

"I hope the library is quiet."

11. 「日本のホームステイの家族がいい人達だ<u>といいですね</u>。」

"I hope your host family in Japan will be nice people."

12. 「私の<u>悩み</u>を聞いて下さい。」

"Please listen to my worry (troubles)."

13. 「君と人生の<u>喜び</u>も<u>悲しみ</u>も分け合いたい。」

"I want to share both the pleasures and sorrows of life with you."

14. 「この<u>まま</u>にしておいて下さい。」

"Please leave it like this."

15. 「今の<u>まま</u>で、私は幸福です。」

"I am happy as I am now."

文法

16.　「缶に飲み物を残した<u>まま</u>、捨てないで下さい。」

"Please do not throw away cans while they still have some of the drinks left in them."

17.　「試験に名前を書かない<u>まま</u>、出してしまった。」

"I turned in my exam without writing my name."

18.　「宿題をする<u>こと</u>」

"Do your homework."

19.　「宿題を忘れない<u>こと</u>」

"Don't forget your homework.

I. 動詞 Verbs, いAdjectives and なAdjectives

[The Roman numerals preceding each word indicate the volume in which the word was introduced. I = Lev. 1, II = Level 2, III = Level 3, IV = Level 4. Arabic numerals indicate the lesson where the word was first introduced.]

A. Verbs
Group 1 Verbs

-む	-ぬ	-ぶ	-う	-つ
I-4　のむ	I-12 しぬ	I-15　あそぶ	I-13　いう	I-12　かつ
I-4　よむ		IV-1　よぶ	I-12　あう（会）	I-13　たつ
I-12　やすむ		IV-3　よろこぶ	I-13　かう	I-13　まつ
II-2　すむ		IV-4　とぶ	I-15　うたう	II-2　もつ
II-3　かむ		IV-6　えらぶ	I-15　もらう	IV-9 やくにたつ
II-13　こむ		IV-8　ならぶ	II-2　ならう	
III-6　たのしむ			II-2　ちがう	
IV-2　ぬすむ			II-3　すう	
IV-3　やむ			II-5　はらう	
IV-7　なやむ			II-7　あらう	
			II-7　てつだう	
			II-9　ちがう	
			II-11　(TE)しまう	
			II-11　おもう	
			II-13　うかがう	
			II-15　わらう	
			III-1　つかう	
			III-2　かよう	
			III-6　つきあう	
			IV-2　いわう	
			IV-2　たたかう	
			IV-3　(Stem)あう	
			IV-3　ふへいをいう	
			IV-6　あじわう	
			IV-9　ひろう	

[The Roman numerals preceding each word indicate the volume in which the word was introduced. I = Lev. 1, II = Level 2, III = Level 3, IV = Level 4. Arabic numerals indicate the lesson where the word was first introduced.]

-る		-く	-ぐ	-す
I-1 おわる	III-2 やる do	I-4 きく	I-15 およぐ	I-4 はなす
I-2 わかる	III-3 (ふろに)はいる	I-4 かく （書）	III-2 ぬぐ	I-13 だす
I-2 しる	III-3 はる （貼）	I-7 行く		I-14 かす
I-6 ふとる	III-3 うけとる	I-7 あるく		II-4 スピードをだす
I-6 とる	III-3 こまる	II-2 はたらく		II-5 かえす
I-7 かえる	III-4 (〜が)みつかる	II-3 はく		II-7 ゴミをだす
I-10 ある	III-4 (stem)おわる	II-4 つく		II-11 かくす
I-12 がんばる	III-6 おどる	II-5 おく put, leave		II-11 ふきとばす
I-12 はしる	III-6 にんきがある	II-6 (かぜを)ひく		II-15 あいす
I-13 すわる	III-6 なくなる	II-6 (ピアノを)ひく		III-4 さがす
I-15 やる	III-7 かざる	II-10 むかえに行く		III-4 おもいだす
I-15 つくる	III-7 あがる	II-10 とりに行く		III-4 やくす
II-3 かぶる	III-8 いのる	II-11 うごく		III-7 こわす
II-4 とまる （止）	III-8 かわった	II-13 すく		III-7 なおす
II-4 まがる	III-9 まいごになる	II-15 かく （描）		III-9 くりかえす
II-4 のる	IV-1 めしあがる	II-15 なく		IV-1 わたす
II-6 いらっしゃる	IV-1 いらっしゃる	III-2 (はを)みがく		IV-1 もうす
II-6 かわる	IV-1 ごらんになる	III-4 (じしょを)ひく		IV-1 いたす
II-7 おくる （送）	IV-1 おっしゃる	III-6 (トランペット を)ふく		IV-2 ひっこす
II-7 ふる （降）	IV-1 なさる	III-6 (ドラムを)たたく		IV-3 (stem)だす
II-9 かかる	IV-1 おやすみになる	III-7 おちつく		IV-4 おとす
II-9 うる	IV-1 まいる	III-8 (〜て)おく		IV-4 (じこを)おこす
II-10 はじまる	IV-1 おる be	III-8 やく		IV-4 おす
II-10 おわる	IV-2 なぐる	IV-1 いただく		IV-4 ころす
II-10 とりにかえる	IV-2 きまる	IV-2 おどろく		IV-6 まわす
II-10 むかえにかえる	IV-3 まもる	IV-4 あく		
II-10 よる （寄）	IV-3 あつまる	IV-4 (でんきが)つく		
II-12 なる	IV-4 しまる	IV-4 ひく （引）		
II-13 わたる	IV-4 ほしがる	IV-6 さく		
II-14 きる （切）	IV-7 いばる	IV-6 つづく		
II-15 おこる （怒）	IV-7 あやまる	IV-8 かわく		
II-15 しかる	IV-7 ふる jilt			
IV-8 とまる （泊）				
IV-8 のぼる				
IV-9 (〜が)のこる				

Group 2 Verbs

-E	One ひらがな	Special	
I-1　はじめる	III-1 かえる	I-4　みる	I-7　おきる get up
I-2　みえる	III-2 はきかえる	I-7　ねる	II-3　かりる
I-2　きこえる	III-2 やめる	I-10 いる	II-4　おりる（降）
I-4　たべる	III-2 (パーマを)かける	II-3　きる	II-6　できる
I-6　やせる	III-3 (しけんを)うける	II-4　でる	II-14- すぎる
I-12　つかれる	III-4 まちがえる	III-6 (part of body)	III-3 (シャワーを)あびる
I-12　まける	III-4 (〜を)みつける	をしている	III-7　おりる（下）
I-13　みせる	III-4 (Stem)はじめる	III-8 にる（煮）	IV-2 いきる
I-13　あける	III-4 (Stem)つづける	IV-4 (ちが)でる	IV-4 おちる
I-13　しめる	III-4 しらべる		IV-4 おきる happen
I-14　わすれる	III-6 わかれる		IV-6 かんじる
I-15　くれる	III-7 かける		
I-15　あげる	III-7 (〜が)こわれる		
II-2　うまれる	III-7 たてる		
II-2　つとめる	III-8 つける（漬）		
II-2　こたえる	III-8 かける		
II-3 (めがねを)かける	IV-2 そだてる		
II-3　(ごみを)すてる	IV-2 ほめる		
II-3　きをつける	IV-2 もうける		
II-4　おしえる	IV-2 きめる		
II-4　でかける	IV-3 しらせる		
II-6 (でんわを)かける	IV-3 あつめる		
II-6　まちがえる	IV-4 きえる		
II-6　おぼえる	IV-4 にげる		
II-9　さしあげる	IV-6(えいきょうを)あたえる		
II-9　くらべる	IV-6(えいきょうを)うける		
II-9　いれる	IV-7 あきらめる		
II-14　つける	IV-8 ぬれる		
II-14　かたづける	IV-9 もえる		
II-15　たすける	IV-9 わける		

[The Roman numerals preceding each word indicate the volume in which the word was introduced. I = Lev. 1, II = Level 2, III = Level 3, IV = Level 4. Arabic numerals indicate the lesson where the word was first introduced.]

Group 3 Irregular Verbs

I-7　くる II-10　むかえにくる II-10　とりにくる	II-15 さんぽ(を)する II-15 りこん(を)する II-15 かんしゃ(を)する III-1 そつぎょう(を)する III-1 せんこう(を)する III-2 りゅうがく(を)する	IV-6 だいじにする IV-7 きふ(を)する IV-7 どりょく(を)する IV-7 きょうりょく(を)する IV-7 こい(を)する IV-7 かんどう(を)する
I-4　する I-4　べんきょう(を)する I-4　タイプ(を)する I-7　りょこう(を)する I-7　かいもの(を)する I-7　しょくじ(を)する I-7　でんわ(を)する I-12　れんしゅう(を)する II-2　アルバイト(を)する II-2　けっこん(を)する II-2　ホームステイ(を)する II-2　しょうかい(を)する II-2　じこしょうかい(を)する II-2　しつもん(を)する II-3　アクセサリーをする II-3　うんてん(を)する II-4　しんぱい(を)する II-4　シートベルトをする II-4　けんか(を)する II-5　(thing に)する II-5　よやく(を)する II-5　ちゅうもん(を)する II-5　ごちそう(を)する II-7　そうじ(を)する II-7　せんたく(を)する II-7　りょうり(を)する II-10　うんどう(を)する II-10　おうえん(を)する II-10　ゆうしょう(を)する II-12　げきをする II-14　あつくする II-14　きれいにする	III-2 (お)けしょう(を)する III-3 せわ(を)する III-3 はっぴょう(を)する III-3 そうだん(を)する III-4 はつおん(を)する III-6 せいこう(を)する III-7 けいけん(を)する III-7 せいざ(を)する III-8 まる(を)する III-8 えんりょ(を)する III-9 せつめい(を)する III-9 やくそく(を)する IV-1 あいさつ(を)する IV-1 ほうもん(を)する IV-1 はいけん(を)する IV-2 くろう(を)する IV-2 にんしん(を)する IV-2 さいこん(を)する IV-2 たいしょく(を)する IV-3 めいれい(を)する IV-3 ちゅうしゃ(を)する(駐車) IV-3 こうげき(を)する IV-3 さべつ(を)する IV-3 じゅんび(を)する IV-3 おしゃべり(を)する IV-3 たいけん(を)する IV-4 さんせい(を)する IV-4 はんたい(を)する IV-4 やけど(を)する IV-4 けが(を)する IV-6 けんちく(を)する IV-6 たいせつにする	IV-8 きんちょう(を)する IV-8 あんしん(を)する IV-8 しゅっぱつ(を)する IV-8 とうちゃく(を)する IV-8 けんぶつ(を)する IV-8 かんこう(を)する IV-8 あんない(を)する IV-9 すいせん(を)する IV-9 ごうかく(を)する IV-9 さんか(を)する

Japanese 1 Verbs

[The Roman numerals preceding each word indicate the volume in which the word was introduced. I = Lev. 1, II = Level 2, III = Level 3, IV = Level 4. Arabic numerals indicate the lesson and section in which the word was introduced.]

I-1-4 はじめます	to begin; start	I-10-1 います	exist (animate)
I-1-4 おわります	to finish	I-10-1 あります	exist (inanimate)
I-2-1 わかります	to understand	I-11-2 あります	to have
I-2-1 しりません	do not know	I-12-1 しにます	to die
I-2-1 みえます	can see	I-12-2 やすみます	to rest; be absent
I-2-1 きこえます	can hear	I-12-2 (くすりを)のみます	to take (medicine)
I-2-1 いいます	to say	I-12-2 つかれています	to be tired
I-4-1 はなします	to speak; talk	I-12-3 かちます	to win
I-4-2 たべます	to eat	I-12-3 まけます	to lose
I-4-2 のみます	to drink	I-12-4 がんばります	to do one's best
I-4-4 よみます	to read	I-12-5 あいます	to meet
I-4-4 เกิด ききます	to listen; hear; ask	I-12-5 れんしゅう(を)します	to practice
I-4-4 します	to do	I-12-5 はしります	to run
I-4-4 べんきょう(を)します	to study	I-13-2 すわります	to sit
I-4-5 みます	to see; watch; look	I-13-2 たちます	to stand
I-4-5 かきます	to write	I-13-2 だします	to turn in
I-4-5 タイプ(を)します	to type	I-13-2 みせます	to show
I-6-4 ふとっています	is fat	I-13-2 あけます	to open
I-6-4 やせています	is thin	I-13-2 しめます	to close
I-6-4 としを とっています	is old (age)	I-13-2 しずかにします	to quiet (down)
I-7-3 いきます	to go	I-13-2 いいます	to say
I-7-3 きます	to come	I-13-2 まちます	to wait
I-7-3 かえります	to return (place)	I-13-2 かいます	to buy
I-7-3 おきます	to get up; wake up	I-14-3 わすれます	to forget
I-7-3 ねます	to go to bed; sleep	I-14-3 (〜が)いります	need 〜
I-7-4 あるいて いきます	to go on foot	I-14-3 かします	to lend
I-7-4 あるいて きます	to come on foot	I-15-1 うたいます	to sing
I-7-4 あるいて かえります	to return on foot	I-15-2 くれます	to give (me)
I-7-5 スポーツを します	to play sports	I-15-2 もらいます	to receive, get
I-7-5 パーティーをします	to have a party	I-15-3 あげます	to give (to equal)
I-7-5 りょこう(を)します	to travel	I-15-3 やります	to give (to inferior)
I-7-5 かいもの(を)します	to shop	I-15-5 あそびます	to play (for fun)
I-7-5 しょくじ(を)します	to have a meal, dine	I-15-5 およぎます	to swim
I-7-5 でんわ(を)します	to make a phone call	I-15-5 ゲームをします	to play a game
		I-15-5 つくります	to make
		I-15-5 (しゃしんを)とります	to take (picture)

Japanese 2 Verbs

[The Roman numerals preceding each word indicate the volume in which the word was introduced. I = Lev. 1, II = Level 2, III = Level 3, IV = Level 4. Arabic numerals indicate the lesson and section in which the word was introduced.]

II-2-1 Place で　うまれる	V2	to be born in (place)
II-2-1 Place に　すんで　いる	V1	to be living in (place)
II-2-1 Place に　つとめて　いる	V2	to be employed at (place)
II-2-1 Place で　はたらく	V1	to work at (place)
II-2-1 Place で　アルバイト（を）する	V3	to work part-time at (place)
II-2-1 Person と　けっこん（を）する	V3	to marry (a person)
II-2-1 もって　いる	V1	to have
II-2-1 しっている	V1	to know
II-2-1 しらない	V1	do not know
II-2-1 ならう	V1	to learn
II-2-1 ホームステイを　する	V3	to do a homestay
II-2-3 しょうかい（を）する	V3	to introduce
II-2-3 じこしょうかい（を）する	V3	to introduce oneself
II-2-4 ちがう	V1	to differ; is wrong
II-2-4 しつもん（を）する	V3	to ask a question
II-2-4 こたえる	V2	to answer
II-3-1 きる	V2	to wear [above the waist]
II-3-1 はく	V1	to wear [at or below the waist]
II-3-1 する	V3	to wear [accessories]
II-3-1 かぶる	V1	to wear [on the head]
II-3-1 かける	V2	to wear [glasses]
II-3-2 いけません	V2	won't do; must not do
II-3-2 かまいません	V1	I do not mind if . . .
II-3-2 たばこを　すう	V1	to smoke cigarettes
II-3-2 ガムを　かむ	V1	to chew gum
II-3-2 ごみを　すてる	V2	to litter; throw away garbage
II-3-2 うんてん（を）する	V3	to drive
II-3-2 Person に　あう	V1	to meet (a person)
II-3-2 Person に　聞く	V1	to ask (a person)
II-3-3 かりる	V2	to borrow
II-3-3 きを　つける	V2	to be careful
II-3-4 Thing が　見える	V2	(Thing) can be seen
II-3-4 Thing が　聞こえる	V2	(Thing) can be heard
II-4-1 おしえる	V2	to teach
II-4-2 とまる	V1	to stop
II-4-2 まがる	V1	to turn

Summary

146

II-4-2	スピードを　だす	V1	to speed
II-4-2	しんぱい（を）する	V3	to worry
II-4-3	Vehicle に　のる	V1	to ride (vehicle); to get on
II-4-3	Vehicle から／を　おりる	V2	to get off; to get out (vehicle)
II-4-3	シートベルトを　する	V3	to wear a seatbelt
II-4-3	出かける	V2	to go out
II-4-3	Place を　出る	V2	to leave (a place)
II-4-3	Place に　つく	V1	to arrive (at a place)
II-4-4	けんか（を）する	V3	to fight
II-5-1	Thing に　する	V3	to decide on (thing)
II-5-2	よやく（を）する	V3	to make a reservation
II-5-2	ちゅうもん（を）する	V3	to order
II-5-2	おく	V1	to put; leave
II-5-2	はらう	V1	to pay
II-5-3	ごちそう（を）する	V3	to treat someone
II-5-3	かえす	V1	to return (something)
II-6-1	かぜを　ひく	V1	to catch a cold
II-6-1	ひく	V1	to play (string instrument)
II-6-1	Thing が　出来る	V2	can do (thing)
II-6-2	（でんわを）かける	V2	to make a phone call
II-6-2	いらっしゃいます［いらっしゃる］	V1	to exist [polite equiv. of います]
II-6-2	まちがえる	V2	to make a mistake
II-6-2	かわりました［かわる］	V1	It's me. [lit., We've changed over.]
II-6-3	クラス／うんてんめんきょを　とる	V1	to take (a class); get (a driver's license)
II-6-3	おぼえる	V2	to memorize
II-7-1	おくる	V1	to send; mail
II-7-2	（あめ／ゆきが）ふる	V1	to (rain/snow) fall
II-7-3	そうじ（を）する	V3	to clean (house, room)
II-7-3	せんたく（を）する	V3	to do laundry
II-7-3	りょうり（を）する	V3	to cook
II-7-3	あらう	V1	to wash
II-7-3	てつだう	V1	to help
II-7-3	ごみを　だす	V1	to take out the garbage
II-9-1	Person に　さしあげる	V2	to give (to a superior)
II-9-2	くらべる	V2	to compare
II-9-2	ちがう	V1	is different; is wrong
II-9-4	いれる	V2	to put in ～
II-9-4	かかる	V1	to require (tax); to take (time)

147

[The Roman numerals preceding each word indicate the volume in which the word was introduced. I = Lev. 1, II = Level 2, III = Level 3, IV = Level 4. Arabic numerals indicate the lesson and section in which the word was introduced.]

II-9-4	うる	V1	to sell
II-10-1	うんどう（を）する	V3	to exercise
II-10-1	（しあいに）出る	V2	to play (a game)
II-10-1	おうえん（を）する	V3	to cheer
II-10-1	（〜が）はじまる	V1	(something) begins; starts
II-10-1	（〜が）おわる	V1	(something) finishes; ends
II-10-2	（Placeに）よる	V1	to stop by; drop by (a place)
II-10-2	（Person を）むかえに行く	V1	to go to pick up (a person)
II-10-2	（Person を）むかえに来る	V3	to come to pick up (a person)
II-10-2	（Person を）むかえにかえる	V1	to return to pick up (a person)
II-10-2	（Object を）とりに行く	V1	to go to pick up (an object)
II-10-2	（Object を）とりに来る	V3	to come to pick up (an object)
II-10-2	（Object を）とりにかえる	V1	to return to pick up (an object)
II-10-3	ゆうしょう（を）する	V3	to win a championship
II-10-4	ドキドキしている	V3	to be excited, be nervous
II-11-2	（Thing を）かくす	V1	to hide (a thing)
II-11-2	ふきとばす	V1	to blow away
II-11-2	（Thing が）うごく	V1	(thing) moves
II-11-2	Verb (TE) しまう	V1	to do 〜 completely
II-11-4	おもう	V1	to think
II-12-1	げきをする	V3	to give (put on) a (stage) play
II-12-1	〜に　なる	V1	to become 〜
II-13-1	うかがう	V1	to ask; inquire [Polite equiv. of きく]
II-13-2	〜を　わたる	V1	to cross; go over 〜
II-13-4	こんでいる	V1	to be crowded
II-13-4	すいている	V1	not to be crowded; is empty
II-14-2	きる	V1	to cut
II-14-2	あつくする	V3	to make hot; to heat
II-14-2	きれいにする	V3	to make clean; to clean
II-14-4	〜すぎる	V2	to exceed; too 〜
II-14-4	〜が　出来た	V2	〜 is ready; 〜 is done
II-14-4	（Object を）（Thing に）つける	V2	to dip (object) in (thing)
II-14-4	かたづける	V2	to clean up; put away
II-15-1	さんぽ（を）する	V3	to take a walk
II-15-1	わらう	V1	to smile; laugh
II-15-1	なく	V1	to cry
II-15-1	おこる	V1	to become angry
II-15-1	しかる	V1	to scold

Summary

148

[The Roman numerals preceding each word indicate the volume in which the word was introduced. I = Lev. 1, II = Level 2, III = Level 3, IV = Level 4. Arabic numerals indicate the lesson and section in which the word was introduced.]

II-15-1	りこん（を）する	V3	to divorce
II-15-3	たすける	V2	to rescue; help
II-15-4	かんしゃ（を）する	V3	to appreciate; thank
II-15-4	あいしている	V1	to love (someone)

149

Japanese 3 Verbs

[The Roman numerals preceding each word indicate the volume in which the word was introduced. I = Lev. 1, II = Level 2, III = Level 3, IV = Level 4. Arabic numerals indicate the lesson in which the word was introduced.]

III-1	そつぎょう(を)する	V3	to graduate
III-1	(Subject を)せんこう(を)する	V3	to major in (a subject)
III-1	食べよう	V2	let's eat
III-1	かえる	V2	to change (something)
III-1	つかう	V1	to use
III-2	かよう	V1	to commute
III-2	りゅうがく(を)する	V3	to study abroad
III-2	やる	V1	to do [informal form of する]
III-2	パーマをかける	V2	to perm (one's hair)
III-2	(お)けしょう(を)する	V3	to apply make-up
III-2	ぬぐ	V1	to remove clothing [i.e., shoes, dress, hat]
III-2	はきかえる	V2	to change [i.e., shoes, pants, etc.]
III-2	やめる	V2	to quit; discontinue
III-3	(はを)みがく	V1	to brush teeth
III-3	(シャワーを)あびる	V2	to take a shower
III-3	(ふろに)はいる	V1	to take a bath
III-3	はる	V1	to paste; glue; attach
III-3	うけとる	V1	to receive
III-3	せわをする	V3	to take care of
III-3	はっぴょう(を)する	V3	to present; announce
III-3	(しけんを)うける	V2	to take (an exam)
III-3	そうだん(を)する	V3	to consult
III-3	こまる	V1	to be troubled
III-3	(ペットを)かう	V1	to raise a pet
III-3	そんけい(を)する	V3	to respect
III-4	まちがえる	V2	to make mistakes
III-4	(じしょを)ひく	V1	to look up a word (in a dictionary)
III-4	さがす	V1	to look for; search for
III-4	(〜が)見つかる	V1	(something) is found [intransitive]
III-4	(〜を)見つける	V2	to find (an object) [transitive]
III-4	Verb stem + はじめる	V2	to begin doing 〜
III-4	Verb stem + おわる	V1	to finish doing 〜
III-4	Verb stem + つづける	V2	to continue/keep doing 〜
III-4	しらべる	V2	to check; investigate
III-4	おもいだす	V1	to recall
III-4	やくす	V1	to translate
III-4	はつおん(を)する	V3	to pronounce

Summary

150

[The Roman numerals preceding each word indicate the volume in which the word was introduced. I = Lev. 1, II = Level 2, III = Level 3, IV = Level 4. Arabic numerals indicate the lesson in which the word was introduced.]

III-6	おどる	V1	to dance
III-6	(トランペットを)ふく	V1	to blow (a trumpet)
III-6	(ドラムを)たたく	V1	to beat (a drum)
III-6	(part of body を)している	V2	to have (part of body)
III-6	にんきがある	V1	to be popular
III-6	せいこう(を)する	V3	to succeed
III-6	わかれる	V2	to separate
III-6	なくなる	V1	to pass away; die [polite form of しぬ]
III-6	たのしむ	V1	to enjoy
III-6	(〜と)つきあう	V1	to associate with 〜
III-7	けいけん(を)する	V3	to experience
III-7	かける	V2	to hang
III-7	かざる	V1	to decorate
III-7	(〜が)こわれる	V2	(something) breaks [intransitive]
III-7	(〜を)こわす	V1	to break (object) [transitive]
III-7	なおす	V1	to fix
III-7	あがる	V1	to step up
III-7	おりる	V2	to go down
III-7	おちつく	V1	to become calm
III-7	せいざ(を)する	V3	to sit properly
III-7	たてる	V2	to build
III-8	つける	V2	to soak; dip
III-8	(〜て)おく	V1	to do (something in advance)
III-8	にる	V2	to boil (in broth); simmer
III-8	やく	V1	to grill; roast; bake; toast; fry
III-8	まるをする	V3	to circle
III-8	かける	V2	to pour over; sprinkle
III-8	いのる	V1	to pray
III-8	えんりょ(を)する	V3	to hesitate; be reserved
III-9	まいごになる	V1	to get lost

151

Summary

Japanese 4 Verbs

[The Roman numerals preceding each word indicate the volume in which the word was introduced. I = Lev. 1,
II = Level 2, III = Level 3, IV = Level 4. Arabic numerals indicate the lesson in which the word was introduced.]

IV-1	めしあがる	V1	to eat; drink [honorific equiv. of 食べる, 飲む]
IV-1	いらっしゃる／いらっしゃいます		
		V1	to come; go; (animate) exist [honorific equiv. of 来る, 行く, いる]
IV-1	ごらんになる	V1	to look [honorific equiv. of 見る]
IV-1	おっしゃる／おっしゃいます	V1	to say [honorific equiv. of 言う]
IV-1	なさる／なさいます	V1	to do [honorific equiv. of する]
IV-1	あいさつ(を)する	V3	to greet
IV-1	ほうもん(を)する	V3	to visit
IV-1	わたす	V1	to hand over
IV-1	いただく	V1	to eat; drink; receive [humble equiv. of 食べる, 飲む, もらう]
IV-1	いたす	V1	to do [humble equiv. of する]
IV-1	まいる	V1	to come; go [humble equiv. of 来る, 行く]
IV-1	おる	V1	to be [humble equiv. of いる]
IV-1	もうす	V1	to say [humble equiv. of 言う]
IV-1	はいけんする	V3	to look; see [humble equiv. of 見る]
IV-2	いわう	V1	to celebrate; congratulate
IV-2	ぬすむ	V1	to steal
IV-2	なぐる	V1	to hit (someone); beat (someone)
IV-2	そだてる	V2	to raise (a person/pet)
IV-2	ほめる	V2	to praise
IV-2	いきる	V2	to live
IV-2	もうける	V2	to earn/make (money)
IV-2	くろう(を)する	V3	to suffer; have a hard time; struggle
IV-2	きめる	V2	to decide
IV-2	きまる	V1	to be decided
IV-2	ひっこす	V1	to move (one's residence)
IV-2	ひっこし(を)する	V3	to move (one's residence)
IV-2	おどろく	V1	to be surprised; be shocked
IV-2	にんしん(を)する	V3	to get pregnant
IV-2	さいこん(を)する	V3	to remarry
IV-2	たたかう	V1	to fight a battle; battle
IV-2	たいしょく(を)する	V3	to retire (from a job)
IV-2	こもり(を)する	V3	to babysit
IV-2	しんじる	V2	to believe; trust
IV-2	がまん(を)する	V3	to be patient; endure
IV-3	めいれい(を)する	V3	to command; order

[The Roman numerals preceding each word indicate the volume in which the word was introduced. I = Lev. 1, II = Level 2, III = Level 3, IV = Level 4. Arabic numerals indicate the lesson in which the word was introduced.]

IV-3	ちゅう車(を)する	V3	to park
IV-3	こうげき(を)する	V3	to attack
IV-3	さべつ(を)する	V3	to descriminate
IV-3	よろこぶ	V1	to be glad; be pleased
IV-3	じゅんび(を)する	V3	to prepare
IV-3	はなしあう	V1	to talk each other; discuss
IV-3	しらせる	V2	to report; inform
IV-3	ふへいをいう	V1	to complain
IV-3	おしゃべり(を)する	V3	to chat
IV-3	まもる	V1	to protect; follow (the rules)
IV-3	たいけん(を)する	V3	to experience
IV-3	(Stem) だす	V1	to start ~
IV-3	(〜が)やむ	V1	to stop [intransitive]
IV-4	(〜が)あく	V1	(something; someplace) opens [intransitive]
IV-4	(〜が)しまる	V1	(something; someplace) closes [intransitive]
IV-4	(〜が)つく	V1	(something) turns on [intransitive]
IV-4	(〜が)きえる	V1	(something) turns off [intransitive]
IV-4	(〜を)おとす	V1	to drop (something) [transitive]
IV-4	(〜が)おちる	V2	(something) drops; falls [intransitive]
IV-4	(〜を)おこす	V1	to cause (something) [transitive]
IV-4	(〜が)おきる	V2	(something) happens [intransitive]
IV-4	おす	V1	to push
IV-4	ひく	V1	to pull
IV-4	ころす	V1	to kill
IV-4	にげる	V2	to escape; run away
IV-4	とぶ	V1	to fly
IV-4	ほしがる	V1	(someone else) wants
IV-4	さんせい(を)する	V3	to agree
IV-4	はんたい(を)する	V3	to disagree
IV-4	やけど(を)する	V3	to get burned
IV-4	けが(を)する	V3	to get injured
IV-6	さく	V1	to bloom
IV-6	かんじる	V2	to feel
IV-6	けんちく(を)する	V3	to build (a house or a building)
IV-6	(かんきょうを)あたえる	V2	to influence
IV-6	(かんきょうを)うける	V2	to be influenced
IV-6	あじわう	V1	to taste
IV-6	(〜で／から)できている	V2	is made of/from ~

153

Summary

[The Roman numerals preceding each word indicate the volume in which the word was introduced. I = Lev. 1, II = Level 2, III = Level 3, IV = Level 4. Arabic numerals indicate the lesson in which the word was introduced.]

IV-6	(〜が)つづく	V1	(something) continues [intransitive]
IV-6	(〜を)たいせつにする	V3	to value; take good care of ~
IV-6	(〜を)だいじにする	V3	to value; take good care of ~
IV-6	まわす	V1	to turn (something) around; circulate
IV-7	きふ(を)する	V3	to donate
IV-7	どりょく(を)する	V3	to make efforts
IV-7	きょうりょく(を)する	V3	to cooperate
IV-7	いばる	V1	to brag; be arrogant
IV-7	あきらめる	V2	to give up
IV-7	あやまる	V1	to apologize
IV-7	(〜を)ふる	V1	to jilt; leave/reject (a boyfriend/girlfriend)
IV-7	(〜に)こい(を)する	V3	to fall in love (with person)
IV-7	なやむ	V1	to be troubled; be worried [personal]
IV-7	かんどう(を)する	V3	to be impressed (with ~); be touched (by ~)
IV-8	きんちょう(を)する	V3	to become nurvous
IV-8	あんしん(を)する	V3	to become relieved
IV-8	(placeに)とまる（泊）	V1	to stay overnight (at ~)
IV-8	けいかく(を)する	V3	to plan
IV-8	しゅっぱつ(を)する	V3	to depart
IV-8	とうちゃく(を)する	V3	to arrive
IV-8	けんぶつ(を)する	V3	to sightsee
IV-8	かんこう(を)する	V3	to tour
IV-8	あんない(を)する	V3	to guide
IV-8	のぼる	V1	to climb
IV-8	(〜が)ならぶ	V1	(someone/something) lines up [intransitive]
IV-8	ぬれる	V2	(someone/something) gets wet [intransitive]
IV-8	かわく	V3	(someone/something) gets dry [intransitive]
IV-9	ひろう	V1	to pick up
IV-9	ごうかく(を)する	V3	to pass an exam; be accepted (by school)
IV-9	(〜が)のこる	V1	(something) remains [intransitive]
IV-9	やくにたつ	V1	to be useful
IV-9	さんか(を)する	V3	to participate

B. いAdjectives

[The Roman numerals preceding each word indicate the volume and the arabic numerals indicate the lesson in which the word was introduced.]

Japanese 1 いAdjectives

I-1 あつい	hot		I-10 うつくしい	beautiful
I-1 さむい	cold		I-10 ひろい	spacious, wide
I-1 ずずしい	cool		I-10 せまい	narrow, small (space)
I-2 いい	good		I-10 ちかい	near
I-6 たかい	tall, high		I-10 とおい	far
I-6 ひくい	short (height), low		I-11 むずかしい	difficult
I-6 よい	good		I-11 やさしい	easy
I-6 わるい	bad		I-11 たのしい	fun, enjoyable
I-6 おおきい	big		I-11 おもしろい	interesting
I-6 ちいさい	small		I-11 つまらない	boring, uninteresting
I-6 ながい	long		I-11 ひどい	terrible
I-6 みじかい	short (length)		I-11 うれしい	happy
I-6 あかい	red		I-11 かなしい	sad
I-6 しろい	white		I-11 おおい	many
I-6 くろい	black		I-11 すくない	few, a little
I-6 あおい	blue		I-11 (〜が)ほしい	want (something)
I-6 きいろい	yellow		I-12 いたい	sore, painful
I-6 ちゃいろい	brown		I-12 ねむい	sleepy
I-6 わかい	young		I-12 つよい	strong
I-6 きびしい	strict		I-12 よわい	weak
I-6 やさしい	kind, nice		I-12 たかい	expensive
I-6 きたない	dirty		I-12 やすい	cheap
I-6 かわいい	cute		I-12 おいしい	delicious, tasty
I-6 うるさい	noisy		I-12 まずい	unappetizing
I-7 はやい	early		I-12 すごい	terrific, terrible
I-7 おそい	late		I-12 すばらしい	wonderful
I-7 いそがしい	busy		I-14 つめたい	cold (drink)
I-10 あたらしい	new		I-14 あたたかい	warm
I-10 ふるい	old (not for age)			

Japanese 2 いAdjectives

II-2 ただしい	correct; right		II-14 あつい（厚）	thick
II-4 あぶない	dangerous		II-14 あまい	sweet
II-4 こわい	scary		II-14 しおからい	salty
II-11 あかるい	bright		II-14 からい	salty; spicy
II-11 くらい	dark		II-14 すっぱい	sour
II-11 えらい	great (for people)		II-14 きもちがわるい	unpleasant; uncomfortable
II-14 うすい	thin (for objects)		II-14 きもちがいい	pleasant; comfortable

[The Roman numerals preceding each word indicate the volume and the arabic numerals indicate the lesson in which the word was introduced.]

Japanese 3 い Adjectives

III-3	つらい	hard; bitter; painful	III-8	くさい	smelly
III-4	V-stemやすい	easy to do ~	III-8	しかくい	square (shaped)
III-4	V-stemにくい	hard to do ~	III-8	まるい	round
III-5	さびしい	lonely	III-8	ふとい	thick (in width, size)
III-5	なつかしい	nostalgic	III-8	ほそい	thin; slender
III-5	うらやましい	envious	III-8	ほそながい	long and thin
III-7	おもい	heavy	III-8	かたい	hard; tough
III-7	かるい	light (in weight)	III-8	やわらかい	soft; tender
III-8	にがい	bitter	III-8	めずらしい	rare; unusual

Japanese 4 い Adjectives

IV-1	よろしい	good [polite equiv. of いい]	IV-2	がまんづよい	patient
IV-2	うんがいい	lucky	IV-3	まずしい	poor [formal]
IV-2	うんがわるい	unlucky	IV-7	なかがいい	be on good terms with ~
IV-2	くるしい	painful; have difficulty; hard	IV-7	なかがわるい	be on bad terms with ~

Conjugation of い Adjectives

Function	Formal form	Informal form	Meaning
nonpast	あついです	あつい	is hot
neg. nonpast	あつくないです or あつくありません	あつくない	is not hot
past	あつかったです	あつかった	was hot
neg. past	あつくなかったです or あつくありませんでした	あつくなかった	was not hot
pre-noun	あつい　おちゃ		hot tea
conjunction	あつくて、おいしいです。		It is hot and tasty.

[The Roman numerals preceding each word indicate the volume and the arabic numerals indicate the lesson in which the word was introduced.]

Conjugation of irregular い Adjective: いい

Function	Formal form	Informal form	Meaning
nonpast	いいです	いい	is good
neg. nonpast	よくないです or よくありません	よくない	is not good
past	よかったです	よかった	was good
neg. past	よくなかったです or よくありませんでした	よくなかった	was not good
pre-noun	いい　ひと		good person
conjunction	あたまが　よくて、せが　たかいです。		He is smart and tall.

C. な Adjectives

Japanese 1 な Adjectives

I-1	げんき	healthy; fine	I-1	にがて	be weak in
I-1	だめ	no good	I-1	きれい	pretty; clean; neat
I-1	すき	like	I-1	しずか	quiet
I-1	だいすき	like very much; love	I-1	じゃま	is a hindrance; is a nuisance; is in my way
I-1	きらい	dislike			
I-1	だいきらい	dislike a lot; hate	I-1	ゆうめい	famous
I-1	じょうず	skillful; be good at	I-1	たいへん	hard
I-1	へた	unskillful; be poor at	I-1	だいじょうぶ	all right
I-1	とくい	be strong in; can do well	I-1	だいじ	important

Japanese 2 な Adjectives

II-3	じゆう	free; liberal	II-9	いろいろ	various
II-4	あんぜん	safe	II-11	びんぼう	poor
II-6	へん	strange; weird; unusual	II-15	ひま	free (time)

Japanese 3 な Adjectives

III-3	へいわ	peaceful	III-3	しあわせ	happy; fortunate
III-3	とくべつ	special	III-3	にぎやか	lively
III-3	らく	comfortable	III-3	とうようてき	Eastern style
III-3	かんたん	simple	III-3	せいようてき	Western style
III-3	ふくざつ	complicated	III-3	でんとうてき	traditional
III-3	めちゃくちゃ	messy; confusing; incorrect	III-3	けんこうてき	healthy

Summary

[The Roman numerals preceding each word indicate the volume and the arabic numerals indicate the lesson in which the word was introduced.]

Japanese 4 な Adjectives

IV-1	ていねい	polite	IV-7	こうふく	happy; fortunate
IV-2	おやこうこう	filial piety	IV-7	ふこう	unhappy; unfortunate
IV-2	むせきにん	irresponsible	IV-7	どうとくてき	moral
IV-3	いんしょうてき	impressive	IV-7	ふどうとく	immoral
IV-6	ひつよう	necessary	IV-7	しょうじき	honest
IV-6	てきとう	proper; appropriate	IV-7	せいじつ	sincere
IV-6	ふてきとう	improper; inappropriate	IV-7	けんきょ	humble
IV-7	じょうぶ	strong; healthy; durable	IV-8	きょうりょくてき	cooperative
IV-7	よくばり	greedy (person)	IV-9	じゅうぶん	enough; ample
IV-7	わがまま	selfish; self-centered	IV-9	ゆたか	abundant; rich (life)
IV-7	ぜいたく	luxurious; extravagant			

Conjugation of な Adjectives

Function	Formal form	Informal form	Meaning
nonpast	すきです	すきだ	like
neg. nonpast	すきではありません or すきじゃありません	すきではない or すきじゃない	do not like
past	すきでした	すきだった	liked
neg. past	すきではありませんでした or すきじゃありませんでした	すきではなかった or すきじゃなかった	did not like
pre-noun	すきなひと		person I like
conjoining	すきで、まいにち たべます。		I like it and eat it every day.

Summary   158

II. Adverbs, question words, sentence interjectives, particles, clause particles, copula (plain form), dependent nouns, expressions, counters.

[The Roman numerals preceding each word indicate the volume and the arabic numerals indicate the lesson in which the word was introduced.]

A. Adverbs

I-4	よく + Verb	well; often		II-7	ぜひ	by all means
I-4	すこし	a little		II-9	もっと	more
I-4	ちょっと	a little		II-9	ずっと	by far
I-4	ときどき	sometimes		II-9	りょう方〔ほう〕	both
I-4	たいてい	usually		II-9	一番	the most
I-4	いつも	always		II-10	そのころ	around that time
I-5	とても	very		II-11	ガリガリ	chew away; gnaw
I-5	まあまあ	so, so		II-11	いっしょうけんめい	with one's utmost effort
I-5	あまり + Neg.	(not) very		II-11	とうとう	finally; at last
I-5	ぜんぜん + Neg.	(not) at all		II-13	まっすぐ	straight
I-10	また	again		II-14	うすく	thin
I-10	たくさん	a lot; many		II-14	あつく	thick
I-10	すこし	a few; a little		II-14	はんぶんに	in half
I-12	はやく	early		II-14	まず	first of all
I-12	おそく	late		II-14	はじめに	at the beginning
I-14	もう + Positive	already		II-14	つぎに	next
I-14	まだ + Neg.	(not) yet		II-14	おわりに	at the end
I-14	ぜんぶ	everything		II-15	ニコニコ	smilingly
I-14	もう(いっぱい)	(one) more (cup)		II-15	ずっと	throughout; all the time
I-15	もうすぐ	very soon		II-15	たまに	occasionally; once in a while
II-2	まだ + Aff.	still		II-15	そのとき	at that time
II-2	もう + Neg.	(not) any more		III-2	ほとんど	almost; mostly
II-2	とくに	especially		III-3	ずいぶん	quite; fairly
II-3	ぜったい(に)	absolutely		III-4	なかなか + Neg.	(not) easily
II-3	本当〔ほんとう〕に	truly; really		III-4	さいきん	recently
II-4	はやく	fast; early		III-7	もし	if
II-4	きゅうに	suddenly		III-8	さいしょに	at first
II-4	けっして + Neg.	never		III-8	さいごに	at last; finally
II-5	だいたい	roughly		III-8	さいこうに	the most
II-5	ほかに	besides		IV-2	うんよく	luckily; fortunately
II-6	何度〔なんど〕も	many times		IV-2	うんわるく	unluckily; unfortunately
II-6	もちろん	of course		IV-3	とつぜん	suddenly; enexpectedly

Summary

[The Roman numerals preceding each word indicate the volume and the arabic numerals indicate the lesson in which the word was introduced.]

IV-3	やっと	at last; finally		IV-8	きっと	surely; most certainly
IV-4	だんだん	step by step; gradually		IV-8	しばらく	for a while
IV-4	どんどん	rapidly		IV-9	べつ(べつ)に	separately
IV-6	もっとも	the most		IV-9	じゅうぶん	enough
IV-6	すくなくとも	at least		IV-9	いつまでも	forever
IV-7	できるだけ(はやく)	as (soon) as possible				

B. Interrogatives (Question Words)

I-1	なに, なん	what?	I-7	いつ	when?
I-2	なんまい	how many (sheets)?	I-7	なんじ	what time?
I-2	いくつ	how many (general things)?	I-7	なんぷん	how many minutes?
I-3	だれ	who?	I-11	なぜ, どうして	why?
I-3	なんにん	how many (people)?	I-13	(お)いくら	how much?
I-3	なんさい	how old?	I-13	どれ	which one?
I-3	(お)いくつ	how old?	I-13	どの〜	which 〜 ?
I-3	なんねんせい	what grade?	I-13	いかが	how? [Formal]
I-3	どこ	where?	II-5	どちら	which way? [Formal]
I-3	なにじん	what nationality?	II-6	どのぐらい	how much? how long?
I-3	なんがつ	what month?	II-9	どっち	which (one of two)? [Informal]
I-4	なにご	what language?	II-9	どちら	which (one of two)? [Formal]
I-5	どんな〜	what kind of 〜 ?	II-9	どれ	which one (of three or more)?
I-5	なにいろ	what color?	III-9	どうやって	how? [Informal]
I-7	なんようび	what day of the week?	IV-2	なんせい	what generation?

[The Roman numerals preceding each word indicate the volume and the arabic numerals indicate the lesson in which the word was introduced.]

C. Sentence Conjunctives and Interjectives

I-1	はい	Here! [In response to roll call.]	II-4	ううん	No [Informal]
I-1	はい or ええ	Yes	II-5	う〜ん	Yummm . . .
I-1	いいえ	No	II-9	さあ	Well . . .
I-2	ええと...	Let me see . . .	II-11	えっ	What?
I-2	あのう	Well . . .	II-11	いや（っ）	No [Stronger negation than いいえ.]
I-3	そして	And	II-11	だから	Therefore [Informal]
I-4	でも	But	II-11	ですから	Therefore [Formal]
I-6	それとも	Q1 or Q2?	II-13	ああ	Oh!
I-7	それから	And then	II-15	しかし	However [Formal equiv. of でも]
I-11	それに	Besides, moreover	III-3	たとえば	For example
I-14	これから	From now (on)	IV-2	なぜなら	That's because
I-14	じゃ、	Well then [informal]	IV-8	やはり or やっぱり	Indeed! Just as I thought.
I-14	では、	Well then [formal]	IV-9	へ〜え	Really! [informal]
II-3	ところで	By the way			
II-4	うん	Yes [Informal]			

D. Particles

I-1	は	Topic particle
I-1	Sentence ＋ か。	Question-ending particle
I-1	Sentence ＋ ねえ。	Sentence final particle expressing admiration, surprise or exclamation
I-3	の	Possessive and descriptive particle
I-3	と	and [Noun <u>and</u> Noun only]
I-3	も	also; too [replaces を, が, は]
I-4	で	at; in (place) [with action verb]
I-4	と（いっしょに）	(together) with
I-4	tool ＋ で	by; with; on; in
I-6	Sentence ＋ ね。	Sentence final particle for seeking agreement or confirmation
I-6	Sentence ＋ よ。	Sentence final particle for emphasis or exclamation
I-7	specific time ＋ に	at; on
I-7	place ＋ へ／に	to [with direction verb]
I-7	activity ＋ に	to; for (activity)
I-7	transportation ＋ で	by [with direction verb]
I-10	Location ＋ に ＋ Existence Verb	in; at
I-11	〜から〜まで	from 〜 to 〜

161

[The Roman numerals preceding each word indicate the volume and the arabic numerals indicate the lesson in which the word was introduced.]

I-14　（ふたつ）で	for (two) [totalizing particle]
I-14　（フォーク）で	with; by; by means of
I-15　〜や〜（など）	〜 and 〜, etc.
II-2　〜について [P+V]	about 〜
II-3　〜だけ	only
II-4　を	along; through
II-5　〜に〜	〜 and 〜 (as a set)
II-6　S1 + け(れ)ど、S2.	Although; Though S1, S2.
II-6　Sentence + が	[Softens the statement.]
II-6　〜で	because of 〜
II-6　に	per
II-6　も	as many/long as
II-9　AとBで	between A and B
II-9　〜より	more than 〜
II-9　〜ほど + Neg.	(not) as 〜 as
II-9　（〜の中）で	among 〜
II-10　(time) までに	by (a certain time)
II-11　「　」と	[Quotation particle]
III-1　N1 という N2 [P+V]	N2 called N1
III-1　〜しか + Neg.	only; nothing but 〜
III-1　〜って	[informal form of quotation particle と]
III-1　Sentence + の？	[female sentence ending particle]
III-1　Sentence + なの？	[female sentence ending particle]
III-1　Sentence + か？	[male informal sentence ending particle]
III-1　Sentence + かい？	[male informal sentence ending particle]
III-2　Sentence + かな。	I wonder if 〜. [used by male and female]
III-2　Sentence + かしら。	I wonder if 〜. [used by female]
III-2　N1 とか N2	N1 and N2 (among others)
III-2　〜として [P+V]	as 〜; for 〜
III-6　〜によると [P+V+P]	according to 〜
III-6　N1 のような N2 [P+N]	N2 like N1
III-8　〜ばかり	only 〜
IV-1　〜でも	(〜 or) something
IV-2　（〜の)ために	for the sake of 〜
IV-3　〜のように	like 〜
IV-3　〜さえ	even 〜

[The Roman numerals preceding each word indicate the volume and the arabic numerals indicate the lesson in which the word was introduced.]

IV-3	Question word (counter) も	many 〜
IV-6	(topic) って	[informal form of topic particle は]
IV-6	〜によって + passive	by〜 [formal equiv. of 〜に]
IV-6	〜だけでなく〜も	not only 〜, but also 〜
IV-7	〜と（わかった）	(understand) that 〜
IV-7	(counter) も + Neg.	(not) even (〜)
IV-8	〜によって	depending on 〜
IV-9	〜なんか	and so on; and the like; for example; things like 〜 [informal use of など]

E. Clause Particles

I-5	〜が、〜	〜, but 〜
I-11	〜から、〜	〜, so 〜
III-3	〜ので、	since 〜; because 〜
III-3	〜のに、	in spite of 〜; although 〜
III-3	〜し、	besides; what's more
III-3	〜て（から）、	after 〜
III-6	〜あいだに、	while 〜
III-6	(Verb stem form) ながら、	while 〜 (a person's simultaneous or concurrent actions]
III-6	(Verb dic. form) まえに、	before 〜
III-6	(Verb TA form) あとで、	after 〜
IV-2	(Verb dic./NAI form) ために、	in order to do/not to do 〜
IV-9	(Verb TA/NAI/この) まま、	as it is; unchanged

F. Copula (Plain & polite form)

II-11	(Noun/なAdj.) だ	[Plain form of です]
II-11	(Noun/なAdj.) だった	[Plain form of でした]
III-1	(Noun/なAdj.) だろう	probably is [Plain form of でしょう]
IV-1	(Noun) でございます	[Polite form of です]

G. Sentence Endings

III-1	〜てくれ	[male informal form of 一て下さい]
III-3	〜てくださいます	(superior) do 〜 for me
III-6	[Plain form]そうだ	I heard that 〜
III-7	[Plain form]かもしれない	might; may 〜
III-8	[Plain form]らしい	It seems that 〜

163

Summary

[The Roman numerals preceding each word indicate the volume and the arabic numerals indicate the lesson in which the word was introduced.]

III-8 [OO form] と思っている	I am thinking of doing 〜
IV-1 [TE form] くださいませんか	Would/Won't you do 〜 for me? [request form to a superior]
IV-1 [TE form] いただけませんか	Would/Won't you do 〜 for me? [request form to a superior]
IV-2 [Dic./NAI form] ことにする/ことにきめる	decide to do 〜
IV-2 [Dic./NAI form] ことになる/ことにきまる	It will be decided that 〜
IV-3 Noun のようだ	It is like 〜
IV-3 [Dic./NAI form] ようにする	try to (make efforts to) do 〜
IV-4 [Dic./NAI form] ようになる	come to do 〜/come not to do 〜
IV-4 [Dic. form] べきだ	should do 〜
IV-4 [Dic. form] べきではない	should not to do 〜
IV-6 [plain form] ような気がする	feel like 〜
IV-7 [plain form] じゃない？	〜, isn't it? [emphasis and confirmation]
IV-8 [plain form] にちがいない	must be 〜; without doubt
IV-8 [plain form] みたい (だ)	seem 〜 [informal equiv. of よう (だ)]
IV-8 [Dic./NAI form] ように言う	say that 〜
IV-9 [plain form] んだって	I heard that 〜 [informal]
IV-9 [plain form] といい (です)	I hope/wish that 〜

H. Dependent Nouns (Suffixes)

I-1 〜せんせい	Mr./Mrs./Ms./Dr.
I-1 〜さん	Mr./Mrs./Ms.
I-3 〜がつうまれ	born in (month)
I-7 〜はん	half past 〜
I-7 〜ころ、ごろ	about 〜 (time)
I-7 〜まえ	before 〜
I-7 〜すぎ	after 〜
I-12 〜たち	[plural for animate objects]
I-13 〜くらい, ぐらい	about [not for specific time]
I-15 〜ねんうまれ	born in (year)
II-2 〜ちゃん	used instead of 〜さん for small, cute children or animals
II-13 〜がわ	〜 side
II-14 〜かた	how to 〜
II-15 〜まえ	〜 ago
IV-2 (1970)ねんだい	1970's

I. Dependent Nouns (Suffixes)

I-2 この〜	this 〜
I-2 その〜	that 〜
I-2 あの〜	that 〜 over there
I-3 ご〜	[polite]
I-3 お〜	[polite]
II-10 あと〜	〜 more
II-11 ある〜	a certain 〜
IV-1 だい〜	[sequential numbers]

IV-2 〜せい	[generation]
IV-4 〜ずつ	〜 each
IV-4 〜いじょう	more than 〜
IV-4 〜いか	less than 〜

[The Roman numerals preceding each word indicate the volume and the arabic numerals indicate the lesson in which the word was introduced.]

J. Expressions

I-1	はじめまして。	How do you do?
I-1	どうぞよろしく。	Nice to meet you.
I-1	おはよう。	Good morning.
I-1	おはようございます。	Good morning. [Polite]
I-1	こんにちは。	Hello. Hi.
I-1	さようなら。	Good-bye.
I-1	はじめましょう。	Let's begin.
I-1	きりつ。	Stand. [used at ceremonies]
I-1	れい。	Bow. [used at ceremonies]
I-1	ちゃくせき。	Sit. [used at ceremonies]
I-1	(お)やすみです。	〜 is absent.
I-1	ちこくです。	〜 is tardy.
I-1	はやく。	Hurry!
I-1	おわりましょう。	Let's finish.
I-1	すみません。もういちどおねがいします。	Excuse me. One more time please.
I-1	すみません。ゆっくりおねがいします。	Excuse me. Slowly please.
I-1	ちょっとまってください。	Please wait a minute.
I-1	どうもありがとうございます。	Thank you very much.
I-1	どういたしまして。	You are welcome.
I-1	はい、そうです。	Yes, it is.
I-1	いいえ、そうではありません。 or いいえ、そうじゃありません。	No, it is not.
I-1	あついですねえ。	It's hot!
I-1	さむいですねえ。	It's cold!
I-1	すずしいですねえ。	It is cool!
I-1	そうですねえ。	Yes, it is!
I-1	おげんきですか。	How are you?
I-1	はい、げんきです。	Yes, I am fine.
I-2	わかりますか。	Do you understand?
I-2	しりません。	I do not know.
I-2	見えません。	I cannot see.
I-2	聞こえません。	I cannot hear.
I-2	Treeは　日本語で何と言いますか。	How do you say "tree" in Japanese?
I-2	〜を　ください。	Please give me 〜.

[The Roman numerals preceding each word indicate the volume and the arabic numerals indicate the lesson in which the word was introduced.]

I-2	はい、どうぞ。	Here, please (take it).
I-3	そうですか。	Is that so?
I-3	〜は？	How about 〜?
I-5	そうですねえ...	Let me see . . .
I-7	こんばんは。	Good evening.
I-11	どうですか。	How is it?
I-11	それはいいですねえ。	How nice! [for a future event]
I-11	それはよかったですねえ。	How nice! [for a past event]
I-11	それはざんねんですねえ。	How disappointing! [for a future event]
I-11	それはざんねんでしたねえ。	How disappointing! [for a past event]
I-12	どうしましたか。	What happened?
I-12	かわいそうに。	How pitiful! [to inferior]
I-12	がんばって。	Do your best. Good luck.
I-13	すわってください。	Please sit down.
I-13	たってください。	Please stand up.
I-13	だしてください。	Please turn (it) in.
I-13	みせてください。	Please show (it) to me.
I-13	まどをあけてください。	Please open the window.
I-13	ドアをしめてください。	Please close the door.
I-13	しずかにしてください。	Please be quiet.
I-13	もういちど言ってください。	Please say it one more time.
I-13	ちょっと待ってください。	Please wait a minute.
I-13	すみません。	Excuse me. [to get attention]
I-13	いくらですか。	How much is it?
I-13	いかがですか。	How is it? [polite]
I-13	わあ！	Wow!
I-14	おなかがすきました／ペコペコです。	I am hungry.
I-14	のどがかわきました／カラカラです。	I am thirsty.
I-14	いいえ、まだです。	No, not yet.
I-14	いいえ、けっこうです。	No, thank you.
I-14	〜を　かしてください。	Please lend me 〜.
I-14	いただきます。	[expression before meal]
I-14	ごちそうさま。	[expression after meal]
I-14	おなかがいっぱいです。	I am full.
I-14	じゃ、またあとで。	Well then, see you later.

Summary

166

[The Roman numerals preceding each word indicate the volume and the arabic numerals indicate the lesson in which the word was introduced.]

I-14	バイバイ。	Bye-bye.
I-15	(お)たんじょうびおめでとう(ございます)。	Happy Birthday!
I-15	おめでとう(ございます)。	Congratulations!
I-15	(〜を)たのしみにしています。	I am looking forward to (something).
I-15	はい、チーズ。	Say "cheese."
I-15	はい、ピース。	Say "peace."
II-5	いらっしゃいませ。	Welcome.
II-5	どうぞ　こちらへ。	This way, please.
II-5	ほかに　何か。	Anything else?
II-5	それだけです。	That is all.
II-5	すみません。	Excuse me.
II-6	ぐあいが　わるいです。	I don't feel well.
II-6	ストレスが　いっぱいです。	I am stressed.
II-6	(お)きのどくに。	I'm sorry. [Sympathy]
II-6	もしもし	Hello. [Telephone]
II-6	るすです。	No one is at home.
II-6	はなし中 [ちゅう]です。	The line is busy.
II-6	しかたが　ありません。	It can't be helped.
II-7	あけまして　おめでとうございます。	Happy New Year!
II-9	お好きですか。	Do you like it? [Polite expression of 好きですか]
II-9	何を　さしあげましょうか。	May I help you? [lit., What shall I give you?]
II-9	ありがとうございました。	Thank you very much. [Used after a deed has been done]
II-9	また　どうぞ。	Please come again.
II-10	それは　いいかんがえです。	That's a good idea.
II-10	うそです（よ）。	It is a lie (you know).
II-10	うそでしょう？	Are you kidding? Are you serious?
II-10	じょうだんです（よ）。	It's a joke (you know). I'm just kidding.
II-10	やったあ！	We did it!
II-10	ばんざい！	Hurray!
II-10	かった！　かった！	(We) won! (We) won!
II-11	とんでもない（です）。	How ridiculous! That's impossible!
II-11	なるほど。	Indeed! I see!
II-13	あのう...ちょっとうかがいますが...	Excuse me . . . I have a question.
II-13	どのぐらい　かかりますか。	How long does it take? [time]
II-13	どのぐらい　ありますか。	How far is it? [distance]
II-14	〜が　出来ました。	〜 is ready. 〜 is done.

167

Summary

[The Roman numerals preceding each word indicate the volume and the arabic numerals indicate the lesson in which the word was introduced.]

III-1	こちらこそ。	It is I, not you. [emphasis]
III-1	いってきます。	[Used by a family member who leaves home for the day.]
III-1	いってらっしゃい。	[Used by a family member who sends off another family member for the day.]
III-1	ただいま。	I'm home. [Used by a family member who has come home.]
III-1	お帰りなさい。	Welcome home. [Used by a family member who welcomes another family member home.]
III-1	おやすみ（なさい）。	Good night.
III-1	おさきに。	Excuse me for going/doing something first.
III-1	しつれいします。	Excuse me, I must be going now.
		[Used when one must leave a place. lit., I will be rude.]
III-1	しつれいしました。	I am sorry to have inconvenienced you, or for a rude act I have committed.
III-3	どうしたら、いいですか。	What should I do?
III-3	おひさしぶりです。	I have not seen you for a long time.
III-3	おかげさまで。	Thanks to you . . .
III-3	おせわになりました。	Thank you for your kind help.
III-4	どういういみですか。	What does it mean?
III-4	～といういみです。	It means ～.
III-8	かんぱい。	Cheers!
III-8	ごえんりょなく、どうぞ。	Without reservation/hesitation, please.
III-8	おかわりは？	Will you have seconds?
III-8	～をとってください。	Excuse me. Please pass me ～.
IV-1	ごぞんじですか。	Do you know? [honorific form of 知っていますか。]
IV-1	おはいりください。	Please come in. [more polite than はいってください。]
IV-1	おあがりください。	Please step up. [more polite than あがってください。]
IV-1	しょうしょうおまちください。	Just a minute, please.
		[more polite than ちょっとまってください。]
IV-1	ごらんください。	Please look. [more polite than 見てください。]
IV-1	いらっしゃい。	Welcome.
IV-1	おじゃまします。	Excuse me.
IV-1	おじゃましました。	Thank you for allowing me to trouble you.
IV-1	これはすこしですが...	This is a small gift.
IV-1	そろそろしつれいします。	It's almost time (for me) to leave.
IV-1	また、いらしてください。	Please come again. [more polite than また来てください。]
IV-1	かしこまりました。	Certainly, Sir/Madam.
IV-1	もうしわけございません。	I am sorry. [polite equiv. of ごめんなさい。]
IV-1	とんでもございません。	Don't mention it.

Summary
168

IV-9	ごくろうさま。	Thank you very much (for your service).
IV-9	おつかれさま。	Thank you very much (for your hard work).
IV-9	もったいない。	It's a waste.

K. Onomatopoetic & *Kasanekotoba* expressions

I-5	まあまあ	so, so
I-14	（のどが）からから（です）。	I am thirsty.
I-14	（おなかが）ぺこぺこ（です）。	I am hungry
II-6	もしもし	Hello. [on the phone]
II-10	ドキドキ	excited
II-11	ガリガリ	chew away; gnaw
II-15	ニコニコ	smilingly
III-4	めちゃくちゃ	messy; confusing; incorrect
III-4	なかなか+Neg.	(not) easily
IV-1	ぺらぺら	fluent
IV-1	ちゃんと	properly, in the right way
IV-1	さっさと	quickly
IV-1	ばらばらに	separately, scattered
IV-1	きょろきょろ	looking curiously around
IV-2	びっくり	surprise
IV-2	がっかり	disappointment
IV-2	やれやれ	relief after experiencing a challenging situation
IV-2	あつあつ	in love
IV-2	ぼろぼろ	worn out
IV-3	ハ（ッ）クション	Ahchoo!
IV-3	ゴホンゴホン	Cough, cough
IV-3	ザーザー	a very heavy rain
IV-3	ぶつぶつ	grumpy, complaining
IV-3	ぺちゃくちゃ	chattering in a noisy, animated way
IV-4	ピカッ（と）	flashes suddenly and instantaneously
IV-4	ドーン（と）	a loud boom
IV-4	くたくた	a person who is worn out from exhaustion
IV-4	そっくり	looks exactly like another person
IV-4	よいしょ（こらしょどっこいしょ）	used when one carries something heavy
IV-6	わくわくする	excitement and expectation
IV-6	わいわいがやがや	a loud chatter of people's talk

169

Summary

[The Roman numerals preceding each word indicate the volume and the arabic numerals indicate the lesson in which the word was introduced.]

IV-6 のんびりする	a leisurely, relaxed manner
IV-6 じっと	a motionlessness state
IV-6 シーンとする	a sudden silencing of sound
IV-7 こつこつ	diligent and steady manner
IV-7 にっこり	a broad smile
IV-7 ゆうゆう（と）	a calm, unruffled appearance
IV-7 ぼーっ（と）	the action of blankly staring or gazing into nothingness
IV-7 おろおろ	uncertainty
IV-8 ぶらぶら	aimless, idle wandering
IV-8 てくてく	walking around in a trudging or plodding manner
IV-8 じろじろ	a concentrated manner of watching or looking
IV-8 むしむし	a humid, sticky feeling
IV-8 すやすや	in deep sleep
IV-9 のろのろ	a slow moving pace
IV-9 ずけずけ	the action of saying unpleasant things to someone's face.
IV-9 よぼよぼ	decrepit; tottering
IV-9 チンする	warms up things with a microwave oven
IV-9 ガミガミ	a snapping, critical or nagging manner

L. Proverbs & Sayings

I-5　じゅうにんといろ＜十人十色＞	Ten men, ten colors.
I-10　かえるの子はかえる	A frog's child is a frog.
I-10　ねこにこばん	To give a gold coin to a cat.
I-10　さるも木からおちる	Even monkeys fall from trees.
I-11　みっかぼうず	A three days monk.
I-12　ばかにつけるくすりはない	There is no medicine for stupidity.
II-2　いしのうえにもさんねん	Sitting on a stone for as long as three years makes anything possible.
II-2　となりのはなはあかい	Flowers next door are red.
II-9　はなよりだんご	Sweet rice dumplings rather than flowers.
II-10　まけるがかち	Defeat is a win.
II-15　うみよりふかい母のあい	Mother's love is deeper than the ocean.
III-1　ちりもつもれば山となる	Dust amassed will make a mountain.
III-2　二度あることは三度ある	If something happens twice, it will happen three times.
III-7　ごうにいれば、ごうにしたがえ	When in a village, follow do as the villagers do. (When in Rome, do as the Romans do.)
III-8　いっせきにちょう	Killing two birds with one stone.

Summary   170

[The Roman numerals preceding each word indicate the volume and the arabic numerals indicate the lesson in which the word was introduced.]

IV-1	好きこそ物の上手なれ	What one likes, one does well.
IV-1	のうあるたかはつめをかくす	A wise hawk hides its claws.
IV-1	れいもすぎればぶれいとなる	When one is too polite, it borders on rudeness.
IV-1	みのるほどこうべをたれるいなほかな	As the grains of the rice plant ripen, the head of the stem of the rice plant bows lower.
IV-2	下手なてっぽうもかずうてばあたる	Even a poor shot hits his target if he shoots often enough.
IV-2	つった魚にえさはやらぬ	A caught fish is not fed.
IV-2	よらばたいじゅのかげ	When in need of shelter, seek a big tree's shade.
IV-2	ほそく長く	Slender and long.
IV-2	人の一生は重きにもつをおってとおき道を歩くがごとし	Life is like carrying a heavy load over a long journey.
IV-3	雨降ってじかたまる	The ground becomes firm after rain.
IV-3	えんの下の力持ち	A strong man under the veranda.
IV-3	ろんよりしょうこ	Proof is stronger than argument.
IV-3	楽あればくあり	After pleasure comes pain.
IV-4	ふこうちゅうのさいわい	To have good luck in the midst of bad luck.
IV-4	りょうやく口ににがし	Good medicine is bitter to the mouth.
IV-4	やまいは気から	Illness starts from the spirit.
IV-4	ゆだんたいてき	Carelessness is a great enemy.
IV-6	けんえんのなか	Like dog and monkey.
IV-6	もちはもち屋	Leave mochi-making to the mochi-maker.
IV-6	るいはともをよぶ	Like kinds gather together.
IV-6	でるくぎはうたれる	A protruding nail is hammered down.
IV-6	いちごいちえ	Treasure every meeting, for it will never reoccur.
IV-7	口はわざわいのもと	The mouth is the gate of disaster or ruin.
IV-7	ぬかにくぎ	Pounding nails into rice bran.
IV-7	目からうろこ（がおちる）	The scales drop from one's eyes.
IV-7	わらうかどにはふくきたる	Good fortune enters through a gate of laughter.
IV-8	聞くはいっときのはじ、聞かぬはまつだいのはじ	To ask may be a moment's shame, but not to ask and to remain ignorant is an everlasting shame.
IV-8	ひゃくぶんはいっけんにしかず	One look is better than one hundred "listens."
IV-8	おわりよければすべてよし	If it ends well, all is good.
IV-9	ぜんはいそげ	Be quick to do good.
IV-9	そんしてとくとれ	Take profit from a loss.
IV-9	ただよりたかいものはない	Receiving a free gift is sometimes more costly than not receiving one at all.
IV-9	むようのちょうぶつ	A useless long object.

171

M. Counters

[The numbers in the upper corner indicate the volume and lesson in which the counter was introduced.]

	II-5	II-5 %	II-9 Floors	I-2	I-2	I-3
1	いっこ	いっパーセント	いっかい	いちまい	ひとつ	ひとり
2	にこ	にパーセント	にかい	にまい	ふたつ	ふたり
3	さんこ	さんパーセント	さんがい	さんまい	みっつ	さんにん
4	よんこ	よんパーセント	よんかい	よんまい	よっつ	よにん
5	ごこ	ごパーセント	ごかい	ごまい	いつつ	ごにん
6	ろっこ	ろくパーセント	ろっかい	ろくまい	むっつ	ろくにん
7	ななこ	ななパーセント	ななかい	ななまい	ななつ	ななにん
8	はっこ	はっパーセント	はっかい	はちまい	やっつ	はちにん
9	きゅうこ	きゅうパーセント	きゅうかい	きゅうまい	ここのつ	きゅうにん
10	じ(ゅ)っこ	じ(ゅ)っパーセント	じ(ゅ)っかい	じゅうまい	とお	じゅうにん
?	なんこ？	なんパーセント？	なんがい？	なんまい？	いくつ？	なんにん？

	Age I-3	Months I-3	Grade I-3	Hours I-7	Minutes I-7	Points II-10
1	いっさい	いちがつ	いちねんせい	いちじ	いっぷん	いってん
2	にさい	にがつ	にねんせい	にじ	にふん	にてん
3	さんさい	さんがつ	さんねんせい	さんじ	さんぷん	さんてん
4	よんさい	しがつ	よねんせい	よじ	よんふん	よんてん
5	ごさい	ごがつ		ごじ	ごふん	ごてん
6	ろくさい	ろくがつ		ろくじ	ろっぷん	ろくてん
7	ななさい	しちがつ		な-なじ	ななふん	ななてん
8	はっさい	はちがつ		はちじ	はっぷん	はってん
9	きゅうさい	くがつ		くじ	きゅうふん	きゅうてん
10	じ(ゅ)っさい	じゅうがつ		じゅうじ	じ(ゅ)っぷん	じ(ゅ)ってん
11		じゅういちがつ		じゅういちじ		
12	20 はたち	じゅうにがつ		じゅうにじ		
?	なんさい？	なんがつ？	なんねんせい？	なんじ？	なんぷん？	なんてん？

Summary

172

	Degree(s); time(s) ～ど II-6	No. of minute(s) ～分（間） II-6	No. of hour(s) ～時間 II-6	No. of day(s) ～日（間） II-6
1	いちど	いっぷん（かん）	いちじかん	いちにち
2	にど	にふん（かん）	にじかん	ふつか（かん）
3	さんど	さんぷん（かん）	さんじかん	みっか（かん）
4	よんど	よんふん（かん）	よじかん	よっか（かん）
5	ごど	ごふん（かん）	ごじかん	いつか（かん）
6	ろくど	ろっぷん（かん）	ろくじかん	むいか（かん）
7	ななど	ななふん（かん）	ななじかん	なのか（かん）
8	はちど	はっぷん（かん）	はちじかん	ようか（かん）
9	きゅうど	きゅうふん（かん）	くじかん	ここのか（かん）
10	じゅうど	じ(ゅ)っぷん（かん）	じゅうかん	とおか（かん）
?	なんど？	なんぷん（かん）？	なんじかん？	なんにち（かん）？

	No. of week(s) ～週間 II-6	No. of month(s) ～か月 II-6	No. of year(s) ～年（間） II-6	No. ～ ～ばん II-10
1	いっしゅうかん	いっかげつ	いちねん（かん）	いちばん
2	にしゅうかん	にかげつ	にねん（かん）	にばん
3	さんしゅうかん	さんかげつ	さんねん（かん）	さんばん
4	よんしゅうかん	よんかげつ	よねん（かん）	よんばん
5	ごしゅうかん	ごかげつ	ごねん（かん）	ごばん
6	ろくしゅうかん	ろっかげつ	ろくねん（かん）	ろくばん
7	ななしゅうかん	ななかげつ	ななねん（かん）	ななばん
8	はっしゅうかん	はっかげつ	はちねん（かん）	はちばん
9	きゅうしゅうかん	きゅうかげつ	きゅうねん（かん）	きゅうばん
10	じ(ゅ)っしゅうかん	じ(ゅ)っかげつ	じゅうねん（かん）	じゅうばん
?	なんしゅうかん？	なんかげつ？	なんねん（かん）？	なんばん？

Summary

[The numbers in the right corner indicate the volume and lesson in which the counter was introduced.]

	rank 〜い II-10	〜 stroke(s) 〜かく III-3	〜 time(s) 〜かい III-4	〜 tatami 〜じょう III-7
1	いちい	いっかく	いっかい	いちじょう
2	にい	にかく	にかい	にじょう
3	さんい	さんかく	さんかい	さんじょう
4	よい	よんかく	よんかい	よじょう
5	ごい	ごかく	ごかい	ごじょう
6	ろくい	ろっかく	ろっかい	ろくじょう
7	なない	ななかく	ななかい	ななじょう
8	はちい	はっかく	はっかい	はちじょう
9	きゅうい	きゅうかく	きゅうかい	きゅうじょう
10	じゅうい	じ(ゅ)っかく	じ(ゅ)っかい	じゅうじょう
?	なんい？	なんかく？	なんかい？	なんじょう？

	〜 night(s) (stay) 〜ぱく IV-8
1	いっぱく
2	にはく
3	さんぱく
4	よんはく
5	ごはく
6	ろっぱく
7	ななはく
8	はっぱく
9	きゅうはく
10	じゅっぱく
?	なんぱく？

漢字リスト　*Kanji* List

Hiragana is used for *KUN* (Japanese) readings and *katakana* for *ON* (Chinese) readings.

I-13課　　☆ Special reading　　＊ Previously introduced.　　＊＊ For recognition only.

1. 一　one　　　ひと　　　一つ〔ひとつ〕one (general object)

　　　　　　　　　イチ　　　一月〔いちがつ〕January

　　　　　　　　　☆　　　　一日〔ついたち〕the first day of the month

2. 二　two　　　ふた　　　二つ〔ふたつ〕two (general objects)

　　　　　　　　　ニ　　　　二月〔にがつ〕February

　　　　　　　　　☆　　　　二日〔ふつか〕the second day of the month

3. 三　three　　みっ　　　三つ〔みっつ〕three (general objects)

　　　　　　　　　　　　　　三日〔みっか〕the third day of the month

　　　　　　　　　サン　　　三月〔さんがつ〕March

4. 四　four　　　よ（っ）　四つ〔よっつ〕four (general objects)

　　　　　　　　　　　　　　四日〔よっか〕the fourth day of the month

　　　　　　　　　よん　　　四本〔よんほん〕four (long objects)

　　　　　　　　　シ　　　　四月〔しがつ〕April

5. 五　five　　　いつ　　　五つ〔いつつ〕five (general objects)

　　　　　　　　　　　　　　五日〔いつか〕the fifth day of the month

　　　　　　　　　ゴ　　　　五月〔ごがつ〕May

I-14課

6. 六　six　　　むっ　　　六つ〔むっつ〕six (general objects)

　　　　　　　　　☆　　　　六日〔むいか〕the sixth day of the month

　　　　　　　　　ロク　　　六月〔ろくがつ〕June

7. 七　seven　　なな　　　七つ〔ななつ〕seven (general objects)

　　　　　　　　　なの　　　七日〔なのか〕the seventh day of the month

175

漢字

			シチ	七月 〔しちがつ〕 July
8.	八	eight	やっ	八つ 〔やっつ〕 eight (general objects)
			よう	八日 〔ようか〕 the eighth day of the month
			ハチ	八月 〔はちがつ〕 August
9.	九	nine	ここの	九つ 〔ここのつ〕 nine (general objects)
				九日 〔ここのか〕 the ninth of the month
			キュウ	九十 〔きゅうじゅう〕 90
			ク	九月 〔くがつ〕 September
10.	十	10	とお	十日 〔とおか〕 the 10th day of the month
			ジュウ	十月 〔じゅうがつ〕 October

			ガツ	一月 〔いちがつ〕 January
11.	月	moon	ゲツ	月曜日 〔げつようび〕 Monday
12.	日	sun; day	ひ	その日 〔ひ〕 that day
			び	月曜日 〔げつようび〕 Monday
			か	十四日 〔じゅうよっか〕 the 14th of the month
			ニチ	日曜日 〔にちようび〕 Sunday
13.	火	fire	カ	火曜日 〔かようび〕 Tuesday
14.	水	water	みず	お水 〔みず〕 water
			スイ	水曜日 〔すいようび〕 Wednesday
15.	木	tree	き	おおきい木 a big tree
			モク	木曜日 〔もくようび〕 Thursday
16.	金	gold	かね	お金 money
			キン	金曜日 〔きんようび〕 Friday
17.	土	soil	ド	土曜日 〔どようび〕 Saturday

18. 口　mouth　　　　くち, ぐち

19. 目　eye　　　　　め

20. 人　person　　　ひと　　　あの人 that person

　　　　　　　　　　ニン　　　三人〔さんにん〕three people

　　　　　　　　　　ジン　　　アメリカ人 American

　　　　　　　　　　☆　　　　一人〔ひとり〕one (person)

　　　　　　　　　　　　　　　二人〔ふたり〕two (persons)

21. 本　origin; book　もと　　　山本〔やまもと〕さん

　　　　　　　　　　　　　　　中本〔なかもと〕さん

　　　　　　　　　　　　　　　川本〔かわもと〕さん

　　　　　　　　　　　　　　　木本〔きもと〕さん

　　　　　　　　　　ホン　　　本をよむ to read a book

　　　　　　　　　　　　　　　日本〔にほん or にっぽん〕Japan

　　　　　　　　　　ポン　　　一本〔いっぽん〕one (long object)

　　　　　　　　　　ボン　　　三本〔さんぼん〕three (long objects)

22. 今　now　　　　いま　　　今、一時です。It's now 1 o'clock.

　　　　　　　　　　　　　　　今田〔いまだ〕さん

　　　　　　　　　　コン　　　今月〔こんげつ〕this month

　　　　　　　　　　　　　　　今週〔こんしゅう〕this week

　　　　　　　　　　☆　　　　今日〔きょう〕today

　　　　　　　　　　　　　　　今年〔ことし〕this year

23. 年　year　　　　とし　　　今年〔ことし〕this year

　　　　　　　　　　　　　　　毎年〔まいとし〕every year

　　　　　　　　　　ネン　　　毎年〔まいねん〕every year

　　　　　　　　　　　　　　　来年〔らいねん〕next year

177

漢字

去年〔きょねん〕last year

一年〔いちねん〕 one year

四年生〔よねんせい〕fourth grader

二〇〇三年〔にせんさんねん〕the year 2003

24. 私　I; me　　　わたし　　　私は　中本です。I am Nakamoto.
　　　　　　　　　わたくし

25. 曜　day of the week　よう　　日曜日〔にちようび〕Sunday

月曜日〔げつようび〕Monday

火曜日〔かようび〕Tuesday

水曜日〔すいようび〕Wednesday

木曜日〔もくようび〕Thursday

金曜日〔きんようび〕Friday

土曜日〔どようび〕Saturday

何曜日〔なんようび〕What day of the week?

Ⅱ-3課

26. 上　above　　　うえ　　　上田〔うえだ〕さん

目上〔めうえ〕の人 superiors

27. 下　under　　　した　　　木下〔きのした〕さん

くだ　　　食べて下さい。Please eat.

28. 大　big　　　おお　　　大きい人 a big person

大下〔おおした〕さん

大月〔おおつき〕さん

タイ　　　大変〔たいへん〕hard; difficult; very

ダイ　　　大学〔だいがく〕college

大好き to like very much

29. 小　small　　ちい(さい)　小さい人 a small person

漢字

178

| | | ショウ | 小学生 <ruby>小学生<rt>がくせい</rt></ruby> elementary school student |
| | | | 小学校 <ruby>小学校<rt>がっこう</rt></ruby> elementary school |

30. 夕　early evening　　ゆう　　　夕方 <ruby>夕方<rt>がた</rt></ruby> late afternoon, early evening

31. 何　what　　なに　　　何人〔なにじん〕 What nationality?

　　　　　　　　なん　　　何人〔なんにん〕 How many people?

　　　　　　　　　　　　　何月〔なんがつ〕 What month?

　　　　　　　　　　　　　何曜日〔なんようび〕 What day of the week?

　　　　　　　　　　　　　何日〔なんにち〕 What day of the month?

32. 中　inside; middle　　なか　　　中本〔なかもと〕さん

　　　　　　　　　　　　　中口〔なかぐち〕さん

　　　　　　　　　　　　　今中〔いまなか〕さん

　　　　　　　　チュウ　　　中学〔ちゅうがく〕 junior high school

　　　　　　　　　　　　　中学生〔ちゅうがくせい〕 junior high school student

　　　　　　　　　　　　　中国〔ちゅうごく〕 China

　　　　　　　　　　　　　中国人〔ちゅうごくじん〕 Chinese person

33. 外　outside　　そと　　　家の外 outside the house

　　　　　　　　ガイ　　　外国〔がいこく〕 foreign country

　　　　　　　　　　　　　外国人〔がいこくじん〕 foreigner

　　　　　　　　　　　　　外国語〔がいこくご〕 foreign language

II - 4課

34. 行　go　　い（く）　　　行きます to go

　　　　　　　コウ　　　旅行〔りょこう〕します to travel

　　　　　　　　　　　　銀行〔ぎんこう〕 bank

35. 来　come　　き（ます）　　来て下さい。 Please come.

　　　　　　　　　　　　よく出来ました。 He/she/they did well.

漢字

		く（る）	来る to come
		こ（ない）	来ないで下さい。 Please do not come.
		ライ	来年〔らいねん〕next year
			来月〔らいげつ〕next month
			来週〔らいしゅう〕next week
36.	子 child	こ	子ども child
37.	車 vehicle	くるま	車にのる to ride in a car
		シャ	自動車 car
			自転車 bicycle
			電車 electric train
			外車〔がいしゃ〕foreign car
38.	学 study	ガク	学生〔がくせい〕college student
			小学生〔しょうがくせい〕elementary school student
			中学生〔ちゅうがくせい〕junior high school student
			大学〔だいがく〕college
		ガッ	学校〔がっこう〕school
39.	校 school	コウ	学校〔がっこう〕school
			中学校〔ちゅうがっこう〕junior high school
			小学校〔しょうがっこう〕elementary school
			高校〔こうこう〕high school
			高校生〔こうこうせい〕high school student
40.	見 look; see	み（る）	見ます to look
41.	良 is good	よい	良くないです is not good
42.	食 eat	た（べる）	食べましょう。 Let's eat.
		ショク	食事をします to have a meal
			夕食〔ゆうしょく〕supper

漢字

180

外食〔がいしょく〕eating out

43. 川 river   かわ   川口〔かわぐち〕さん

                   がわ   小川〔おがわ〕さん

44. 山 mountain   やま   山口〔やまぐち〕さん

                                 山本〔やまもと〕さん

                                 大山〔おおやま〕さん

                                 小山〔こやま〕さん

                                 中山〔なかやま〕さん

                                 山下〔やました〕さん

                   サン   富士山〔ふじさん or ふじやま〕Mt. Fuji

45. 出 go out   で（る）   出かけます to leave

                                 出て下さい。Please go out.

                                 よく出来ました。 He/she/they did well.

                                 出口〔でぐち〕exit

                   だ（す）   出して下さい。Please turn it in.

                                 スピードを出す to speed up

46. 先 first; previous   セン   先生 teacher

                                 先月〔せんげつ〕last month

                                 先週 last week

47. 生 be born   う（まれる）   生まれました was born

     person   セイ   先生〔せんせい〕teacher

                                 学生〔がくせい〕college student

                                 生徒〔せいと〕K-12 student

48. 父 father   ちち   父 one's own father

                   とう   お父さん someone else's father

漢字

49.	母	mother	はは	母 one's own mother
			かあ	お母さん someone else's mother
50.	毎	every	マイ	毎日〔まいにち〕every day
				毎月〔まいつき〕every month
				毎年〔まいねん or まいとし〕every year
				毎週 every week
				毎食〔まいしょく〕every meal
51.	書	write	か（く）	書いて下さい。Please write.
		writing	ショ	教科書 textbook
				辞書 dictionary
				図書館 library
				書道 calligraphy

II-6課

52.	手	hand	て	右手 right hand
				左手 left hand
				苦手 is weak at
			☆	上手〔じょうず〕skillful
				下手〔へた〕unskillful
53.	耳	ear	みみ	右耳 right ear
				左耳 left ear
				小さい耳 small ears
54.	門	gate	モン	学校〔がっこう〕の門 school gate
				家の門 gateway to a house
55.	聞	listen; hear	き（く）	聞きます to listen; hear; ask
			ブン	新聞 newspaper
56.	女	female	おんな	女の人〔おんなのひと〕woman; lady

女の子〔おんなのこ〕girl

女の学生〔おんなのがくせい〕female student

57.	好 like	す（き）	大好〔だいす〕き like very much
58.	田 rice field	た	田中〔たなか〕さん
			中田〔なかた〕さん
			田口〔たぐち〕さん
		だ	金田〔かねだ〕さん
			山田〔やまだ〕さん
			上田〔うえだ〕さん

59. 男 male　おとこ

男の人 man

男の子 boy

男の学生〔がくせい〕male student

II-7課

60. 言 say　い（う）　もう一度言って下さい。 Please say it again.

61. 語 language　ゴ

日本語〔にほんご〕Japanese language

英語〔えいご〕English language

外国語〔がいこくご〕foreign language

中国語〔ちゅうごくご〕Chinese language

何語〔なにご〕What language?

語学〔ごがく〕language study

62. 寺 temple　てら

寺に行く to go to the temple

寺田〔てらだ〕さん

寺山〔てらやま〕さん

寺本〔てらもと〕さん

でら　山寺〔やまでら〕temple in the mountains

ジ　本願寺〔ほんがんじ〕Honganji Temple

漢字

63.	時	time; o'clock	とき	時々〔ときどき〕sometimes
			ジ	何時〔なんじ〕What time?
				一時間〔いちじかん〕one hour
64.	間	between; among; interval	あいだ	学校〔がっこう〕と家〔いえ〕の間 between school and my house.
			カン	時間〔じかん〕time
				一時間〔いちじかん〕one hour
65.	分	minute	わ(かる)	分かりません。I do not understand.
			フン	二分〔にふん〕two minutes
			プン	六分〔ろっぷん〕six minutes
			ブン	半分〔はんぶん〕a half
66.	正	correct	ただ（しい）	正しいです is correct
			ショウ	お正月〔しょうがつ〕New Year
				正田〔しょうだ〕さん
67.	家	house	いえ	大きい家 a big house
			カ	家族 family
68.	々	[pluralizer]		時々〔ときどき〕sometimes
				木々〔きぎ〕trees
				山々〔やまやま〕mountains
				日々〔ひび〕days
				人々〔ひとびと〕people
				家々〔いえいえ〕houses

II-9課

69.	白	white	しろ	白いシャツ a white shirt
				白木屋〔しろきや〕Shirokiya Department Store
			ハク	白人〔はくじん〕Caucasian

漢字

70. 百 hundred	ヒャク	百人〔ひゃくにん〕100 people
	ビャク	三百〔さんびゃく〕300
	ピャク	六百〔ろっぴゃく〕600
		八百〔はっぴゃく〕800

71. 千 thousand	セン	二千〔にせん〕2,000
		八千〔はっせん〕8,000
	ゼン	三千〔さんぜん〕3,000

72. 万 ten thousand	マン	一万〔いちまん〕10,000
		十万〔じゅうまん〕100,000
		百万〔ひゃくまん〕one million

73. 方 person [polite]	かた	あの方 that person [polite]
alternative	ホウ	この方が好きです。I like this better.
		両方〔りょうほう〕both

74. 玉 ball; coin	たま	玉田〔たまだ〕さん
		玉川〔たまかわ〕さん
		玉城〔たましろ〕さん
	だま	お年玉〔としだま〕New Year's monetary gift
		十円玉〔じゅうえんだま〕10 yen coin
		目玉〔めだま〕eyeball

75. 国 country	くに, ぐに	どこの国 Which country?
		国本〔くにもと〕さん
	コク, ゴク	外国〔がいこく〕foreign country
		韓国〔かんこく〕Korea
		中国〔ちゅうごく〕China

| 76. 安 cheap | やす（い） | 安い本 a cheap book |
| | | 安田〔やすだ〕さん |

185

77.	高	expensive; high	たか（い）	高い家〔たかいいえ〕an expensive house
				高田〔たかた/たかだ〕さん
				高山〔たかやま〕さん
				高木〔たかき/たかぎ〕さん
			コウ	高校〔こうこう〕high school
				高校生〔こうこうせい〕high school student

Ⅱ－10課

78.	牛	cow	うし	牛がいる。There are cows.
			ギュウ	牛肉〔ぎゅうにく〕beef
				牛乳〔ぎゅうにゅう〕milk (cow)
79.	半	half	ハン	半分〔はんぶん〕a half
				五時半〔ごじはん〕5:30 (time)
*3.	手	hand	て*	大きい手 big hands
			シュ	バスケット選手 basketball player
			☆*	上手〔じょうず〕skillful
				下手〔へた〕unskillful
80.	友	friend	とも	友達〔ともだち〕friend
				友子〔ともこ〕さん
81.	帰	return	かえ（る）	家〔いえ〕へ帰る return home
82.	待	wait	ま（つ）	待って下さい。 Please wait.
83.	持	have; hold	も（つ）	持っています。I have it.
84.	米	rice	こめ	米を買う to buy rice
				米屋 rice shop
85.	番	number	バン	一番〔いちばん〕No. 1
86.	事	matter	こと	どんな事 What kind of things?
			ごと	仕事〔しごと〕job

漢字

186

		ジ	食事〔しょくじ〕meal
			大事〔だいじ〕important
			事務所〔じむしょ〕office

II - 11課

87.	雨	rain	あめ	雨がふっています。 It is raining.
88.	電	electricity	デン	電話 telephone
				電気 electricity
				電車〔でんしゃ〕electric train
89.	天	heaven	テン	天ぷら tenpura
				天どん tenpura donburi
90.	気	spirit	キ	天気〔てんき〕weather
				病気 illness
				合気道 aikido
				お気の毒に。 I'm sorry. [sympathy]
91.	会	meet	あ（う）	会いましょう。Let's meet.
			カイ	会社〔かいしゃ〕company
				社会〔しゃかい〕social studies; society
				教会〔きょうかい〕church
92.	話	talk	はな（す）	話して下さい。 Please speak.
			はなし	お話 story
			ばなし	昔話〔むかしばなし〕folk tale
			ワ	電話〔でんわ〕telephone
				会話〔かいわ〕conversation
93.	売	sell	う（る）	売っていますか。Are they selling?
94.	読	read	よ（む）	本を読む to read a book

95. 右　right　　みぎ　　右手〔みぎて〕right hand

右目〔みぎめ〕right eye

右耳〔みぎみみ〕left ear

右田〔みぎた〕さん

96. 左　left　　ひだり　　左手〔ひだりて〕left hand

左目〔ひだりめ〕left eye

左耳〔ひだりみみ〕left ear

97. 入　put in　　い（れる）　入れて下さい。Please put it in.

　　　enter　　はい（る）　入って下さい。Please enter.

　　　　　いり　　入口〔いりぐち〕entrance

98. 物　thing　　もの　　食べ物〔たべもの〕food

飲み物 a drink

建物 building

着物 *kimono* (things to wear)

買い物 shopping

読み物〔よみもの〕things to read

ブツ　　動物 animal

動物園 zoo

99. 名　name　　な　　名前 name

メイ　有名〔ゆうめい〕famous

100. 前　front; before　　まえ　　名前〔なまえ〕name

家の前〔いえのまえ〕front of the house

前田〔まえだ〕さん

前川〔まえかわ〕さん

ゼン　午前〔ごぜん〕a.m.

101. 戸　door　　　と　　　　　　戸を閉^しめて下さい。 Please close the door.

戸田〔とだ〕さん

戸口〔とぐち〕さん

戸川〔とがわ〕さん

ど　　　　　　木戸〔きど〕さん

102. 所　place　　ところ　　　　しずかな所 a quiet place

どころ　　　　田所〔たどころ〕さん

ショ　　　　　住所^{じゅう}〔じゅうしょ〕address

事務所^む〔じむしょ〕office

103. 近　near　　ちか（い）　　近い所〔ところ〕a nearby place

川近〔かわちか〕さん

Ⅱ-14課

104. 立　stand　　た（つ）　　　立って下さい。 Please stand.

リツ　　　　　起立^き〔きりつ〕Stand up.

105. 作　make　　つく（る）　　作って下さい。 Please make (it).

サク　　　　　作文^{ぶん} composition

作田〔さくだ〕さん

作本〔さくもと〕さん

106. 肉　meat　　にく　　　　　肉を食べる〔にくをたべる〕to eat meat

牛肉〔ぎゅうにく〕beef

豚肉^{ぶた}〔ぶたにく〕pork

鳥肉^{とり}〔とりにく〕chicken

焼き肉^や〔やきにく〕*yakiniku*

筋肉^{きん}〔きんにく〕muscle

107. 魚　fish　　　さかな

108. 多　many　　おお（い）　　人が多いです。 There are many people.

189

漢字

			タ	多分〔たぶん〕 probably
109.	少	few	すく（ない）	人が少ないです。There are few people.
			すこ（し）	少し食べました。I ate a little.
110.	古	old	ふる（い）	古い車〔くるま〕 old car
				古川〔ふるかわ〕さん
				古本〔ふるもと〕さん
				古田〔ふるた〕さん
111.	新	new	あたら（しい）	新しい本〔ほん〕 a new book
			シン	新聞〔しんぶん〕 newspaper
				新幹線〔しんかんせん〕 bullet train
*47.	生	be born	う（まれる）*	日本で生まれました。 I was born in Japan.
			なま	生卵〔なまたまご〕 raw egg
			セイ*	先生〔せんせい〕 teacher
				学生〔がくせい〕 college student

Ⅱ-15課

112.	才	～years old	サイ	十六才〔じゅうろくさい〕16 years old
113.	心	heart; mind	こころ	心がきれいです good-hearted
			シン	心配しないで下さい。Please do not worry.
114.	思	think	おも（う）	いいと思います。I think it is good.
115.	休	rest; absent	やす（む）	学校を休んでいます is absent from school
				お休み holiday; day off
116.	買	buy	か（う）	買いたいです。I want to buy it.
				買い物〔かいもの〕 shopping
117.	早	early	はや（い）	早い is early
				早見〔はやみ〕さん

漢字　　　　　　　　　190

早川〔はやかわ〕さん

118.	自	oneself	ジ	自分〔じぶん〕の車 one's own car
				自動車〔じどうしゃ〕car
				自転車〔じてんしゃ〕bicycle
				自由〔じゆう〕free
119.	犬	dog	いぬ	白〔しろ〕い犬 a white dog
120.	太	fat	ふと（る）	太っています is fat
121.	屋	store	や	本屋〔ほんや〕bookstore
				パン屋 bakery
				白木屋〔しろきや〕Shirokiya Department Store
				部屋〔へや〕room

III - 1課

122.	漢	China	カン	漢字 Chinese characters
123.	字	character; writing	ジ	漢字〔かんじ〕Chinese characters
124.	姉	older sister	あね	姉の本 my older sister's book
			ねえ	お姉さん (someone's) older sister
125.	妹	younger sister	いもうと	妹の名前 my younger sister's name
				妹さん someone else's younger sister
126.	兄	older brother	あに	兄の車 my older brother's car
			にい	お兄さん someone's older brother
127.	弟	younger brother	おとうと	弟の本 my younger brother's book
				弟さん someone else's younger brother
			☆	兄弟〔きょうだい〕siblings
128.	朝	morning	あさ	朝御飯〔あさごはん〕breakfast
				毎朝〔まいあさ〕every morning
				朝日新聞〔あさひしんぶん〕Asahi Newspaper

		チョウ	朝食〔ちょうしょく〕breakfast
		☆	今朝〔けさ〕this morning
129. 昼	daytime	ひる	昼御飯〔ひるごはん〕lunch
		チュウ	昼食〔ちゅうしょく〕lunch
130. 明	is bright	あか（るい）	明るい所〔あかるいところ〕a bright place
		☆	明日〔あした〕tomorrow
131. 去	past	キョ	去年〔きょねん〕last year
132. 銀	silver	ギン	銀行〔ぎんこう〕bank
			銀のネックレス a silver necklace
133. 仕	to serve	シ	仕事〔しごと〕job
			仕方〔しかた〕がない It cannot be helped.
*48. 父	father	ちち*	父の仕事〔しごと〕my father's job
		とう*	お父さん someone else's father
		フ	祖父 my own grandfather
*49. 母	mother	はは*	母の名前〔なまえ〕my mother's name
		かあ*	お母さん someone else's mother
		ボ	祖母 my own grandmother
*46. 先	first, previous	セン*	先生〔せんせい〕teacher
			先月〔せんげつ〕last month
		さき	お先に。 Excuse me for going/doing something first.
**1. 家族	かぞく	family
**2. 友達	ともだち	friend
**3. 質問	しつもん	question
**4. 答え	こたえ	answer
**5. 宿題	しゅくだい	homework

漢字

192

**6. 試験　　　しけん　　　exam

**7. 昨日　　　きのう　　　yesterday

III-2課

134. 公 public　　　コウ　　　公園 park

　　　　　　　　　　　　　　公立〔こうりつ〕public

135. 文 writing; composition　ブン　　　文化〔ぶんか〕culture

　　　　　　　　　　　　　　作文〔さくぶん〕composition

　　　　　　　　　　　　　　文学〔ぶんがく〕literature

136. 化 to take the form of　カ　　　化学〔かがく〕chemistry

　　　　　　　　　　　　　　文化〔ぶんか〕culture

　　　　　　　　　ケ　　　化粧する to apply make-up

137. 花 flower　　　はな　　　花屋〔はなや〕flower shop

138. 海 ocean; sea; beach　うみ　　　海へ行く to go to the beach

　　　　　　　　　カイ　　　海外〔かいがい〕overseas

　　　　　　　　　　　　　　日本海〔にほんかい〕Sea of Japan

139. 旅 travel　　　リョ　　　旅行〔りょこう〕travel

　　　　　　　　　　　　　　海外旅行〔かいがいりょこう〕overseas travel

　　　　　　　　　　　　　　修学旅行〔しゅうがくりょこう〕study tour

140. 教 to teach　　　おし（える）　教えて下さい。 Please teach me.

　　　　　　　　　キョウ　　　教室 classroom

　　　　　　　　　　　　　　教科書〔きょうかしょ〕textbook

　　　　　　　　　　　　　　教会〔きょうかい〕church

　　　　　　　　　　　　　　キリスト教 Christianity

141. 室 room　　　シツ　　　教室〔きょうしつ〕classroom

142. 後 behind; after　うし（ろ）　車〔くるま〕の後ろ behind the car

　　　　　　　　　あと　　　学校の後で〔がっこうのあとで〕after school

漢字

		ゴ	午後 p.m.
			放課後 after school
143. 午	noon	ゴ	午前一時〔ごぜんいちじ〕 1:00 a.m.
			午後一時〔ごごいちじ〕 1:00 p.m.
144. 着	to wear	き（る）	シャツを着る to wear a shirt
			着物〔きもの〕Japanese traditional *kimono*
	to arrive	つ（く）	学校に着く to arrive at school
145. 知	to get to know	し（る）	知りません。 I do not know.
*24. 私	I; private	わたし*	私は山本です。 I am Yamamoto.
		わたくし*	
		シ	私立〔しりつ or わたくしりつ〕private
*59. 男	male	おとこ*	男の子〔おとこのこ〕boy
			男の人〔おとこのひと〕man
		ダン	男子〔だんし〕boy
*56. 女	female	おんな*	女の子〔おんなのこ〕girl
			女の人〔おんなのひと〕woman; lady
		ジョ	女子〔じょし〕girl
			男女共学〔だんじょきょうがく〕co-educational
*36. 子	child	こ*	子供 child(ren)
		シ	男子〔だんし〕boy
			女子〔じょし〕girl
*97. 入	to enter;	はい（る）*	入って下さい。 Please enter.
	to put in	い（れる）*	さとうを入れる to put sugar in
		いり*	入口〔いりぐち〕entrance
		ニュウ	入学〔にゅうがく〕to enter a school
*34. 行	to go	い（く）*	学校へ行く to go to school

		コウ*	旅行〔りょこう〕travel
		ギョウ	行事〔ぎょうじ〕event
**8.	生徒	せいと	student [non-college]
**9.	問題	もんだい	problem
**10.	教科書	きょうかしょ	textbook
**11.	公園	こうえん	park
**12.	一度	いちど	one time; once
**13.	図書館	としょかん	library

Ⅲ-3課

146.	春	spring	はる	春休み〔はるやすみ〕spring vacation
				春子さん Haruko
147.	夏	summer	なつ	夏休み〔なつやすみ〕summer vacation
				夏時間〔なつじかん〕summer time
148.	秋	autumn; fall	あき	秋山さん Mr. Akiyama
				秋田さん Mr. Akita
				秋中さん Mr. Akinaka
				秋子さん Akiko (Japanese girl's name)
149.	冬	winter	ふゆ	冬休み〔ふゆやすみ〕winter vacation
				冬時間〔ふゆじかん〕winter time
150.	雪	snow	ゆき	雪がふる to snow
151.	元	healthy	ゲン	元気〔げんき〕fine; be in a good health
152.	飲	to drink	の（む）	飲み物〔のみもの〕a drink
153.	体	body	からだ	大きい体 a big body
			タイ	体育 physical education
				体育館 gym
154.	音	sound	おと	うるさい音 noisy sound

漢字

		オン	音楽 music
155. 楽	enjoyable	たの（しい）	楽しい is enjoyable
	comfortable	らく	楽ないす comfortable chair
		ガク	音楽〔おんがく〕music
156. 糸	thread; string	いと	糸こんにゃく shredded *konnyaku*
157. 紙	paper	かみ	白い紙〔しろいかみ〕white paper
		がみ	手紙〔てがみ〕letter
*47. 生	be born	う（まれる）*	日本で生まれました。 I was born in Japan.
		なま*	生卵〔なまたまご〕raw egg
	person	セイ*	先生〔せんせい〕teacher
			学生〔がくせい〕student
		ショウ	一生懸命〔いっしょうけんめい〕utmost efforts
**14. 世話		せわ	care
**15. 生活		せいかつ	life; living
**16. 体育		たいいく	P.E.
**17. 様		さま	polite equivalent of -さん
**18. 変		へん	strange; weird; unusual
**19. 大変		たいへん	hard; difficult

III - 4 課

158. 英	British;	エイ	英語〔えいご〕English
	excellent		英国〔えいこく〕England
			英文学〔えいぶんがく〕British literature
159. 草	grass	くさ	みどりの草 green grass
160. 林	small forest	はやし	林さん
			林田〔はやしだ〕さん
		ばやし	小林〔こばやし〕さん

漢字

中林〔なかばやし〕さん

外林〔そとばやし〕さん

161. 森 forest　もり　　森さん

森田〔もりた〕さん

小森〔こもり〕さん

大森〔おおもり〕さん

中森〔なかもり〕さん

森本〔もりもと〕さん

162. 台 counter　タイ　　台湾 Taiwan

ダイ　　一台の車〔いちだいのくるま〕one car

台所〔だいどころ〕kitchen

163. 始 start; begin　はじ（める）　始める to begin

164. 終 end; finish　お（わる）　終わりましょう。 Let's finish.

165. 使 to use　つか（う）　車を使う to use a car

辞書の使い方〔じしょのつかいかた〕

166. 勉 to endeavor　ベン　　勉強〔べんきょう〕study

ガリ勉〔ガリべん〕study fervently

167. 強 strong　つよ（い）　強いチーム a strong team

キョウ　　勉強〔べんきょう〕study

168. 回 - time(s)　カイ　　二回〔にかい〕two times

169. 週 week　シュウ　　今週〔こんしゅう〕this week

先週〔せんしゅう〕last week

来週〔らいしゅう〕next week

毎週〔まいしゅう〕every week

週末〔しゅうまつ〕weekend

一週間〔いっしゅうかん〕one week

197　　　　　漢字

*103. 近	near	ちか（い）*	学校〔がっこう〕に近い close to school	
		キン	最近〔さいきん〕recently	
*64. 間	between; among	あいだ*	学校〔がっこう〕と家〔いえ〕の間	
			between school and my house	
	interval	カン*	時間〔じかん〕time	
		ま	間違える to make a mistake	
**20. 本当		ほんとう	true; real	
**21. 最近		さいきん	recent; recently	
**22. 違う		ちがう	is different; is wrong	
**23. 辞書		じしょ	dictionary	
**24. 〜君		〜くん	[a suffix usually attached to boys' names]	
**25. 週末		しゅうまつ	weekend	

III - 6課

170. 映	reflection; projection	エイ	映画 movie
			映画館 movie theater
171. 画	picture	ガ	映画〔えいが〕movie
			漫画〔まんが〕cartoons, comics
	stroke(s)	カク	この漢字は何画〔なんかく〕ですか。
			How many strokes is this *kanji*?
172. 歌	song; to sing	うた	歌を歌う to sing a song
		カ	歌手〔かしゅ〕singer
			校歌〔こうか〕school song
173. 晩	evening; night	ばん	今晩〔こんばん〕tonight
			毎晩〔まいばん〕every night
			晩ご飯〔ばんごはん〕dinner
174. 夜	night	よる	夜 night

漢字

175. 黒 black	くろ	黒い髪の毛（かみけ）black hair	
		白黒映画〔しろくろえいが〕black and white movie	
	コク	黒人〔こくじん〕black person	
		黒板〔こくばん〕blackboard	
176. 茶 tea	チャ	お茶 tea; tea ceremony	
		茶色〔ちゃいろ〕brown	
	サ	喫茶店（きっさてん）coffee shop	
177. 飯 cooked rice	ハン	ご飯 cooked rice; meal	
		朝御飯（あさごはん）breakfast	
		昼御飯（ひるごはん）lunch	
		晩御飯（ばんごはん）dinner	
178. 足 foot	あし	大きい足 big feet	
179. 長 is long	なが（い）	長いお話〔ながいおはなし〕a long story	
		長山〔ながやま〕さん	
chief	チョウ	校長先生〔こうちょうせんせい〕school principal	
		社長〔しゃちょう〕company president	
180. 走 to run	はし（る）	走りました。I ran.	
181. 起 to get up; to wake up	お（きる）	六時〔ろくじ〕に起きました。 I woke up at 6:00.	
182. 寝 to sleep	ね（る）	早〔はや〕く寝ました。I went to sleep early.	
＊＊26. 有名	ゆうめい	famous	
＊＊27. 番組	ばんぐみ	(TV) program	
＊＊28. 女性	じょせい	female	
＊＊29. 男性	だんせい	male	
＊＊30. 曲	きょく	musical piece; song	
＊＊31. 子供	こども	child	

199

漢字

＊＊32. 選手　　せんしゅ　　(sports) player

＊＊33. 彼　　　かれ　　　he; him; boyfriend

＊＊34. 彼女　　かのじょ　　she; her; girlfriend

| III-7課 |

183. 東　east　　ひがし　　東口〔ひがしぐち〕East exit

　　　　　　　　　　　　東山〔ひがしやま〕さん

　　　　　　トウ　　東京〔とうきょう〕Tokyo

184. 西　west　　にし　　西口〔にしぐち〕West exit

　　　　　　　　　　　　西田〔にしだ〕さん

　　　　　　　　　　　　西川〔にしかわ〕さん

　　　　　　セイ　　西洋〔せいよう〕the West

185. 洋　ocean　　ヨウ　　東洋〔とうよう〕the East; Asia

　　　　　　　　　　　　西洋〔せいよう〕the West

　　　　　　　　　　　　洋子〔ようこ〕さん

186. 和　Japanese;　ワ　　和食〔わしょく〕Japanese food

　　　harmony　　　　和室〔わしつ〕Japanese-style room

　　　　　　　　　　和英辞典〔わえいじてん〕Japanese-English dictionary

　　　　　　　　　　英和辞典〔えいわじてん〕English-Japanese dictionary

187. 部　part　　ブ　　全部〔ぜんぶ〕all

　　　club　　　　部活〔ぶかつ〕club activity

　　　　　　ヘ　　部屋〔へや〕room

188. 美　beautiful　うつく(しい)　美しい庭 a beautiful garden

　　　　　　ビ　　美術〔びじゅつ〕fine arts

　　　　　　　　　美人〔びじん〕a beautiful woman

189. 広　is spacious　ひろ(い)　広い家〔いえ〕a spacious house

　　　　　　　　　広島 Hiroshima

| 漢字 |　　　　　　　200

広田〔ひろた〕さん

広中〔ひろなか〕さん

190. 内　inside　　　うち　　　　　　内にお上〔あ〕がり下さい。

内田〔うちだ〕さん

山内〔やまうち〕さん

ナイ　　　　　　家内〔かない〕one's own wife

191. 主　main　　　シュ　　　　　　主人〔しゅじん〕one's own husband

ご主人〔しゅじん〕someone else's husband

192. 住　to live　　　す（む）　　　　日本に住んでいる。I am living in Japan.

ジュウ　　　　　住所〔じゅうしょ〕address

193. 開　to open　　　あ（ける）　　　窓を開けて下さい。Please open the window.

194. 閉　to close　　　し（める）　　　戸〔と〕を閉めて下さい。Please close the

door.

47. 生　be born　　　う（まれる）　日本で生まれました。I was born in Japan.

なま*　　　　　生卵〔なまたまご〕raw egg

person　　セイ*　　　　　先生〔せんせい〕teacher

学生〔がくせい〕student

ショウ*　　　　一生懸命〔いっしょうけんめい〕utmost efforts

arrange (flowers)　い（ける）　　生け花〔いけばな〕flower arrangement

*26. 上　to go up　　あ（がる）　　　階段を上がる　to go up the stairs

top; above　うえ*　　　　　山の上〔やまのうえ〕top of the mountain

ジョウ*　　　　上手〔じょうず〕skillful

*27. 下　to go down　お（りる）　　　山を下りる　to go down the mountain

under　　した*　　　　　車の下〔くるまのした〕under the car

to give　　くだ（さい）*　お水〔みず〕を下さい。Please give me some

water.

へ*　　　　　　下手〔へた〕unskillful

201　　　　　　　　　　　　　　　　　　漢字

＊66. 正 is correct 　セイ 　　　　　　正座〔せいざ〕する　to sit properly

ただ（しい）＊　正しいです It is correct.

ショウ＊　　　お正月〔しょうがつ〕New Year's

＊182. 寝 to sleep 　シン 　　　　　　寝室〔しんしつ〕bedroom

ね（る）＊　　　早〔はや〕く寝ました。I went to sleep early.

＊＊36. ～階 　　～かい／がい　　- floor

＊＊37. ～的 　　～てき 　　　　[suffix for - ic, -al, -ish, - style]

＊＊38. 全部 　　ぜんぶ 　　　　everything

＊＊39. 座る 　　すわる 　　　　to sit

＊＊40. 正座する せいざする 　to sit properly

Ⅲ-8課

195. 竹 bamboo 　たけ 　　　　　　竹の子〔たけのこ〕bamboo shoot

竹田〔たけだ〕さん

竹本〔たけもと〕さん

竹内〔たけうち〕さん

196. 鳥 bird 　　とり 　　　　　　鳥肉〔とりにく〕chicken; poultry

焼き鳥〔やきとり〕grilled chicken on skewers

チョウ 　　　　一石二鳥〔いっせきにちょう〕

Kill two birds with one stone.

197. 色 color 　　いろ 　　　　　　何色〔なにいろ〕what color?

茶色〔ちゃいろ〕brown

198. 赤 red 　　　あか 　　　　　　赤い車〔くるま〕red car

赤ちゃん a baby

199. 青 blue 　　　あお 　　　　　　青い海〔うみ〕blue ocean

青木〔あおき〕さん

青色〔あおいろ〕blue (color)

漢字 　　　　　　　　202

200. 黄　yellow　き　黄色〔きいろ〕yellow (color)

黄色い花〔きいろいはな〕yellow flowers

201. 風　wind　かぜ　強い風〔つよいかぜ〕strong wind

〜 style　フウ　和風〔わふう〕Japanese-style

洋風〔ようふう〕Western-style

台風〔たいふう〕typhoon

フ　風呂〔ふろ〕Japanese bath

202. 味　flavor; taste　あじ　いい味 good taste

味の素 MSG (monosodium glutamate; a

flavor-enhancer for food)

ミ　趣味はテニスです。 My hobby is tennis.

何という意味ですか。 What does it mean?

203. 料　materials　リョウ　料理する　to cook

授業料　tuition

材料〔ざいりょう〕ingredients

調味料〔ちょうみりょう〕seasonings

204. 理　arrangement　リ　日本料理〔にほんりょうり〕Japanese cooking

料理屋〔りょうりや〕(Japanese) restaurant

料理人〔りょうりにん〕a cook

205. 由　a reason　ユウ　自由〔じゆう〕free, liberal

206. 重　is heavy　おも（い）　重い本 heavy books

重〔おも〕さ weight

＊118. 自　oneself　ジ＊　自分の車〔じぶんのくるま〕one's own car

シ　自然〔しぜん〕nature

＊＊40. 自然　しぜん　nature

＊＊41. 焼く　やく　to grill; roast; bake; toast; fry

**42.	苦手	にがて	be weak in
**43.	丸	まる	circle
**44.	三角	さんかく	triangle
**45.	四角	しかく	square
**46.	弁当	べんとう	box lunch
**47.	最〜	さい〜	the most 〜

Ⅲ-9課

207. 北　north　きた　北口〔きたぐち〕North exit

北川〔きたがわ〕さん

ホク　東北大学〔とうほくだいがく〕Tohoku University

ホッ　北海道〔ほっかいどう〕Hokkaido

208. 南　south　みなみ　南口〔みなみぐち〕South exit

南田〔みなみだ〕さん

209. 京　capital　キョウ　東京〔とうきょう〕Tokyo

京都〔きょうと〕Kyoto

210. 駅　train station　エキ　東京駅〔とうきょうえき〕Tokyo Station

駅員〔えきいん〕station employee

211. 乗　to ride　の（る）　電車〔でんしゃ〕に乗る　to ride an electric train

212. 地　ground　チ　地下〔ちか〕underground

地図〔ちず〕map

213. 鉄　iron　テツ　地下鉄〔ちかてつ〕subway

214. 図　chart　ズ　地図〔ちず〕map

ト　図書館〔としょかん〕library

215. 道　road; way　みち　道をまっすぐ行く　to go straight on the road

道子〔みちこ〕さん　Michiko (girl's name)

トウ　神道〔しんとう〕*Shinto* (Japanese religion)

漢字　　　204

	ドウ	北海道〔ほっかいどう〕Hokkaido
		書道〔しょどう〕calligraphy
		剣道〔けんどう〕*kendo*

216. 歩　to walk　ある（く）　歩いて行く　to go by walking

ホ、ポ　散歩〔さんぽ〕する to take a walk

217. 動　to move　うご（く）　車は動きませんでした。The car did not move.

ドウ　自動車〔じどうしゃ〕car

動物園〔どうぶつえん〕zoo

運動会〔うんどうかい〕athletic event

218. 働　to work　はたら（く）　父は銀行で働いています。

My father is working at a bank.

219. 円　yen;　エン　百円玉〔ひゃくえんだま〕one hundred yen coin

circle　千円〔せんえん〕one thousand yen

一万円〔いちまんえん〕ten thousand yen

＊130. 明　is bright　あか（るい）　＊　明るい部屋〔へや〕a bright room

☆＊　明日〔あした〕tomorrow

メイ　説明〔せつめい〕して下さい。Please explain it.

＊93. 売　to sell　う（る）＊　売っています。They are selling it.

バイ　券売機〔けんばいき〕ticket vending machine

＊＊48. 〜線　- せん　〜 line

＊＊49. 橋　はし／- ばし　bridge

＊＊50. 病院　びょういん　hospital

＊＊51. 新幹線　しんかんせん　bullet train

＊＊52. 中央線　ちゅうおうせん　Chuo (Central) Line [orange-colored train line in

Tokyo]

220. 社 company シャ 社長〔しゃちょう〕 company president

ジャ 会社〔かいしゃ〕 company

旅行会社〔りょこうがいしゃ〕 travel agency

社員〔しゃいん〕 company employee

社会〔しゃかい〕 society; social studies

神社〔じんじゃ〕 shrine

221. 員 member; イン 社員〔しゃいん〕 company employee

personnel 店員〔てんいん〕 store clerk

駅員〔えきいん〕 station worker

会員〔かいいん〕 member (of a group)

222. 店 store; shop みせ 店で働〔はたら〕く to work at a store

テン 店員〔てんいん〕 store employee

喫茶店〔きっさてん〕 coffee shop

223. 客 guest; キャク 御客様〔おきゃくさま〕 customer; guest [polite]

customer 客間〔きゃくま〕 room where guests are received

224. 島 island しま 美〔うつく〕しい島 a beautiful island

広島〔ひろしま〕 Hiroshima

島田〔しまだ〕さん

じま 北島〔きたじま〕さん

島々〔しまじま〕 islands

225. 座 to sit すわ（る） 正〔ただ〕しく座る to sit properly

ザ 正座〔せいざ〕する to sit properly

座〔ざ〕ぶとん floor cushion

銀座〔ぎんざ〕 Ginza [place name]

226. 取 to take と（る） 日本語を取る to take Japanese

227. 卒	graduate	ソツ	卒業する to graduate
228. 業	work; business	ギョウ	卒業〔そつぎょう〕する to graduate 授業〔じゅぎょう〕class
229. 同	same	おな（じ）	同じ色〔おなじいろ〕same color
230. 悪	bad	わる（い）	悪い人〔ひと〕a bad person
231. 両	both	リョウ	両方〔りょうほう〕both 両手〔りょうて〕both hands 両足〔りょうあし〕both feet 両親〔りょうしん〕parents
232. 全	all; whole	ゼン	全部〔ぜんぶ〕everything, all 全然〔ぜんぜん〕(not) at all 全国〔ぜんこく〕a whole country 全員〔ぜんいん〕everyone; all people
233. 有	exist; have (inanimate)	ユウ	有名〔ゆうめい〕な歌手〔かしゅ〕famous singer 有名人〔ゆうめいじん〕famous person; celebrity 有名校〔ゆうめいこう〕famous school 有料〔ゆうりょう〕with a fee
234. 当	to hit	トウ	本当〔ほんとう〕true 弁当〔べんとう〕box lunch
* 109. 少	few	すく（ない）* すこ（し）* ショウ	人〔ひと〕が少ないです。 There are few people. 少し食〔た〕べました。I ate a little. 少々〔しょうしょう〕お待〔ま〕ち下〔くだ〕さい。 Please wait a minute. [honorific expression]
** 53. 〜歳		〜さい	〜 years old [original *kanji* form of 才]
** 54. 言葉		ことば	word(s); language

207

55. 失礼	しつれい	rude	
56. 御〜	ご〜／お〜	[polite prefix]	
57. 願い	ねがい	wish; request	
58. 写真	しゃしん	photo	
59. 横浜	よこはま	Yokohama [a major port city near Tokyo]	

IV - 2課

235. 世 world　　セ　　世界〔せかい〕 world

お世話〔せわ〕になりました。

Thank you very much for taking care of me.

セイ　　一世〔いっせい〕 first generation

236. 親 parent　　おや　　父親〔ちちおや〕 father

親孝行〔おやこうこう〕 filial piety

シン　　両親〔りょうしん〕 parents

親戚〔しんせき〕 relatives

237. 病 illness;　　ビョウ　　病気〔びょうき〕 illness

sickness　　病院〔びょういん〕 hospital

238. 院 institute　　イン　　病院〔びょういん〕 hospital

入院〔にゅういん〕する be hospitalized

大学院〔だいがくいん〕 graduate school

院長〔いんちょう〕 hospital director

239. 医 medical　　イ　　医者〔いしゃ〕 doctor

医学〔いがく〕 medical study

医学部〔いがくぶ〕 medical school

240. 者 person　　シャ　　医者〔いしゃ〕 doctor

学者〔がくしゃ〕 scholar

教育者〔きょういくしゃ〕 educator

241. 死 to die　　し（ぬ）　　死ぬ die

死〔し〕 death

242. 亡 to pass away　な（くなる）祖父〔そふ〕が亡くなった。

My grandfather passed away.

243. 忘 to forget　　わす（れる）忘れました。 I forgot.

244. 育 to raise　　そだ（てる）子供〔こども〕を育てる raise children

（a child　　イク　　　教育〔きょういく〕education

or pet)　　　　　　体育〔たいいく〕physical education

245. 降 to fall;　　ふ（る）　雨〔あめ〕が降る to rain

to get off;　お（りる）自動車〔じどうしゃ〕を降りる get out of a car

246. 困 to be troubled　こま（る）困っている is troubled

247. 末 end　　　すえ　　末っ子〔すえっこ〕youngest child (of a family)

四月〔しがつ〕の末 the end of April

マツ　　週末〔しゅうまつ〕weekend

月末〔げつまつ〕end of the month

年末〔ねんまつ〕end of the year

248. 族 group　　ゾク　　家族〔かぞく〕 family

249. 達 [plural for　タチ　　人達〔ひとたち〕people

animate objects]　ダチ　　友達〔ともだち〕a friend

* 59. 男 male　　おとこ*　男の人〔ひと〕 a man

ダン*　　男子校〔だんしこう〕boy's school

ナン　　長男〔ちょうなん〕oldest son

* 47. 生 to be born;　う（まれる）* ここで生まれた was born here

to arrange (flowers); い（ける）* 生け花〔いけばな〕flower arrangement

to live;　い（きる）長〔なが〕く生きた lived long

raw;　なま*　生たまご raw egg

209 漢字

	person	セイ＊	先生〔せんせい〕teacher
			父〔ちち〕の人生〔じんせい〕my father's life
		ショウ＊	一生懸命〔いっしょうけんめい〕utmost effort
＊＊60.	試合	しあい	athletic game
＊＊61.	結婚	けっこん	marriage
＊＊62.	時代	じだい	period; era
＊＊63.	太郎	たろう	Taro [boy's name]
＊＊64.	次郎	じろう	Jiro [second son's name]
＊＊65.	子供	こども	child
＊＊66.	忙しい	いそがしい	busy

IV-3課

250.	村 village	むら	村の人々〔ひとびと〕village people
			中村〔なかむら〕さん
			山村先生〔やまむらせんせい〕
			村田君〔むらたくん〕
		ソン	村長〔そんちょう〕village chief
251.	町 town	まち	町田〔まちだ〕さん
			町子〔まちこ〕さん [a girl's name]
		チョウ	町長〔ちょうちょう〕a mayor of town
252.	船 ship; boat	ふね	船に乗〔の〕る ride a boat
		セン	船長〔せんちょう〕(ship) captain
			客船〔きゃくせん〕passenger boat
253.	州 state	シュウ	ワシントン州 Washington state
			州立大学〔しゅうりつだいがく〕state university
			州知事〔しゅうちじ〕state governor
254.	界 boundary	カイ	世界〔せかい〕world

漢字   210

255. 第　counter for naming sequential numbers

ダイ　　　　第三月曜日〔だいさんげつようび〕

the third Monday

第一課〔だいいっか〕 Lesson 1

256. 次　next　　　つぎ　　　次の人〔ひと〕 next person

ジ　　　　次郎〔じろう〕 Jiro [common boy's first name given

to second sons]

次男〔じなん〕 second son

次女〔じじょ〕 second daughter

257. 戦　to fight　　たたか（う）　戦った fought

セン　　　戦争〔せんそう〕 war

戦前〔せんぜん〕 pre-war

戦中〔せんちゅう〕 during the war

戦後〔せんご〕 post-war

第二次世界大戦〔だいにじせかいたいせん〕

World War II

258. 争　to contend; compete　ソウ　　戦争〔せんそう〕 war

259. 合　to fit;　　　あ（う）　　話〔はな〕し合う to discuss (together)

to do mutually　　　　知〔し〕り合う to acquaint (with one another)

待〔ま〕ち合う to wait for each other

to match;　　アイ　　試合〔しあい〕 (sports) game

260. 止　to stop　　と（まる）　止まれ Stop.

や（む）　　雨〔あめ〕が止んだ。 The rain stopped.

261. 平　flat; calm　　ヘイ　　　平和〔へいわ〕 peace

平日〔へいじつ〕 weekday

太平洋〔たいへいよう〕 Pacific Ocean

211　　　　　　　　　　　　　　　　　　　　　漢字

		ひら	平田〔ひらた〕さん
			大平〔おおひら〕さん
262.	不 not	フ	不便〔ふべん〕 inconvenient
			不平〔ふへい〕を言〔い〕う to complain
			不公平〔ふこうへい〕 unfair
263.	活 active; live	カツ	生活〔せいかつ〕 living; life
			活動〔かつどう〕 activity
			部活〔ぶかつ〕 club activity
264.	送 to send	おく（る）	手紙〔てがみ〕を送る to send a letter
＊84.	米 rice;	こめ＊	米を買〔か〕う to buy rice
	U.S.	ベイ	米国〔べいこく〕 U.S.
			日米〔にちべい〕 Japan and U.S.
			米軍〔べいぐん〕 U.S. military
＊212.	地 ground	チ＊	地下鉄〔ちかてつ〕 subway
			地図〔ちず〕 map
		ジ	地獄〔じごく〕 hell
＊＊67.	日系人	にっけいじん	person of Japanese descent
＊＊68.	祖父	そふ	(own) grandfather
＊＊69.	祖母	そぼ	(own) grandmother
＊＊70.	畑	はたけ	(vegetable) field; garden
＊＊71.	汽車	きしゃ	steam engine train
＊＊72.	単語	たんご	word; vocabulary

IV - 4課

265.	洗 to wash	あら（う）	顔を洗う to wash one's face
		セン	洗濯〔せんたく〕する to do laundry
			洗濯機〔せんたくき〕 washing machine

漢字   212

266. 市 city　　　　シ　　　　広島市〔ひろしまし〕Hiroshima City

市長〔しちょう〕city mayor

市内〔しない〕within the city

市外電話〔しがいでんわ〕long distance call

(outside city limits)

267. 以 to the ~ of　　イ　　　　~以上〔いじょう〕more than ~

~以下〔いか〕less than ~

268. 庭 garden;　　にわ　　庭の花〔はな〕flowers in the garden

　　　yard　　　　　　庭仕事〔にわしごと〕yard work

269. 軍 military　　　グン　　　軍人〔ぐんじん〕military personnel

海軍〔かいぐん〕navy

米軍〔べいぐん〕American military

270. 連 take; bring;　つ（れる）　連れて行〔い〕く to take (someone)

　　　accompany　　　　連れて来〔く〕る to bring (someone)

連れて帰〔かえ〕る to take (someone) home

271. 運 luck;　　　　ウン　　　運動〔うんどう〕physical exercise

運転〔うんてん〕driving

　　　carry　　　　　　運良く〔うんよく〕luckily

運悪く〔うんわるく〕unluckily

272. 都 capital　　　ト　　　　京都〔きょうと〕Kyoto

東京都〔とうきょうと〕Tokyo metropolitan area

都会〔とかい〕metropolis

273. 空 sky;　　　　そら　　　青〔あお〕い空 blue sky

　　　　　　　　　　ぞら　　　青空〔あおぞら〕blue sky

　　　empty　　　　から　　　空手〔からて〕karate

　　　　　　　　　　クウ　　　空港〔くうこう〕airport

213

漢字

空軍〔くうぐん〕Air Force

空気〔くうき〕air

274.	暑 hot (weather)	あつ（い）	暑い夏〔なつ〕hot summer
275.	寒 cold (weather)	さむ（い）	寒い冬〔ふゆ〕cold winter
276.	泣 cry	な（く）	泣かないで。 Please don't cry.
277.	笑 smile; laugh	わら（う）	ニコニコ笑っている。 She is smiling.
278.	薬 medicine	くすり	薬を飲〔の〕む to take medicine
		ヤク	麻薬〔まやく〕drugs
279.	館 big building	カン	映画館〔えいがかん〕movie theater
			図書館〔としょかん〕library
			体育館〔たいいくかん〕gym
			博物館〔はくぶつかん〕museum
			美術館〔びじゅつかん〕art museum
* 18.	口 mouth	くち*	大〔おお〕きい口 big mouth
		コウ	人口〔じんこう〕population
* 13.	火 fire	ひ	火をつける set a fire
		カ*	火曜日〔かようび〕Tuesday
			火事〔かじ〕fire
* 198.	赤 red	あか*	赤い紙〔かみ〕red paper
		カ	真っ赤〔まっか〕bright red
**73.	押す	おす	to push
**74.	引く	ひく	to pull
**75.	皆	みんな, みな（さん）	everybody
**76.	和子	かずこ	Kazuko [lit., a child of peace]
**77.	普通	ふつう	ordinary; local train (stops at every stop)
**78.	急に	きゅうに	suddenly

漢字

＊＊79. 急行 きゅうこう express train (stops at all major and selected smaller stations)

IV-6課

280. 石 stone; いし 石川〔いしかわ〕さん
rock 石山〔いしやま〕さん
石田〔いしだ〕さん
セキ 石庭〔せきてい〕 rock garden

281. 園 garden エン 庭園〔ていえん〕 garden
公園〔こうえん〕 park
動物園〔どうぶつえん〕 zoo
幼稚園〔ようちえん〕 kindergarten

282. 絵 painting; picture え 美〔うつく〕しい絵 a beautiful painting

283. 葉 leaf は お茶〔ちゃ〕の葉っぱ tea leaves
絵葉書〔えはがき〕 postcard
秋葉原〔あきはばら〕 Akihabara (a city in Tokyo)
ば 言葉〔ことば〕 word; language
千葉〔ちば〕 Chiba [prefecture near Tokyo where the Narita International Airport and Tokyo Disneyland are located.]

284. 度 - time(s); ド もう一度〔いちど〕 one more time
- degree(s) 何度も〔なんども〕 many times
３２度〔さんじゅうにど〕 32 degrees

285. 代 generation ダイ 江戸時代〔えどじだい〕 Edo Period; Edo Era
１９７０年代〔せんきゅうひゃくななじゅうねんだい〕 1970's

286. 然 be as is; ゼン 自然〔しぜん〕 nature
suffix for forming modifiers 全然〔ぜんぜん〕 (not) at all

215

漢字

突然〔とつぜん〕suddenly; unexpectedly

287. 意　meaning;　　イ　　　意味〔いみ〕meaning

　　　　　mind　　　　　　　　　意見〔いけん〕opinion

288. 最　most　　もっと（も）　最も新〔あたら〕しい newest

　　　　　　　　　サイ　　　　最高〔さいこう〕the best

　　　　　　　　　　　　　　　最近〔さいきん〕recent; recently

　　　　　　　　　　　　　　　最初〔さいしょ〕first

　　　　　　　　　　　　　　　最後〔さいご〕last

289. 切　to cut　き（る）　　紙〔かみ〕を切る to cut papers

　　　　　　　　きっ　　　　切手〔きって〕postage stamp

　　　　　　　　セツ　　　　大切〔たいせつ〕important

290. 習　to learn　なら（う）　日本語〔にほんご〕を習う to learn Japanese

　　　　　　　　シュウ　　　練習〔れんしゅう〕する to practice

　　　　　　　　　　　　　　復習〔ふくしゅう〕する to review

　　　　　　　　　　　　　　習字〔しゅうじ〕calligraphy

291. 続　to continue　つづ（く）　続き continuation

　　　　　　　　つづ（ける）勉強〔べんきょう〕し続ける to continue studying

292. 苦　suffering;　ク　　　苦労〔くろう〕する to suffer

　　　　　painful;　くる（しい）苦しい生活〔せいかつ〕hard life

　　　　　bitter　　にが（い）　苦いお茶〔ちゃ〕bitter tea

　　　　　　　　　　　　　　苦手〔にがて〕to be poor at

293. 痛　sore; pain　いた（い）　頭が痛い to have a headache

294. 静　quiet　しず（か）　静かな村〔むら〕a quiet village

295. 的　suffix attached to テキ　伝統的〔でんとうてき〕traditional

　　　　nouns to create a なAdjective　印象的〔いんしょうてき〕impressive

* 142. 後　after; later　うし（ろ）　* 車〔くるま〕の後ろ behind a car

漢字　　　　　216

		あと*	では、また後で。 Well then, see you later.
		ご*	午後〔ごご〕p.m.
		のち	後に later [formal]
*268.	庭 yard; garden	にわ*	庭仕事〔にわしごと〕yard work
		テイ	庭園〔ていえん〕garden
*168.	回 - time(s); to turn around; to circulate	カイ*	一回〔いっかい〕one time
		まわ(す)	茶碗を右〔みぎ〕に回す to turn a tea cup to the right
			紙〔かみ〕を回す to circulate a paper
**80.	江戸	えど	Edo [former name of Tokyo]
**81.	刀	かたな	sword
**82.	畳	たたみ	*tatami* mat
**83.	-畳	-じょう	[counter for *tatami* mat]
**84.	僕	ぼく	I; me [used by males]
**85.	数学	すうがく	mathematics
**86.	数	かず	amount

IV - 7課

296.	神 God	かみ	神様〔かみさま〕God
		シン	神道〔しんとう〕Shintoism
		ジン	神社〔じんじゃ〕shrine
297.	仏 Buddha	ブツ	大仏〔だいぶつ〕Large image of Buddha
		ブッ	仏教〔ぶっきょう〕Buddhism
298.	顔 face	かお	美〔うつく〕しい顔 beautiful face
299.	頭 head	あたま	頭が良〔よ〕くない not smart
300.	幸 happy	しあわ(せ)	幸せ happy; fortunate
		コウ	幸福 happiness
			不幸〔ふこう〕unhappy; unfortunate

漢字

301.	福 fortune	フク	幸福〔こうふく〕happiness
			福田〔ふくだ〕さん
			福山市〔ふくやまし〕Fukuyama City
302.	建 to build	た（てる）	家〔いえ〕を建てる build a house
			建物〔たてもの〕building
		ケン	建築家〔けんちくか〕architect
303.	考 to think; consider	かんが（える）	よく考える to think hard; to consider well
			いい考え a good idea
304.	助 to help; save; rescue	たす（ける）	助けて！Help!
305.	変 to change	か（える）	円〔えん〕をドルに変える
			to change yen to dollars
		か（わる）	天気〔てんき〕が変わった
			The weather has changed.
	strange	ヘン	大変〔たいへん〕な生活〔せいかつ〕a difficult life
			変な音楽〔おんがく〕strange music
306.	喜 to be happy; to be pleased	よろこ(ぶ)	喜んでいる is pleased
307.	嬉 happy	うれ(しい)	嬉しい happy
308.	悲 sad	かな(しい)	悲しい sad
309.	愛 love; affection	あい	家族〔かぞく〕の愛 family's love
		あい(する)	愛しています (I) love (you).
310.	恋 love	こい	恋をしている I am in love.
		レン	恋愛結婚〔れんあいけっこん〕love marriage
* 84.	米 (uncooked) rice	こめ*	白〔しろ〕いお米 white rice
	U. S.	ベイ	日米〔にちべい〕Japan-U. S.
		マイ	玄米〔げんまい〕brown rice

漢字

218

＊240. 者　person　もの　なまけ者 a lazy person

シャ＊　医者〔いしゃ〕doctor

学者〔がくしゃ〕scholar

＊＊87. 松　まつ　pine tree

＊＊88. 井　い　(water) well

＊＊89. 仲がいい　なかがいい　have good relations/ relationship

＊＊90. 甘い　あま（い）　sweet

＊＊91. 野菜　やさい　vegetables

＊＊92. 果物　くだもの　fruits

＊＊93. 協力(を)する　きょうりょく(を)する　to cooperate

IV - 8課

311. 宗　religion　シュウ　宗教〔しゅうきょう〕religion

312. 原　a field　はら　野原〔のはら〕a field

原田〔はらだ〕さん

原本〔はらもと〕さん

ばら　秋葉原〔あきはばら〕Akihabara (a city in Tokyo)

ゲン　原爆〔げんばく〕atomic bomb

313. 窓　window　まど　窓を開〔あ〕ける to open a window

みどりの窓口〔まどぐち〕JR ticket window

314. 服　cloth;　フク　服を着〔き〕る to wear clothes

dress　正〔ただ〕しい服装〔そう〕 proper dress

洋服〔ようふく〕 western clothing

和服〔わふく〕 traditional Japanese clothing; _kimono_

315. 港　harbor; port　みなと　港の船〔ふね〕a ship in port

コウ　空港〔くうこう〕airport

漢字

316. 晴　clear (weather);　は（れ）　天気〔てんき〕は晴れだ。

The weather will be clear.

　　　become clear　は（れる）　明日〔あした〕は晴れるでしょう。

It will probably clear up tomorrow.

317. 雲　cloud　くも　白〔しろ〕い雲 white cloud

318. 曇　become cloudy;　くも（る）　今日〔きょう〕は曇っている。 It's cloudy today.

　　　cloudy (weather)　くも（り）　天気〔てんき〕は曇りだ。

The weather is cloudy.

曇り後〔のち〕晴〔は〕れ cloudy, later clear

曇り一時〔いちじ〕晴〔は〕れ

cloudy, with occasionally clear (weather)

319. 交　to mix　コウ　交際する to associate with ~

交通 transportation

320. 通　to go along;　とお（る）　この道〔みち〕を通る。

　　　pass through;　　　　　　　to go along this street

　　　to commute　かよ（う）　学校〔がっこう〕に通う。 commute to school

　　　　　　　　　ツウ　交通事故〔こうつうじこ〕traffic accident

321. 泊　stay overnight　と（まる）　旅館〔りょかん〕に泊まる。

stay overnight at a Japanese inn

　　　　　　　　　ハク　京都旅館〔きょうとりょかん〕泊

stay over at Kyoto Inn

　　　　　　　　　パク　一泊二日〔いっぱくふつか〕one night, two days

322. 発　to leave　ハツ　東京発〔とうきょうはつ〕departing from Tokyo

　　　　　　　　ハッ　発表する to present (orally)

　　　　　　　　パツ　出発〔しゅっぱつ〕する to depart

出発時間〔しゅっぱつじかん〕departure time

漢字

323. 感 to feel　　　　カン　　　　感〔かん〕じる to feel

感謝〔かんしゃ〕する to appreciate

感動〔かんどう〕する to be moved

感想文〔かんそうぶん〕(written) reflection

324. 関 border　　　　せき　　　　関さん Seki [last name]

ぜき　　　　大関〔おおぜき〕the second highest *sumo* rank

カン　　　　玄関 entrance way; foyer

関東〔かんとう〕Kanto area [Tokyo region]

関西〔かんさい〕Kansai area [Osaka, Kyoto region]

関西空港〔かんさいくうこう〕Kansai Airport

325. 特 special　　　　トク　　　　特〔とく〕に especially

特別〔とくべつ〕special

トッ　　　　特急〔とっきゅう〕limited express

144. 着 to wear　　　　き（る）　　　シャツを着る wear a shirt

着物〔きもの〕*kimono*; Japanese clothing

つ（く）*　　駅〔えき〕に着く arrive at a station

チャク　　　京都着〔きょうとちゃく〕arrival in Kyoto

197. 色 color　　　　いろ　　　黄色〔きいろ〕yellow

赤色〔あかいろ〕red color

シキ　　　　景色〔けしき〕view; scenery

**94. 富士山　　　ふじさん or ふじやま　Mt. Fuji

**95. 成田　　　　なりた　　　Narita [site of one of Japan's major international

airports, located in Chiba Prefecture]

**96. 新宿　　　　しんじゅく　　Shinjuku

**97. 奈良　　　　なら　　　　Nara

**98. 大阪　　　　おおさか　　　Osaka

漢字

99. 歴史	れきし	history	
100. 風呂	ふろ	bath	
101. 到着	とうちゃく	arrival	
102. 飛行機	ひこうき	airplane	
103. 席	せき	seat	

IV-9課

326. 受 to receive	う（ける）	試験〔しけん〕を受ける。 take an exam	
327. 池 pond	いけ	池田〔いけだ〕さん Mr. Ikeda	
	チ	電池〔でんち〕 battery	
328. 箱 box	はこ	箱に入〔い〕れる to put in a box	
		箱根 resort area near Mt. Fuji	
	ばこ	ゴミ箱 garbage can	
329. 冷 is cold (to the touch)	つめ（たい）	冷たい水 cold water	
	レイ	冷蔵庫 refrigerator	
330. 場 place	バ	場所〔ばしょ〕place; location	
		自転車置き場〔じてんしゃおきば〕 parking area for bicycles	
	ジョウ	運動場〔うんどうじょう〕athletic field	
		会場〔かいじょう〕meeting space	
331. 野 field	の	野村〔のむら〕さん Mr. Nomura	
		野口〔のぐち〕さん Mr. Noguchi	
		野田〔のだ〕さん Mr. Noda	
		川野〔かわの〕さん Mr. Kawano	
	ヤ	野菜〔やさい〕 vegetables	
		野球〔やきゅう〕baseball	
332. 球 ball	たま	黄色〔きいろ〕い球 yellow ball	

漢字

222

		キュウ	野球〔やきゅう〕baseball
			水球〔すいきゅう〕water polo
			地球〔ちきゅう〕Earth
333.	問 to ask	モン	問題 problem
			質問〔しつもん〕question
334.	題 title; topic	ダイ	作文〔さくぶん〕の題 title of a composition
			問題〔もんだい〕problem
			宿題〔しゅくだい〕homework
335.	若 young	わか（い）	若い医者〔いしゃ〕young doctor
			若山〔わかやま〕さん Mr. Wakayama
			若竹〔わかたけ〕さん Mr. Wakatake
			若松〔わかまつ〕さん Mr. Wakamatsu
336.	寄 to stop by	よ（る）	病院〔びょういん〕に寄る。to stop in at a hospital
			お年寄り〔おとしより〕elderly people
		キ	寄付をする to donate
337.	無 do not exist	な（い）	[Hiragana is more commonly used.]
		ム	無料〔むりょう〕free of charge
			無責任〔むせきにん〕irresponsible
338.	集 to collect	あつ（める）	お金を集める to collect money
	to gather	あつ（まる）	集まる時間〔じかん〕time to gather
339.	決 to decide	き（め/まる）	大学〔だいがく〕を決める。decide on a college
		ケツ	解決〔かいけつ〕する to solve
		ケッ	決して忘〔わす〕れない。never forget
340.	信 to believe;	しん（じる）	仏教〔ぶっきょう〕を信じる。 to believe in Buddhism
	to trust	シン	自信〔じしん〕を持〔も〕つ。to gain confidence

223

漢字

* 233. 有 to exist   あ（る）   [*Hiragana* is more commonly used.]

 あり   有森〔ありもり〕さん

ユウ *   有名〔ゆうめい〕 famous

有料駐車場〔ゆうりょうちゅうしゃじょう〕

toll parking lot

* 273. 空 sky   そら *   青い空〔あおいそら〕 blue sky

クウ *   空港〔くうこう〕 airport

あ（き）   空き缶〔かん〕 empty can

から   空の箱〔はこ〕 empty box

* 65. 分 to understand;   わ（かる）*   分かりました。 I understand.

to divide; to sort   わ（ける）   ごみを分ける。 to sort the garbage

minute(s)   フン *   五分〔ごふん〕 five minutes

プン *   一分〔いっぷん〕 one minute

ブン *   半分〔はんぶん〕 a half

* 259. 合 to fit;   あ（う）*   話〔はな〕し合う to discuss (together)

to do mutually;   待〔ま〕ち合う to wait for each other

to match;   アイ *   試合〔しあい〕 (sports) game

ゴウ   合格する to be accepted (by school)

** 104. 缶   かん   (a) can

** 105. 袋、紙袋   ふくろ、かみぶくろ   bag, paper bag

** 106. 猫   ねこ   cat

** 107. 牛乳   ぎゅうにゅう (cow) milk

** 108. 置く   おく   to put; to leave (something)

ひらがな表　*HIRAGANA* CHART

n	W	R	Y	M	H	N	T	S	K	
ん	わ	ら	や	ま	は	な	た	さ	か	あ / A
		り		み	ひ	に	ち (chi)	し (shi)	き	い / I
		る	ゆ	む	ふ	ぬ	つ (tsu)	す	く	う / U
		れ		め	へ	ね	て	せ	け	え / E
	を (o)	ろ	よ	も	ほ	の	と	そ	こ	お / O

(particle)

P	B	D	Z	G	
ぱ	ば	だ	ざ	が	A
ぴ	び	ぢ (ji)	じ (ji)	ぎ	I
ぷ	ぶ	づ (zu)	ず (zu)	ぐ	U
ぺ	べ	で	ぜ	げ	E
ぽ	ぼ	ど	ぞ	ご	O

225

ひらがな

	W	R	Y	M	H	N	T	S	K		
ン n	ワ	ラ	ヤ	マ	ハ	ナ	タ	サ	カ	ア	A
		リ		ミ	ヒ	ニ	チ chi	シ shi	キ	イ	I
		ル	ユ	ム	フ	ヌ	ツ tsu	ス	ク	ウ	U
		レ		メ	ヘ	ネ	テ	セ	ケ	エ	E
	ヲ o	ロ	ヨ	モ	ホ	ノ	ト	ソ	コ	オ	O

(particle)

P	B		D	Z	G	
パ	バ		ダ	ザ	ガ	A
ピ	ビ		ヂ ji	ジ ji	ギ	I
プ	ブ		ヅ zu	ズ zu	グ	U
ペ	ベ		デ	ゼ	ゲ	E
ポ	ボ		ド	ゾ	ゴ	O

I	一 いち, ひと(つ)	二 に, ふた(つ)	三 さん, みっ(つ)	四 し,よ, よん, よっ(つ)	五 ご, いつ(つ)				
	六 ろく, むっ(つ)	七 しち,なの, なな(つ)	八 はち,よう, やっ(つ)	九 きゅう,く, ここの(つ)	十 じゅう,じっ, じゅっ,とお				
	月 がつ, げつ	日 にち,ひ, [び],か	火 か	水 みず, すい	木 き, もく	金 かね, きん	土 ど		
II 2 課	口 くち, [ぐち]	目 め	人 ひと, にん,じん	本 もと, ほん,[ぽん], [ぼん]	今 いま, こん	年 とし, ねん	私 わたし, わたくし	曜 よう	
II 3 課	上 うえ	下 した, くだ(さい)	大 おお(きい), たい,だい	小 ちい(さい), しょう	夕 ゆう	何 なに,なん	中 なか, ちゅう	外 そと, がい	
II 4 課	行 い(く), こう	来 き(ます), く(る), こ(ない), らい	子 こ	車 くるま, しゃ	学 がく, [がっ]	校 こう	見 み(る)	良 よ(い)	食 た(べる), しょく
II 5 課	川 かわ, [がわ]	山 やま, さん	出 で(る), だ(す)	先 せん	生 う(まれる), せい	父 ちち, とう	母 はは, かあ	毎 まい	書 か(く), しょ
II 6 課	手 て	耳 みみ	門 もん	聞 き(く), ぶん	女 おんな	好 す(き)	田 た, [だ]	男 おとこ	
II 7 課	言 い(う)	語 ご	寺 てら,[でら], じ	時 とき, じ	間 あいだ, かん	分 わ(かる), ふん,[ぷん], [ぶん]	正 ただ(しい), しょう	家 いえ, か	々 [repeat]

漢字

課										
二 9課	白 しろ, はく	百 ひゃく, [びゃく], [ぴゃく]	千 せん, [ぜん]	万 まん	方 かた, ほう	玉 たま, [だま]	国 くに,[ぐに] こく,[ごく]	安 やす(い)	高 たか(い), こう	
二 10課	牛 うし, ぎゅう	半 はん	*手 て, しゅ	友 とも	帰 かえ(る)	待 ま(つ)	持 も(つ)	米 こめ	番 ばん	事 こと, [ごと], じ
二 11課	雨 あめ	電 でん	天 てん	気 き	会 あ(う), かい	話 はな(す), はなし, [ばなし], わ	売 う(る)	読 よ(む)		
二 13課	右 みぎ	左 ひだり	入 い(れる), はい(る), [いり]	物 もの, ぶつ	名 な, めい	前 まえ, ぜん	戸 と, [ど]	所 ところ, [どころ] しょ	近 ちか(い)	
二 14課	立 た(つ), りっ	作 つく(る), さく	肉 にく	魚 さかな	多 おお(い), た	少 すく(ない), すこ(し)	古 ふる(い)	新 あたら(しい), しん	*生 う(まれる), せい, なま	
二 15課	才 さい	心 こころ, しん	思 おも(う)	休 やす(み)	買 か(う)	早 はや(い)	自 じ	犬 いぬ	太 ふと(る)	屋 や

* Previously introduced.

III 1課	漢 かん	字 じ	姉 あね, ねえ	妹 いもうと	兄 あに, にい	弟 おとうと	朝 あさ, ちょう	昼 ひる, ちゅう
	明 あか(るい)	去 きょ	銀 ぎん	仕 し	*父 ちち, とう, ふ	*母 はは, かあ, ぼ	*先 せん, さき	家族 かぞく
	友達 ともだち	質問 しつもん	答え こたえ	宿題 しゅくだい	試験 しけん	昨日 きのう		
III 2課	公 こう	文 ぶん	化 か, け	花 はな	海 うみ, かい	旅 りょ	教 おし(える), きょう	室 しつ
	後 うし(ろ), あと, ご	午 ご	着 き(る), つ(く)	知 し(る)	*私 わたし, わたくし, し	*男 おとこ, だん	*女 おんな, じょ	*子 こ, し
	*入 はい(る), い(れる), いり, にゅう	*行 い(く), こう, ぎょう	生徒 せいと	問題 もんだい	教科書 きょうかしょ	公園 こうえん	一度 いちど	図書館 としょかん
III 3課	春 はる	夏 なつ	秋 あき	冬 ふゆ	雪 ゆき	元 げん	飲 の(む)	体 からだ, たい
	音 おと, おん	楽 たの(しい), らく, がく	糸 いと	紙 かみ, [がみ]	*生 う(まれる), なま, せい, しょう	世話 せわ	生活 せいかつ	体育 たいいく
	様 さま	変 へん	大変 たいへん					

* Previously introduced.

Underlined *kanji* are for recognition only.

漢字

III 4課	英 えい	草 くさ	林 はやし,[ばやし]	森 もり	台 たい,[だい]	始 はじ(める)	終 お(わる)	使 つか(う)
	勉 べん	強 つよ(い),きょう	回 かい	週 しゅう	*近 ちか(い),きん	*間 あいだ,かん,ま	本当 ほんとう	最近 さいきん
	違う ちがう	辞書 じしょ	～君 -くん	週末 しゅうまつ				
III 6課	映 えい	画 が,かく	歌 うた,か	晩 ばん	夜 よる	黒 くろ,こく	茶 ちゃ,さ	飯 はん
	足 あし	長 なが(い),ちょう	走 はし(る)	起 お(きる)	寝 ね(る)	有名 ゆうめい	番組 ばんぐみ	女性 じょせい
	男性 だんせい	曲 きょく	子供 こども	選手 せんしゅ	彼 かれ	彼女 かのじょ		
III 7課	東 ひがし,とう	西 にし,せい	洋 よう	和 わ	部 ぶ,へ	美 うつく(しい),び	広 ひろ(い)	内 うち,ない
	主 しゅ	住 す(む),じゅう	開 あ(ける)	閉 し(める)	*生 う(まれる),なま,せい,しょう,い(ける)	*上 あ(がる),うえ,じょう	*下 お(りる),した,くだ(さい),へ	*正 せい,ただ(しい),しょう
	*寝 ね(る),しん	～階 -かい,[-がい]	～的 -てき	全部 ぜんぶ	座る すわる	正座 せいざ		

＊ Previously introduced.

Underlined *kanji* are for recognition only.

III 8課	竹 たけ	鳥 とり, ちょう	色 いろ	赤 あか	青 あお	黄 き	風 かぜ, ふう, [ふ]	味 あじ, み
	料 りょう	理 り	由 ゆう	重 おも(い)	*自 し, [じ]	自然 しぜん	焼く やく	苦手 にがて
	丸 まる	三角 さんかく	四角 しかく	弁当 べんとう	最～ さい～			
III 9課	北 きた, ほく, [ほっ]	南 みなみ	京 きょう	駅 えき	乗 の (る)	地 ち	鉄 てつ	図 ず, と
	道 みち, とう, [どう]	歩 ある(く), ほ, [ぽ]	動 うご(く), どう	働 はたら(く)	円 えん	*明 あか(るい), めい	*売 う(る), ばい	～線 - せん
	橋 はし, [ばし]	病院 びょういん	新幹線 しんかんせん	中央線 ちゅうおうせん				

＊ Previously introduced.

Underlined *kanji* are for recognition only.

漢字

日本語4

IV 1課	社 しゃ,[じゃ]	員 いん	店 みせ,てん	客 きゃく	島 しま,[じま]	座 すわ(る),ざ	取 と(る)	卒 そつ
	業 ぎょう	同 おな(じ)	悪 わる(い)	両 りょう	全 ぜん	有 ゆう	当 とう	*少 すく(ない), すこ(し), しょう
	～歳 ～さい	言葉 ことば	失礼 しつれい	御～ ご～,お～	願い ねがい	写真 しゃしん	横浜 よこはま	
IV 2課	世 せ,せい	親 おや,しん	病 びょう	院 いん	医 い	者 しゃ	死 し(ぬ)	亡 な(くなる)
	忘 わす(れる)	育 そだ(てる), いく	降 ふ(る), お(りる)	困 こま(る)	末 すえ, まつ	族 ぞく	達 たち, [だち]	*男 おとこ, だん,なん
	*生 う(まれる), い(ける), い(きる), なま,せい, しょう	試合 しあい	結婚 けっこん	時代 じだい	太郎 たろう	次郎 じろう	子供 こども	忙 いそが(しい)
IV 3課	村 むら,そん	町 まち, ちょう	船 ふね, せん	州 しゅう	界 かい	第 だい	次 つぎ, じ	戦 たたか((う), せん
	争 そう	合 あ(う), あい	止 と(まる), や(む)	平 へい, ひら	不 ふ	活 かつ	送 おく(る)	*米 こめ, べい
	*地 ち,じ	日系人 にっけいじん	祖父 そふ	祖母 そぼ	畑 はたけ	汽車 きしゃ	単語 たんご	

*Previously introduced.

Underlined *kanji* are for recognition only.

漢字

IV 4課	洗 あら(う), せん	市 し	以 い	庭 にわ	軍 ぐん	連 つ(れる)	運 うん	都 と
	空 そら, [ぞら], から, くう	暑 あつ(い)	寒 さむ(い)	泣 な(く)	笑 わら(う)	薬 くすり, やく	館 かん	*口 くち, こう
	*火 ひ, か	*赤 あか, か	押 お(す)	引 ひ(く)	皆 みな(さん), みんな	和子 かずこ	普通 ふつう	急行 きゅうこう
IV 6課	石 いし, せき	園 えん	絵 え	葉 は, [ば]	度 ど	代 だい	然 ぜん	意 い
	最 もっと(も), さい	切 き(る), [きっ], せつ	習 なら(う), しゅう	続 つづ(く), つづ(ける)	苦 く, くる(しい), にが(い)	痛 いた(い)	静 しず(か)	的 てき
	*後 うし(ろ), あと, ご, のち	*庭 にわ, てい	*回 かい, まわ(す)	江戸 えど	刀 かたな	畳 たたみ, -じょう	僕 ぼく	数 かず, すう
IV 7課	神 かみ, しん, [じん]	仏 ぶつ, [ぶっ]	顔 かお	頭 あたま	幸 しあわ(せ), こう	福 ふく	建 た(てる), けん	考 かんが(える)
	助 たす(ける)	変 か(える), か(わる), へん	喜 よろこ(ぶ)	嬉 うれ(しい)	悲 かな(しい)	愛 あい	恋 こい, れん	*米 こめ, べい, まい
	*者 もの, しゃ	松 まつ	井 い	仲 なか	甘 あま(い)	野菜 やさい	果物 くだもの	協力 きょうりょく

✻ Previously introduced.

Underlined *kanji* are for recognition only.

漢字

IV 8課	宗 しゅう	原 はら,[ばら], げん	窓 まど	服 ふく	港 みなと, こう	晴 は(れ)	雲 くも	曇 くも(り)
	交 こう	通 かよ(う), とお(る), つう	泊 と(まる), はく,[ぱく]	発 はつ, [はっ], [ぱつ]	感 かん	関 せき,[ぜき], かん	特 とく, [とっ]	*着 き(る), つ(く), ちゃく
	*色 いろ, しき	富士山 ふじさん, ふじやま	成田 なりた	新宿 しんじゅく	奈良 なら	大阪 おおさか	歴史 れきし	風呂 ふろ
	到着 とうちゃく	飛行機 ひこうき	席 せき					
IV 9課	受 う(ける)	池 いけ, ち	箱 はこ,[ばこ]	冷 つめ(たい), れい	場 ば, じょう	野 の, や	球 たま, きゅう	問 もん
	題 だい	若 わか(い)	寄 よ(る), き	無 む	集 あつ(める), あつ(まる)	決 き(める), けつ,[けっ]	信 しん(じる), しん	*有 あり, ゆう
	*空 そら, くう, あ(き), から	*分 わ(かる), わ(ける), ふん,[ぷん] [ぶん]	*合 あ(う), あい, ごう	缶 かん	袋 ふくろ, [ぶくろ]	猫 ねこ	牛乳 ぎゅうにゅう	置 お(く)

＊ Previously introduced.

Underlined *kanji* are for recognition only.

動詞変化表　Verb Conjugations Chart

	NAI form	MASU form	Dic. form	BA form	OO form	TE form	TA form
	informal, neg., nonpast	formal, nonpast	informal, nonpast	conditional	informal, volitional		informal, past
I. Group 1 Verbs							
み	のま ない nomanai	のみ ます nomimasu	のむ nomu	のめば nomeba	のもう nomoo	のんで nonde	のんだ nonda
に	しな ない shinanai	しに ます shinimasu	しぬ shinu	しねば shineba	しのう shinoo	しんで shinde	しんだ shinda
び	あそば ない asobanai	あそび ます asobimasu	あそぶ asobu	あそべば asobeba	あそぼう asoboo	あそんで asonde	あそんだ asonda
い	かわ ない kawanai	かい ます kaimasu	かう kau	かえば kaeba	かおう kaoo	かって katte	かった katta
ち	また ない matanai	まち ます machimasu	まつ matsu	まてば mateba	まとう matoo	まって matte	まった matta
り	かえら ない kaeranai	かえり ます kaerimasu	かえる kaeru	かえれば kaereba	かえろう kaeroo	かえって kaette	かえった kaetta
	＊ない * nai	あり ます arimasu	ある aru	あれば areba		あって atte	あった atta
き	かか ない kakanai	かき ます kakimasu	かく kaku	かけば kakeba	かこう kakoo	かいて kaite	かいた kaita
	いか ない ikanai	いき ます ikimasu	いく iku	いけば ikeba	いこう ikoo	＊いって * itte	＊いった * itta
ぎ	およが ない oyoganai	およぎ ます oyogimasu	およぐ oyogu	およげば oyogeba	およごう oyogoo	およいで oyoide	およいだ oyoida
し	はなさ ない hanasanai	はなし ます hanashimasu	はなす hanasu	はなせば hanaseba	はなそう hanasoo	はなして hanashite	はなした hanashita
II. Group 2 Verbs							
-e	たべ ない tabenai	たべ ます tabemasu	たべる taberu	たべれば tabereba	たべよう tabeyoo	たべて tabete	たべた tabeta
□	みない minai	みます mimasu	みる miru	みれば mireba	みよう miyoo	みて mite	みた mita
Special verbs: おきます get up; happen, かります borrow, おります get off; go down, できます can do, -すぎます too ~, (シャワーを)あびます take a shower, いきます to live, おちます to fall, かんじます to feel							
III. Group 3 Irregular verbs							
する (do)	しない shinai	します shimasu	する suru	すれば sureba	しよう shiyoo	して shite	した shita
くる (come)	こない konai	きます kimasu	くる kuru	くれば kureba	こよう koyoo	きて kite	きた kita

＊Exceptional form.

動詞

Verb Conjugations

	NAKATTA form informal, neg., past	(Honorific-Passive)	Causative Permissive	Polite Command	Neg. Command	Potential (Group 2 verb)	Command
I. Group 1 Verbs							
み	のまなかった nomanakatta	のまれる nomareru	のませる nomaseru	のみなさい nominasai	のむな nomuna	のめる nomeru	のめ nome
に	しななかった shinanakatta	しなれる shinareru	しなせる shinaseru	しになさい shininasai	しぬな shinuna	しねる shineru	しね shine
び	あそばなかった asobanakatta	あそばれる asobareru	あそばせる asobaseru	あそびなさい asobinasai	あそぶな asobuna	あそべる asoberu	あそべ asobe
い	かわなかった kawanakatta	かわれる kawareru	かわせる kawaseru	かいなさい kainasai	かうな kauna	かえる kaeru	かえ kae
ち	またなかった matanakatta	またれる matareru	またせる mataseru	まちなさい machinasai	まつな matsuna	まてる materu	まて mate
り	かえらなかった kaeranakatta *なかった * nakatta	かえられる kaereru	かえらせる kaeraseru	かえりなさい kaerinasai	かえるな kaeruna	かえれる kaereru	かえれ kaere
き	かかなかった kakanakatta いかなかった ikanakatta	かかれる kakareru いかれる ikareru	かかせる kakaseru いかせる ikaseru	かきなさい kakinasai いきなさい ikinasai	かくな kakuna いくな ikuna	かける kakeru いける ikeru	かけ kake いけ ike
ぎ	およがなかった oyoganakatta	およがれる oyogareru	およがせる oyogaseru	およぎなさい oyoginasai	およぐな oyoguna	およげる oyogeru	およげ oyoge
し	はなさなかった hanasanakatta	はなされる hanasareru	はなさせる hanasaseru	はなしなさい hanashinasai	はなすな hanasuna	はなせる hanaseru	はなせ hanase
II. Group 2 Verbs							
-e	たべなかった tabenakatta	たべられる taberareru	たべさせる tabesaseru	たべなさい tabenasai	たべるな taberuna	たべられる taberareru	たべろ tabero
□	みなかった minakatta	みられる mirareru	みさせる misaseru	みなさい minasai	みるな miruna	みられる mirareru	みろ miro
Special verbs: おきます get up; happen, かります borrow, おります get off; go down, できます can do, -すぎます too ~, (シャワーを)あびます take a shower, いきます to live, おちます to fall, かんじます to feel							
III. Group 3 Irregular verbs							
する (do)	しなかった shinakatta	される sareru	させる saseru	しなさい shinasai	するな suruna	できる dekiru	しろ shiro
くる (come)	こなかった konakatta	こられる korareru	こさせる korareru	きなさい kinasai	くるな kuruna	こられる korareru	こい koi

＊Exceptional form.

動詞

236